This book acknowledges the financial support of the Publication Project of the Zhejiang Translation Institute and the Eastern Zhejiang Culture Research Institute, Ningbo University.

Maritime Silk Road: A Cultural Journey from Zhejiang to the World

By Gong Yingyan

Translated by Cong Yingxu, Han Xue, and He Ying

CHICAGO ACADEMIC PRESS

Maritime Silk Road: A Cultural Journey from Zhejiang to the World
Author: Gong Yingyan
Translator: Cong Yingxu, Han Xue, and He Ying
Language: English
Word Count (for space of all pages): 281 Thousand words
Publisher: Chicago Academic Press
Number of Pages: 418
ISBN: 979-8-901-86008-3

Publishing	Chicago Academic Press
	5923 N Artesian Ave
	Chicago IL 60659
Email	contact@chicagoacademicpress.com
Website	http://chicagoacademicpress.com/
Book Size	6X9 inches
First Edition	November, 2025

Translator Profile

Dr. Cong Yingxu is a Chinese-English translator and linguist. He serves as an Associate Professor of Contrastive Linguistics and Director of the Center for Master of Translation and Interpreting Education at Ningbo University. His teaching and research are dedicated to advancing the theory and practice of translation and nurturing future scholars in the field.

Ms. Han Xue, who holds a Master's degree in Translation and Interpreting, teaches Translation and Academic English Writing for graduate students at Ningbo University. Her research and professional practice focus on the precise and culturally nuanced translation of Chinese academic discourse into English, with an emphasis on accuracy, clarity, and intercultural intelligibility.

Dr. He Ying, a distinguished Professor of Translation Studies at Ningbo University, stands as a seasoned translator in China. She holds prestigious roles including Council Member of the Translators Association of China, judge for the National Social Science Fund translation program, and Expert Committee Member for CATTI. Her key translations encompass the acclaimed A History of Reading (2009, Wenjin Book Award), Chinese Gardens (2010), and Learning to Be: A New Vision for Post-School Education in South Africa (2021).

General Preface to the Publications of the Zhejiang Cultural Research Project

Xi Jinping

Some liken culture to a river flowing from the headwaters of ancestry toward the horizons of the future. This metaphor speaks to tradition, an ever-flowing current that is transmitted across generations and diffused across communities, ceaselessly shaping and guiding human existence. Others define culture as the vessel, medium, and method for human thought, wisdom, faith, and emotion—the holistic expression of a way of life passed from one generation to the next. We, however, propose a more foundational view: culture offers the norms, forms, and settings that shape communal life; through its transmission, it lays the foundation for social advancement; and it can both propel and temper the growth of the economy and the evolution of society. The power of culture is deeply forged into the vitality, creativity, and cohesion of our nation.

In the course of its evolution, every culture generates a multitude of internal elements, strata, and typologies. This process of internal differentiation is precisely what gives rise to the diversity and complexity that characterize our shared human heritage.

The vastness and profundity of Chinese culture are born of its vibrant internal pluralism. Its enduring vitality, in turn, is sustained by the dynamic interplay of its constituent elements, strata, and typologies. Through a perpetual process of collision, deconstruction, and fusion, this interplay generates a powerful engine for transformative renewal in both content and form.

Across China's vast and varied landscape, distinct regional cultures have been shaped by profound differences in their natural, economic, and social environments. Like a hundred rivers flowing to the sea, these regional cultures converge to form the grand tradition of Chinese civilization. This tradition, in turn, permeates every region like a nourishing spring rain. Within this dynamic, each regional culture flows onward like a clear mountain stream, sustaining and guiding local economic and social development with its unique character, all while operating within the shared values of the broader Chinese civilization.

A comprehensive, systematic, and rigorous study of a region's culture, both past and present, serves a dual purpose. On one hand, it allows us to catalogue and celebrate local historical traditions and cultural assets, enrich contemporary cultural life, and chart a course for future development. This work enhances cultural soft power, providing the philosophical grounding, spiritual impetus, intellectual resources, and public consensus necessary for building a comprehensively prosperous society and advancing China's modernization. On the other hand, such regional studies offer a vital pathway to understanding, researching, developing, and innovating Chinese culture as a whole. Today, the growing emphasis on regional cultural studies marks a new stage of maturity in our nation's scholarship. It is with this very purpose and significance that we now launch the Zhejiang Cultural Research Project.

Over thousands of years, the people of Zhejiang have accumulated and passed down a profound cultural tradition.The uniqueness of this cultural tradition lies in its astonishingly creative wisdom and vitality.

The creative gene in Zhejiang culture appeared early in the origins of its history. In Zhejiang's most famous Neolithic cultures—Hemudu, Majiabang, Liangzhu, and Kuahuqiao—the ancestors of Zhejiang left remarkable achievements at the cradle of Chinese civilization, imprinting marks of creation and progress.

As the people of Zhejiang have advanced along the trajectory of history, they have upheld this creative cultural tradition, deeply ingrained in their blood, reflected in their actions, and fully embodied in numerous outstanding figures throughout Zhejiang's history. From Yu the Great's adaptive governance and tireless flood control, to King Goujian's "sleeping on brushwood and tasting gall" for perseverance and reform; from the Qian family's safeguarding of borders and peaceful submission to the Song Dynasty, to Hu Ze's principle of benefiting the people during his tenure; from Yue Fei's and Yu Qian's unwavering loyalty to the nation and lifelong integrity, to Fang Xiaoru's and Zhang Cangshui's unyielding righteousness and martyrdom; from Shen Kuo's vast erudition and meticulous research, to Zhu Kezhen's scientific dedication to national salvation and lifelong pursuit of truth;

whether it be Chen Liang and Ye Shi's emphasis on practical governance, or Huang Zongxi's advocacy that "commerce and industry are as fundamental as agriculture"; whether it be Wang Chong and Wang Yangming's critical awareness and self-realization, or Gong Zizhen and Cai Yuanpei's enlightenment and openness—these all demonstrate Zhejiang's profound cultural heritage and embody the pragmatic and creative spirit of its people.

This intergenerational legacy of cultural creativity—in terms of concepts, attitudes, behavioral patterns, and values—has nurtured, formed, and developed Zhejiang's distinctive regional cultural tradition and its forward-looking cultural spirit. It nourishes Zhejiang's vitality, fosters its cohesion, stimulates its creativity, cultivates its competitiveness, and inspires the people of Zhejiang to never become complacent or cease striving, continuously surpassing themselves and forging ahead in entrepreneurship across different historical periods.

The long-standing, profound, and richly nuanced Zhejiang cultural tradition is a precious treasure bestowed by history, as well as a rich resource and inexhaustible driving force for pioneering the future. The practice of promoting Zhejiang's new development since the 16th National Congress of the CPC has made us increasingly aware that the deep reason behind Zhejiang's sustained, rapid, and healthy socioeconomic development, alongside the national policies of reform and opening up, lies in the organic integration of Zhejiang's profound cultural heritage and traditions with the spirit of the times, and in the organic combination of developing advanced productive forces with advanced culture. Whether Zhejiang can continue to lead in building a moderately prosperous society in all respects and accelerating socialist modernization in the coming period will largely depend on our profound recognition of cultural power, our high level of awareness in developing advanced culture, and our efforts in accelerating the construction of a culturally strong province. We must recognize that cultural power can ultimately be transformed into material power, and cultural soft power into economic hard power. Culture is the core element of comprehensive competitiveness, cultural resources are important resources for socioeconomic development, and cultural quality is the primary quality of leaders and workers. Therefore, studying the history and current state of Zhejiang culture, enhancing cultural soft power, and serving Zhejiang's modernization is a common endeavor for the people of Zhejiang, as well as an important mission and responsibility for Zhejiang's Party committees and governments at all levels.

The 8th Plenary Session of the 11th Zhejiang Provincial Committee of the CPC, held in July 2005, adopted the "Decision on Accelerating the Construction of a Culturally Strong Province," which proposed vigorously implementing eight major projects—Civilized Quality Project, Cultural Excellence Project, Cultural Research Project, Cultural Protection Project, Cultural Industry Promotion Project, Cultural Positions Project, Cultural Dissemination Project, and Cultural Talent Project—from the perspectives of enhancing the cohesion of advanced culture, liberating and developing productive forces, and strengthening social public services. It also aimed to implement the strategies of invigorating the country through science, education, and talent, and to accelerate the construction of "four strong provinces" in education, technology, health, and sports. As one of the "eight projects" for cultural construction, the Cultural Research Project is tasked with systematically studying the historical achievements and contemporary development of Zhejiang culture, deeply excavating its cultural heritage, researching the "Zhejiang phenomenon," summarizing the "Zhejiang experience," and guiding Zhejiang's future development.

The Zhejiang Cultural Research Project will focus on four major areas: "contemporary, ancient, people, and literature"—namely, research on contemporary development issues in Zhejiang, thematic studies on Zhejiang's historical culture, studies on Zhejiang's notable figures, and the collation of Zhejiang's historical documents—conducting systematic research and publishing a series of books. In terms of research content, it will deeply excavate Zhejiang's cultural heritage, systematically sort out and analyze the internal structure, evolution patterns, and regional characteristics of Zhejiang's historical culture, and uphold and develop the Zhejiang spirit; it will study the similarities and differences between Zhejiang culture and other regional cultures, clarify Zhejiang culture's position and interrelations within Chinese culture; and, centered on Zhejiang's vivid contemporary practices, it will deeply interpret the Zhejiang phenomenon, summarize the Zhejiang experience, and guide Zhejiang's development. In terms of research forces, through organizing projects, providing publication funding, building key research bases, strengthening cooperation with renowned institutions and universities inside and outside the province, and integrating forces from various localities and departments, it will form an overall synergy of top-down collaboration and academic interaction. In terms of application of results, it will emphasize both the academic and practical value of research outcomes, fully leveraging their important roles in understanding the world, inheriting civilization, innovating theory, advising on policy, educating people, and serving society.

We hope that through implementing the Zhejiang Cultural Research Project, we will use Zhejiang's history to educate its people, its culture to edify them, its spirit to inspire them, and its experience to guide them, further unleashing the boundless wisdom and great creative potential of the people of Zhejiang, and promoting Zhejiang's fast and high-quality development.

Today, treading the river of history and bearing the expectations of our people, we should shoulder our mission with utmost sincerity and dedication, ensuring that our culture endures unbroken and our creativity thrives endlessly.

30 May 2006

Contents

Chapter 1. Introduction: The Historical Development of Zhejiang's Maritime Silk Road

Prior to 1840, the great arteries of commerce and communication connecting China to the outside world were known collectively to scholars as the "Silk Road." This vast network linked disparate civilizations, fostering cultural exchange, strengthening the bonds between peoples, enriching Chinese culture, and profoundly influencing the course of human history. The Silk Road consisted of two main branches: the overland route, which emerged around the 13th century BC, and the maritime route, which appeared around 200 BC. This Maritime Silk Road, in turn, comprised two principal trunk lines: the East Sea Route, connecting China to the Korean Peninsula and the Japanese archipelago, and the South Sea Route, extending to Southeast Asia and the Indian Ocean. After 1500, with the arrival of European mariners, the South Sea Route expanded to become part of a truly global maritime network.

Situated on the western shore of the Pacific, at the midpoint of China's continental coastline, Zhejiang is a vital cradle of Chinese maritime culture and a principal gateway of the Maritime Silk Road. The history of its development can be divided into the following six stages:

Stage 1. Prehistoric Foundations

The discovery between 2013 and 2014 of the Jingtoushan site in Yuyao,

Ningbo, dated to over 8,000 years ago, pushed back the timeline of Zhejiang's maritime activity. As China's earliest known shell-mound settlement, it reveals a sustained and systematic exploitation of marine resources. While no dugout canoes were found, the excavation of a finely crafted and well-preserved wooden paddle proves that the inhabitants were capable of building early watercraft. The oldest known dugout canoe in China was unearthed at the Neolithic site of Kuahuqiao in Xiaoshan, Hangzhou, and has been dated to 7070±155 years before present, making it the earliest such vessel yet found in Asia. The subsequent Hemudu culture (c. 7000–5300 BC) has yielded even more evidence, including eight wooden paddles from the Hemudu site itself, two from the Cihu site, six from the Tianluoshan site, and two ceramic boat models from Hemudu. These findings provide conclusive proof that rudimentary shipbuilding—the essential precondition for overseas exchange—was already established in Zhejiang during the Neolithic era.

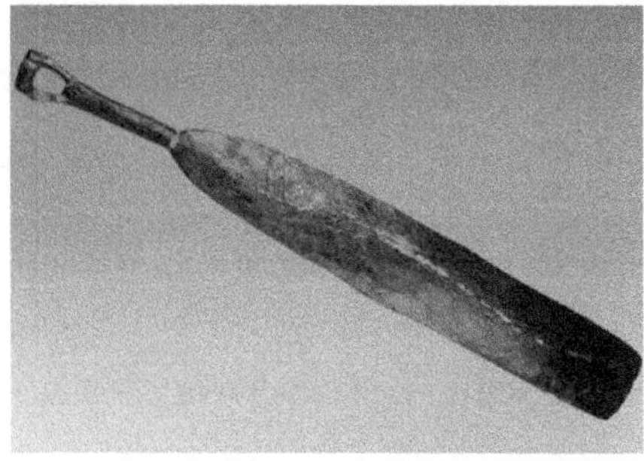

The wooden paddle unearthed from the Jingtou Mountain Site

The canoe unearthed from the Kuahuqiao site

Some scholars have hypothesized that maritime contact between

Zhejiang, the Korean Peninsula, and the Japanese archipelago may have existed in prehistoric times, although such contact has not yet been confirmed by current archaeological evidence. Nevertheless, there is abundant proof of cultural diffusion. The stepped stone adze, a tool found widely across the Western Pacific, originated in the Neolithic coastal cultures of Zhejiang, exemplified by the Hemudu culture. Although this tool was disseminated over a vast period and underwent regional modifications, its fundamental design remained consistent. This technological signature serves as clear evidence that the foundations for Zhejiang's history of overseas exchange were laid in the Neolithic age.

Stage 2. Emergence in the Han and Jin Dynasties

During the Han Dynasty, the main trunk lines of the Maritime Silk Road did not yet terminate in Zhejiang. The South Sea Route originated from the coast of Guangdong, while the East Sea Route to Japan proceeded north along the Shandong Peninsula, followed the western coast of the Korean Peninsula south, and then crossed the Tsushima Strait to northern Japan. Despite this, the influence of these routes radiated indirectly into Zhejiang. Key evidence for this connection comes from foreign-made goods that found their way into the region, such as glass artifacts. For example, a glass bead and two glass earrings dated to the late Western Han or early Eastern Han were discovered in three tombs in Baidu Nan'ao, Fenghua. Similarly, a string of blue glass beads and a blue glass earring from the early Eastern Han (1st century BC) were unearthed from a tomb in Yingluo Village, Beilun.

Toward the end of the Eastern Han, the transformative cultural force of Buddhism began to arrive in Zhejiang. Historical records state that during the reign of Emperor Ling (AD 157–189), the Parthian monk An Shigao came to China as a missionary and is said to have died in Kuaiji (modern-day Shaoxing). A native of Kuaiji, Chen Hui, became one of his most esteemed disciples. As Buddhism took root, temples began to appear. In the fifth year of the Chiwu era of the Eastern Wu dynasty (AD 242), Kan Ze of Cixi donated his residence to found what would become Puji Temple. In the first year of the Taiyuan era of Eastern Wu (AD 251), Liu Yue and others in Gui'an (modern-day Huzhou) established Shizihou Temple. Buddhist motifs from this period can also be found on locally produced ceramics. It is clear, therefore, that during the Han and Jin dynasties, Zhejiang had established a connection with the Maritime Silk Road, even if this connection was still indirect.

Stage 3. Ascendance in the High Tang Dynasty

The 7th century rise of the Silla Kingdom on the Korean Peninsula disrupted traditional northern sea lanes, creating a strategic impetus that Zhejiang's mariners were quick to exploit. Through persistent exploration, navigators forged direct maritime routes from the Zhejiang coast to Japan between the late 7th and 8th centuries. As a result, ports such as Hangzhou, Mingzhou (modern Ningbo), Taizhou, and Wenzhou became China's primary gateways to Japan. Of the sixteen official envoy missions sent from Japan to Tang China, three landed on the coast of Ningbo, in AD 659, AD 752, and AD 804. Even more significant was the rise of private commerce. By the 9th century, merchants were sailing directly from Zhejiang's ports to trade with Japan, as evidenced by records of Li Churen arriving in Wenzhou from Japan in AD 842, Zhang Youxin departing Mingzhou for Japan in AD 847, and Cui Duo setting sail from Taizhou for Japan in AD 877.

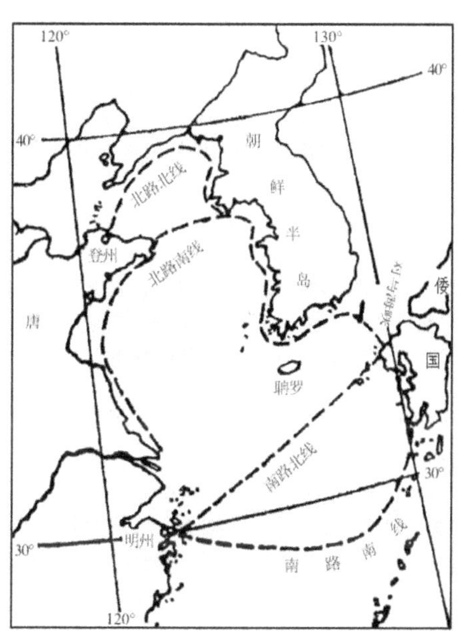

The maritime routes between ancient

Although direct trade between Tang-dynasty Zhejiang and Southeast Asia via the South Sea Route was not yet established, indirect connections flourished. The celebrated Yue ware celadons produced in Zhejiang were transported along the Maritime Silk Road not only to markets in Southeast Asia and across the Indian Ocean but as far as Egypt in North Africa. The discovery of these distinctive ceramics in numerous countries abroad provides a tangible record of Zhejiang's cultural footprint during this era.

It is important to clarify a common misconception. In discussions of the Maritime Silk Road, there is often a debate over which port served as the "original" starting point. This inquiry is misguided, as the Maritime Silk Road was not a single line but a complex network. Every port within this network functioned simultaneously as a point of origin, a destination, and a port of transit. A single, exclusive "first port" never existed. From the Tang Dynasty until 1840, Ningbo was consistently a principal port on China's Maritime Silk Road. At the same time, numerous other ports along the Zhejiang coast—including Hangzhou, Taizhou, Wenzhou, Zhapu, and Zhoushan—played vital roles at different times.

Stage 4. Prosperity in the Song and Yuan Dynasties

The governments of the Song and Yuan dynasties generally adopted an open and encouraging stance toward overseas exchange. This policy propelled Zhejiang's Maritime Silk Road to unprecedented levels of prosperity, a golden age demonstrated by several key developments:

First, the institutionalization of trade through specialized government agencies known as *shibosi* (Maritime Trade Offices). While the Tang Dynasty had only one such office in Guangzhou, the Song established them in nine different locations, four of which—Hangzhou, Ganpu, Wenzhou, and Ningbo—were in Zhejiang. By the Yuan Dynasty, seven official Maritime Trade Offices were set up in Hangzhou, Ganpu, Ningbo, Wenzhou, Shanghai, Quanzhou, and Guangzhou.This indicates that Zhejiang accounted for nearly "half of the empire's maritime trade" during the Song and Yuan dynasties.

Second, the establishment of direct maritime routes to Southeast Asia. In the third year of the Chunhua era of the Northern Song Dynasty (AD 992), during the Northern Song, an envoy from Java (in modern-day Indonesia), guided by the Chinese sea merchant Mao Xu, arrived at the mouth of Ningbo's Yong River after a sixty-day voyage to present tribute. Centuries later, in 1296, the Wenzhou native Zhou Daguan accompanied a Yuan diplomatic mission to Zhenla (modern Cambodia). His party departed from Wenzhou, sailed south along the coasts of Fujian and Guangdong, and reached their destination. Zhou's detailed account, The Customs of Cambodia, remains a vital historical record. The mission returned in August 1297, arriving in Ningbo. These voyages demonstrate that by this time, the sea lanes between Zhejiang and Southeast Asia were well established.

Third, the formation of overseas expatriate communities from Zhejiang. During the late Tang Dynasty, merchants from Zhejiang had already begun engaging in overseas trade. For example, in 819, Zhou Guanghan and Yan Shengze from Yuezhou traveled to Japan on a Silla vessel. However, they returned to China after completing their trade, and no records have been found indicating they settled abroad. During the Song Dynasty, however, some began to settle and raise families abroad. A notable example from the Southern Song is the Ningbo stonemason Yi Xingmo, who was invited to work in Japan, where he married, established a family, and founded a renowned lineage of stonemasons. By the late 11th century, an enclave of Song Chinese residents had formed in Hakata (part of modern Fukuoka). While the total number of Zhejiang natives living there is unknown, records show that between 1233 and 1253, the leader of the Chinese community in Hakata was Xie Guoming, a native of Lin'an Prefecture (modern Hangzhou), whose tomb is preserved to this day.

Fourth, the growth of foreign expatriate enclaves within Zhejiang. As maritime trade flourished, many foreign merchants settled in Zhejiang, forming distinct communities. In Ningbo, near the *shibosi* at the East Gate, Arab and Persian merchants established a market known as the "Persian Guild" and lived in a neighborhood called "Persian Lane." In Hangzhou, Arab traders congregated around the Jianqiao area, where they constructed a landmark eight-story building. A public cemetery for Arabs was located at Jujing Garden, outside the Qingbo Gate. The most compelling physical evidence of this community is the collection of twenty Yuan-dynasty tombstones inscribed in Arabic, which are still preserved at Hangzhou's Phoenix Mosque.

Fifth, the convergence of diverse foreign religions. Foreign communities naturally brought their faiths with them. The most prominent of these was Islam. A Muslim prayer hall (Huihui Tang) was built in Song-dynasty Ningbo, and another was added during the Yuan. In the Yanyou era of the Yuan Dynasty(1314-1320), the Muslim master Alauddin constructed the Zhenjiao (True Religion) Mosque in Hangzhou. Christianity—known during the Yuan period as Yelikewen, a term for the Church of the East (Nestorianism)—also established a presence, with a church named Dapuxing Temple built in Hangzhou. The arrival of Christianity in Wenzhou even led to conflicts with local Daoists over converts. Manichaeism also had a foothold, with temples such as Chongshou Palace in Cixi and Xuanzhen Temple in Wenzhou. The arrival of these foreign faiths created a more pluralistic and vibrant cultural landscape in Zhejiang.

Stage 5. Upheaval in the Ming and Qing Dynasties

The founding of the Ming Dynasty heralded a dramatic shift in policy. The government imposed strict maritime prohibitions (haijin), banning private overseas trade, while simultaneously instituting a tributary system that restricted foreign commerce to officially sanctioned missions. These missions were limited to designated ports: Ningbo was assigned for trade with Japan, Quanzhou for the Ryukyu Kingdom, and Guangzhou for Southeast Asia and the Indian Ocean. This made Ningbo the sole official port for exchange with Japan. Later, after the Qing Dynasty consolidated its rule, it established four maritime customs offices in Guangdong, Fujian, Zhejiang, and Jiangsu, with the Zhejiang office opening in Ningbo in 1686. This multi-port system was short-lived. In 1757, the Qing court reversed course and implemented the "Canton System," restricting all foreign trade to the single port of Guangzhou. This self-imposed policy of isolation made Ningbo and Zhejiang its greatest victims, severely stunting the region's maritime development and causing China to miss a crucial opportunity for global engagement.

Whereas the seas of East Asia had been largely peaceful during the Song and Yuan periods, the Ming era saw the rise of the *wokou*—pirates who ravaged the coastlines of China and Korea. The coast of Zhejiang was one of their most frequent targets. The Ming ban on private trade created a fertile environment for illicit activity. Driven by economic necessity, coastal inhabitants turned to smuggling, often forming symbiotic relationships with pirate groups and operating as pirate-merchants who directly challenged the state's control of the seas. Piracy did not disappear with the consolidation of Qing rule; in fact, it saw a major resurgence around 1800. As the scholar Robert Antony has written, the period from 1520 to 1810 was a veritable "golden age of Chinese piracy," which was "unmatched in scale and scope by pirates anywhere else". Throughout the Ming and Qing dynasties, the development of Zhejiang's maritime networks proceeded under the constant shadow of piracy.

The arrival of Europeans in the late 15th century inaugurated an age of globalization.In late 1497, a Portuguese fleet rounded the Cape of Good Hope and arrived at Calicut on India's west coast in May 1498. This achievement opened a new, direct sea route from the Atlantic to India, which ultimately integrated the South China Sea Route of the Maritime Silk Road into the global maritime network. The Portuguese capture of Malacca in 1511 opened the maritime gateway to China. Soon after, they arrived on

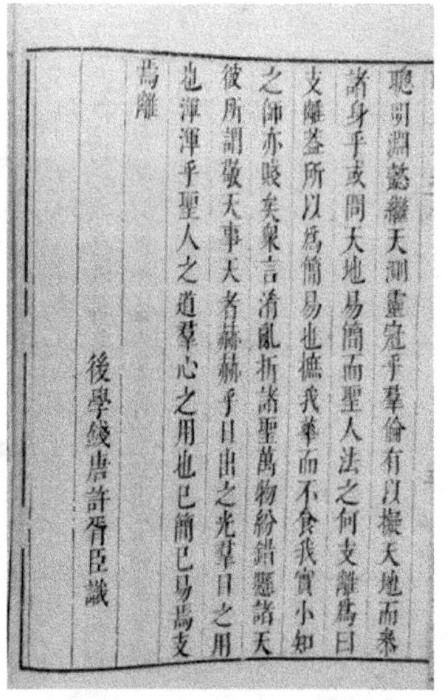

聰明淵懿繼天測靈冠乎羣倫有以擬天地而參
諸身乎或問天地易簡而聖人法之何支離焉曰
支離蓋所以為簡易也撫我華而不食我實小知
之師亦喙矣衆言淆亂折諸聖萬物紛錯懸諸天
彼所謂敬天事天者赫赫乎日出之光羣目之用
也渾渾乎聖人之道羣心之用也已簡已易焉支
焉離
後學錢唐許胥臣識

Partial preface by the Hangzhou scholar Xu Xuchen, in the 1623 Hangzhou edition of *Chronicle of Foreign Lands* by Giulio Aleni

the Chinese coast and, between 1524 and 1548, established a trading post at Shuangyu, an island off the coast of Ningbo. This was Europe's first commercial outpost in East Asia and marked Zhejiang's formal entry into the global trade network. Goods from Zhejiang were shipped to Europe, and some of the province's residents even made their way to Western Europe. By the late 17th century, merchant ships sailed directly from Ningbo to the Spanish-controlled Philippines, and in the 1700s, English traders began frequenting Zhoushan. This new era of global exchange brought a continuous flow of European culture into China, and Zhejiang scholars were at the forefront of studying it. During the Ming-Qing transition, Hangzhou became a center for Sino-Western scholarly exchange, leading international research in fields such as the history of Nestorianism in China.

Zhejiang's integration into global trade routes from the 16th century onward brought an unprecedented influx of products from around the world. Of particular importance were the New World crops introduced from the Americas. Sweet potatoes, maize, potatoes, chili peppers, pumpkins, sunflowers, tomatoes, green beans, and tobacco arrived via various routes, profoundly transforming Zhejiang. They not only diversified the local diet and altered the structure of daily meals but also became deeply integrated into the regional agricultural system, providing a new foundation for sustaining the province's society.

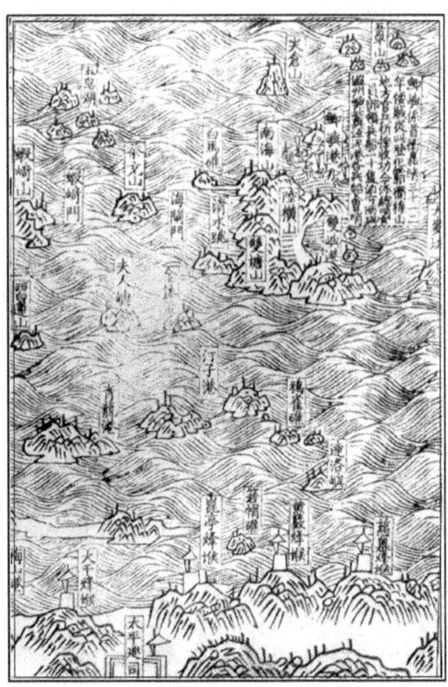

The Shuangyu Port mentioned in the *Classified Examination of Coastal Defense in Jiangsu and Zhejiang* published in 1575

Events that transpired in 16th-century Zhejiang had a profound impact on the broader course of Chinese history. A case in point is the Portuguese experience at Shuangyu. Since beginning their overseas expansion in the late 15th century, the Portuguese had faced relatively weak opposition and had come to rely on military force. Upon reaching China, they attempted the same strategy, seeking to seize a foothold with their superior ships and weapons. However, their first major base, the smugglers' haven of Shuangyu, was decisively destroyed by Ming forces in 1548. This defeat served as a harsh lesson, forcing the Portuguese to recognize that China was a power of a different order. Consequently, they abandoned their strategy of violent seizure and adopted a more diplomatic posture, professing admiration for Chinese civilization and offering tribute, while simultaneously using bribery to curry favor with Ming officials. The Ming, for their part, recognized that these new arrivals, with their advanced arms and commercial acumen, could not be managed with traditional methods. Beijing shifted from a policy of pure suppression to one of accommodation. This mutual adjustment of strategies created the conditions for a unique arrangement: the Ming government permitted the Portuguese to settle in Macao under Chinese sovereignty, provided they paid taxes and land rent, while granting them a degree of autonomy. Macao thus became a pivotal hub for East-West exchange, and the fall of Shuangyu can be seen as the necessary prelude to its rise.

An even more consequential example can be found in the 18th century. After 1700, British merchants began trading frequently at Zhoushan, where they were welcomed by local officials and the populace. The Qianlong Emperor understood that the goods most desired by the British, such as silk and tea, were produced primarily in the Jiangsu-Zhejiang region. He knew that allowing trade at Ningbo would lower costs for the British and stimulate the local economy. Yet, driven by concerns over coastal defense, he issued an edict in 1757 banning British ships from Ningbo. This decision marked the formal shift from a multi-port system to the restrictive "Canton System," which limited all foreign maritime trade to Guangzhou. For the next eight decades, Western powers, led by Great Britain, launched escalating challenges against this single-port policy, a conflict that ultimately culminated in the Opium War of 1840.

In summary, from the founding of the Ming Dynasty to the eve of the Opium War, the history of Zhejiang's Maritime Silk Road was defined by a clash of opposing forces. On one side were the negative pressures of harsh court suppression and the brutal raids of *wokou* pirates. On the other were the positive drivers of a powerful grassroots impulse for overseas trade and the new opportunities created by post-1500 globalization. The collision of these forces produced a history of intense turmoil. This upheaval, in turn, catalyzed profound transformations, which then bred even greater instability. For over four hundred years, the Maritime Silk Road in Zhejiang evolved along this tortuous path of conflict and change, all the while accumulating the energy that would propel it into its next historical stage.

Stage 6. Transformation in the Modern Era

The Opium War, which erupted in 1840, raised the curtain on modern Chinese history. In August 1842, the Qing government was forced to sign the Treaty of Nanking, abandoning the Canton System and opening five cities—Guangzhou, Xiamen, Fuzhou, Ningbo, and Shanghai—to foreign trade. The treaty signaled China's descent into a semi-colonial, semi-feudal society. It also marked the moment when the historical Maritime Silk Road was irrevocably transformed into a network of modern, international shipping lanes.

For two millennia, from its inception around 200 BC, the Maritime Silk Road was the domain of the wooden sailing ship. After 1840, however, the frequent appearance of British warships heralded the dawn of the age of steam. Following the Opium War, foreign steamships arrived in ever-increasing numbers, soon becoming the dominant vessel for ocean transport and ultimately rendering the traditional sailing junk obsolete. The Maritime Silk

Road was fundamentally a network of the age of sail; the international sea lanes that replaced it belonged to the age of steam.

Before the Opium War, the protagonists of the Maritime Silk Road were Chinese; afterward, its successors were dominated by Westerners. Before the war, goods imported into China were primarily luxuries—spices,

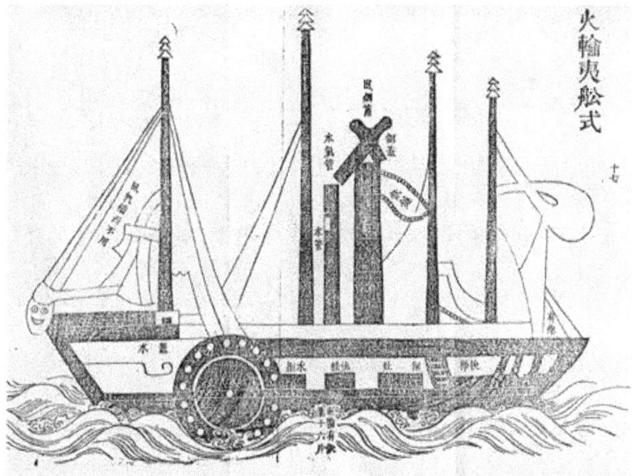

The style of British invading army ships that appeared along the coast of Ningbo during the Opium War

exotic treasures, rare medicines—destined for the elite and having little impact on daily life. After the war, a flood of Western industrial products arrived, profoundly reshaping Chinese society. Matches replaced flint and steel; kerosene lamps replaced oil lamps; glass panes replaced paper windows. Machine-made needles, clocks, soap, and thermoses became common household items. Bicycles became a new mode of transport, and running water, telephones, and flush toilets became symbols of modern luxury. This transformation was not limited to consumer goods. Western machinery, technology, and knowledge, arriving via these new sea lanes, gave birth to

China's modern industry, catalyzed the formation of a modern Chinese culture, and drove unprecedented social change. The pre-Opium War Maritime Silk Road was thus fundamentally different in nature from the modern international sea lanes that followed. The two cannot be conflated. In a very real sense, the history of the Maritime Silk Road came to a definitive close with the Opium War.

Zhejiang was a key battleground of the Opium War and a primary stage for this historic transition. Under the Treaty of Nanking, Ningbo became one of the first five treaty ports, officially opening on January 1, 1844. The ancient port witnessed a rapid evolution from a harbor of sail to a harbor of steam, from a transshipment center for agricultural goods to a hub of industrial commerce, and from a regional East Asian nexus to a node in the global

An Outline of the Theory of the Earth, published by the Hua Hua Bible Study House in Ningbo in 1856

The Chinese telegraph machine designed by Daniel J. Macgowan in the *Bowu Tongshu* (Philosophy of Natural History) and Telegraphy)

shipping network. In this process, Ningbo was a national pioneer. In 1844, the Englishwoman Mary Ann Aldersey founded China's first school for girls in the city. The Hua Hua Bible Press, operating in Ningbo from 1845 to 1860, was the only press in China at the time with four fonts of Chinese movable type and used advanced electroplating techniques to produce them, paving the way for the replacement of traditional woodblock printing. In 1851, the American missionary Daniel J. Macgowan published the Bowu Tongshu (Philosophy of Natural History and Telegraphy) in Ningbo, the first Chinese-language work on electromagnetism, which also proposed the world's first telegraph code for Chinese characters. In 1854, M. Gowan founded *The Chinese and Foreign Gazette* in Ningbo, making it the second newspaper launched in China after the Opium War—preceded only by The Chinese Serial established in Hong Kong in 1853, and predating The Shanghai Serial founded in 1857. In 1855, Ningbo merchants purchased the Paoushun, the first steamship ever introduced into modern China, a vessel of considerable significance in the nation's modern history. Ningbo Port's transformation into a hub of modern international maritime routes also propelled the modernization of the entire Zhejiang region. This development not only laid a solid foundation for Zhejiang to take a leading position in China's march toward modernity, but also left a valuable cultural legacy that continues to inspire the province's active exploration in contemporary modernization.

30 November 1855

$3228.66

The bill of the Baoshun ship in November 1855

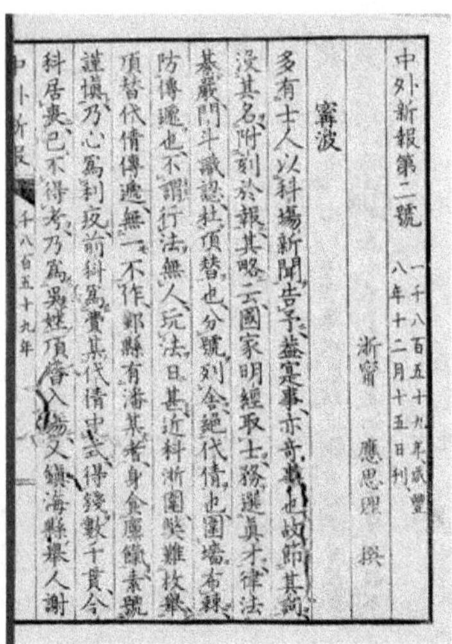
中外新報第二號 一千八百五十九年咸豐八年十二月十五日刊

浙寧 應思理 撰

寧波

多有士人以科場新聞告予蓋寔事亦奇載也故節其詞没其名附刻於報其略云國家明經取士務選真才律法綦嚴門斗識認杜頂替也分號刻坐絕代倩也圍墻布棘防傳遞也不謂行法無人玩法日甚近科浙闈獘難枚舉頂替代倩傳遞無一不作鄞縣有潘某者身食廩餼素號謹愼乃心爲利疚前科爲貴其代倩中式得錢數千貫今科居喪已不得考乃爲易姓頂借入場又鎮海縣舉人謝

中外新報 一千八百五十九年

Chinese and Foreign News (Ningbo Edition), Reproduced in Japana

From the Han and Jin dynasties to the eve of the Opium War, Zhejiang journeyed from the periphery to the center of China's Maritime Silk Road, advancing tortuously through a turbulent world. This history, spanning nearly two millennia, is exceptionally rich, encompassing foreign relations and ocean routes; shipbuilding and navigation; diplomacy and official missions; trade systems and government institutions; private commerce and transnational migration; the movement of goods and people; cultural and technological exchange; and religious beliefs and folk traditions. The totality of the culture formed during this long history can be termed "Zhejiang's Maritime Silk Road Culture." It comprises four main components: Material Culture, including ports, ships, and navigational instruments; Institutional Culture, including government trade regulations, private profit-sharing systems, and crew management practices; Spiritual Culture, including the worship of sea deities, religious faiths, music, and art; and the Human Element, including the merchants, sailors, diplomats, monks, and scholars who were its lifeblood.

The Chinese and foreign figures who braved the stormy seas were the true creators of this culture, and it is they who left its most brilliant legacies. It is with these daring individuals that our story begins.

Part I. The Seafaring People of Zhejiang

The magnificent culture of Zhejiang's Maritime Silk Road was forged over centuries by the collective efforts of its native people, migrants from other Chinese provinces, and foreign visitors. Of these groups, the merchants engaged in international trade were not only the principal pioneers of this sea route but also the primary architects of its vibrant cultural heritage.

Chapter 2. From "Yuezhou Merchants" to Hakata *Gangshou*

2.1 The "Yuezhou Merchants"

Today, vessels that ply the world's oceans, from luxury cruise liners to colossal container ships, are propelled by diesel engines and guided by satellite navigation. But in an age before such technology, how did mariners navigate the vastness of the sea? As early as the Han dynasty (202 BC–AD 220), sailors in East Asian waters had discerned a fundamental pattern in the seasonal winds: powerful southwesterlies dominated the summer, while fierce northeasterlies prevailed in the winter. By harnessing this natural rhythm, they could undertake long voyages, sailing north in the summer and south in the winter to let the wind fill their sails. Whenever possible, they hugged the coastline, using islands, peaks, and river mouths as natural waypoints. Man-made structures like watchtowers and pagodas also served as crucial landmarks, ensuring they did not lose their bearings while allowing for convenient replenishment of fresh water and food from shore.

Before the Tang dynasty, sea routes from Zhejiang traced the coast northward, passing the Shandong Peninsula to reach the western shores of the Korean Peninsula before crossing the Tsushima Strait to Japan. From the late 7th to the late 9th century, the Korean Peninsula was ruled by the kingdom of Silla. Capitalizing on their geographic position, Silla merchants dominated the sea trade between China and Japan, and Zhejiang merchants initially operated under their aegis. The Japanese chronicle *Nihon Kiryaku* records that in the sixth month of AD 819, merchants Zhou Guanghan and Yan Shengze from Yuezhou (modern Shaoxing) of the Great Tang arrived in Japan aboard a Silla vessel. Japanese officials immediately questioned them for news from China. The merchants replied that they were but commoners from remote prefectures and were unaware of the events unfolding in the capital, Chang'an. They had only heard that the military governor Li Shidao had risen in rebellion against the imperial court and that the emperor's armies, despite being sent in force, had failed to quell the uprising, plunging the realm into turmoil. In this way, Zhou Guanghan and his party provided Japanese authorities with the latest intelligence from the mainland. The following year, they departed Japan on a ship carrying an envoy from the Bohai Kingdom.

Zhou Guanghan and Yan Shengze are the earliest Zhejiang merchants known to have appeared on the Maritime Silk Road. The *Nihon Kiryaku* account suggests they were dependent on Silla traders, possessing limited resources and not even their own ships. Their route was not a direct passage from Zhejiang but a coastal journey via the Korean Peninsula. Soon after, however, Chinese merchants grew rapidly in strength, forging their own independent ventures and using their own vessels to trade with Japan. Crucially, they also began to pioneer a new, direct route across the East China Sea from the Zhejiang coast. This breakthrough is exemplified by the merchant Li Churen. In AD 842, after arriving in Japan, he deemed his ship too old for the return journey. He spent three months on the island of Chikanoshima (an ancient name for the Gotō Islands) building a new vessel from local timber. That August, he set sail from Chikanoshima, reaching Wenzhou after a voyage of six days and nights. It was on this new ship that the Japanese monk Eun traveled to China. Eun studied Buddhism in China until the sixth month of AD 847, when he boarded a vessel owned by another Chinese merchant, Zhang Youxin. Departing from the mouth of the Yong River in Mingzhou (modern Ningbo) and aided by strong southwesterly winds, the ship reached Chikanoshima in just three days and nights—a remarkably swift passage for the age of sail. Zhang Youxin was later appointed as an interpreter in the Dazaifu government. In the ninth month of AD 862, he captained a ship from Chikanoshima carrying Japanese monks, including Prince Shinnyo, back to the Ningbo coast. These voyages demonstrate that the direct sea lane between Zhejiang and Japan was becoming firmly established.

When Zhang Youxin's ship arrived in Japan from Ningbo in the sixth month of AD 847, it carried not only Japanese monks like Eun but also a Chinese monk named Yikong. A Chan Buddhist from Yanguan in Zhejiang (part of modern Haining), Yikong had been invited by the Japanese Empress Dowager to propagate the Dharma in her country. Upon his arrival, Yikong received honors from Emperor Ninmyō, and the Empress Dowager installed him as the founding abbot of the newly constructed Danrin-ji Temple in Kyoto. Bolstered by this imperial patronage and his own deep learning, Yikong quickly earned great renown in Japan.

Before his departure from China, Yikong had been close friends with two brothers, Xu Gongzhi and Xu Gongyou. The Xu brothers were likely natives of Suzhou, where they owned property, including houses and land. Xu Gongzhi, the elder, began his career in Wuzhou (modern Jinhua) with the minor official post of Yaqian Sanjiang (a junior local officer), a position he later held in Suzhou as well. His younger brother, Xu Gongyou, was a merchant engaged in the Sino-Japanese trade. A Japanese collection, the Kōya Zappitsushū, preserves eight of their letters: three from Xu Gongzhi and five from Xu Gongyou, all addressed to Yikong. The collection also contains a letter from Xu Gongyou to his nephew Hu Po, Xu Gongzhi's son.

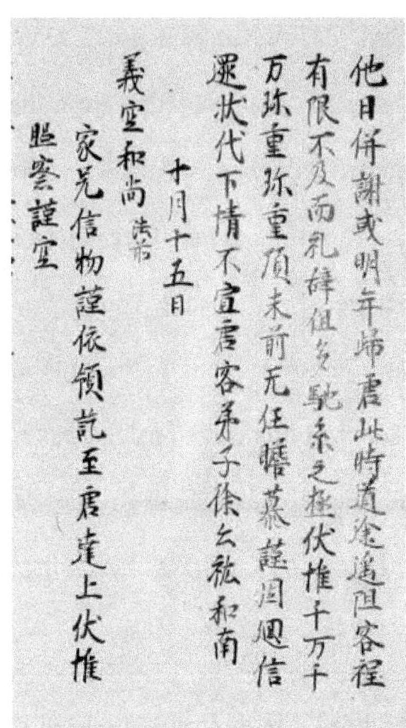

他日併謝或明年歸唐此時道途遙阻客程
有限不及面礼辞但多馳系之極伏惟千万千
万珍重珍重履末前无任攀慕謹因廻信
還狀代下情不宣唐客弟子徐公祐和南
十月十五日
義空和尚 法前
家兄信物謹依領訖至唐達上伏惟
照察謹空

Partial transcription of Xu Gongyou's correspondence with Yikong, preserved in Japan

The letters in the Kōya Zappitsushū reveal that Yikong maintained close contact with the Xu brothers after arriving in Japan. Although only a minor official in the Tang administration, Xu Gongzhi had cultivated an extensive network of officials and monks. His brother Xu Gongyou, a private merchant, relied on this connection for crucial support in his trade with Japan. The brothers were a classic example of the "official-merchant collaboration" (guanshang jiehe) that was widespread at the time. Xu Gongyou plied the route between China and Japan, trading goods and relaying information. On his brother's behalf, he delivered gifts of Zhejiang tea, silk, and porcelain to Yikong. Xu Gongzhi even sent his own son, Hu Po, to Japan to serve as Yikong's attendant. One of Xu Gongyou's voyages to Japan departed from Ningbo in the summer of AD 852. According to his own account, he set sail on the fifth day of the sixth lunar month and reached Dazaifu in Kyushu on the twenty-second, a seventeen-day journey. He carried not only letters and gifts for Yikong but also clothing and other necessities for his nephew, Hu Po. At the time, Japanese regulations required that all imported Chinese goods first be offered to government officials for priority purchase before any private commerce could occur. Furthermore, Chinese merchants were confined to the Kōrokan, a state-run guesthouse in Dazaifu for foreign dignitaries, and were forbidden from trading freely elsewhere. In his letter to Yikong, Xu Gongyou expressed his hope of using connections to sell goods in the capital, Kyoto, where he could fetch higher profits. In essence, he was seeking to bypass Japan's official trade controls and engage in private, unregulated commerce. This reveals that Tang merchants trading with Japan possessed a spirit of enterprise that extended beyond their daring sea voyages to the bold pursuit of new markets abroad.

To expand their network, the Xu brothers also actively cultivated relationships with Japanese monks. In the eighth month of AD 853, the monk Enchin sailed from Chikanoshima to Fuzhou aboard a Tang merchant vessel, from where he traveled onward to Wenzhou, Taizhou, Mount Tiantai, and

Yuezhou (Shaoxing). In AD 855, while journeying from Yuezhou to the Tang capital of Chang'an, Enchin fell ill in Suzhou and was taken in by Xu Gongzhi to recuperate. The following year, upon his return from Chang'an and Luoyang, Enchin once again stayed at Xu Gongzhi's home—a clear testament to the deep trust he placed in his host.

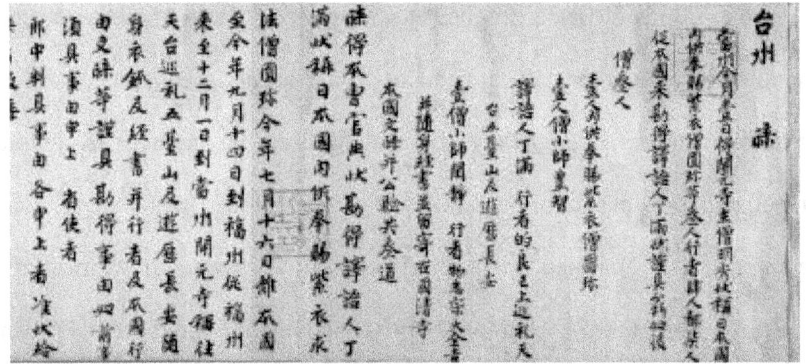

Partial Transit Pass Issued to Japanese Monk Enchin in Taizhou in AD 853

In the early sixth month of AD 858, Enchin departed China from Taizhou aboard a vessel belonging to Li Yanxiao, a merchant from the Bohai Kingdom. Traveling with him were several other Chinese merchants, including two from Zhejiang: Li Da and Zhan Jingquan. According to Japanese historical sources, Li Da's family was originally from Hebei, though he himself was a native of Yongkang in Wuzhou (modern Jinhua). Zhan Jingquan was also from Wuzhou, but because his ancestral home was in Yuezhou, he was sometimes identified as a "Yuezhou merchant." The party, including Enchin, Li Da, and Zhan Jingquan, arrived in Japan later that month.

After returning to Japan, Enchin devoted himself to spreading the teachings of the Tiantai school, and in AD 868, he was appointed its fifth patriarch in Japan. He passed away in AD 891, and in AD 927, the emperor posthumously granted him the title Chishō Daishi ("Great Master of Wisdom and Certification"). Throughout his life, Enchin maintained his connection with Chinese merchants like Li Da and Zhan Jingquan. To this day, Enjō-ji Temple (also known as Mii-dera) in Ōtsu, Shiga Prefecture—the head temple of the Jimon school of Tendai Buddhism—preserves correspondence and poetic exchanges between the three men. One winter, upon arriving in Japan, Li Da promptly wrote to Enchin to pay his respects and sent him gifts, including a pair of socks.

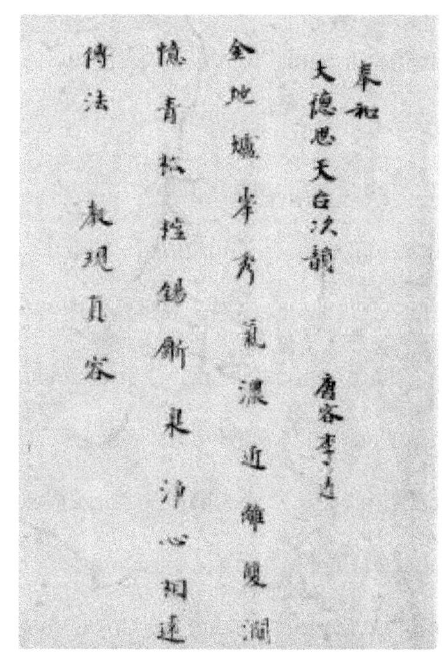

Poetic Exchange by Li Da, Preserved at Japan's Onjō-ji Temple

During his five years in China, apart from travels to Chang'an, Enchin resided primarily on Mount Tiantai, leaving him with a deep affection for the place. After returning to Japan, he often thought of the mountain and composed poetry in its honor. Li Da, a merchant who had grown up nearby, wrote a poem in response. While Enchin's original work is lost, Li Da's poem is preserved at Enjō-ji:

The air of Jindi and Lufeng is rich and sublime;

Leaving the Twin Streams, I long for the green pines.

Striking the spring with a staff, the pure mind appears;

Spreading the Dharma afar, the true form is revealed.

In the poem, "Jindi" (Golden Ground) refers to Jindi Ridge, also called Folong Peak, the site of the stupa containing the remains of Master Zhiyi (AD 538–597), the de facto founder of the Tiantai school. "Lufeng" (Furnace Peak) is Incense Burner Peak, near the Stone Bridge Waterfall on Mount Tiantai. "Twin Streams" alludes to the famous landscape "Twin Streams Meandering" outside Guoqing Temple. According to legend, when Guoqing Temple was first constructed, it was far from any water source, and the monks faced great hardship. A high monk named Puming struck a solid rock with his tin staff, declaring, "How joyous it would be if a spring were to flow from this stone!" A few days later, water miraculously gushed forth, creating the site known as the "Staff-Tapped Spring" (Xizhang Quan). Li Da's line, "Striking the spring with a staff, the pure mind appears," alludes to this very legend. The final line, "Spreading the Dharma afar, the true form is revealed," draws a parallel between Enchin and the miraculous Puming, praising the Japanese monk for bringing the true teachings to his homeland.

More is known about Zhan Jingquan than about Li Da. Records show that by the ninth month of AD 856, Zhan and another "Yuezhou merchant," Liu Shixian, were already conducting business in Japan. Upon returning to China after that trip, Zhan and his party visited Mount Tiantai, where Enchin was overseeing the reconstruction of buildings at Guoqing Temple destroyed during the Huichang Persecution of Buddhism (AD 841–845). Zhan and his fellow merchants donated 4,000 wen in cash to construct three new rooms for the monastery, intended primarily to house visiting monks from abroad who came to study the Dharma. In the sixth month of AD 858, Zhan Jingquan and Li Da traveled with Enchin from Taizhou to Japan. The Chinese merchants took up lodging at the Kōrokan in Dazaifu, while Enchin stayed at the

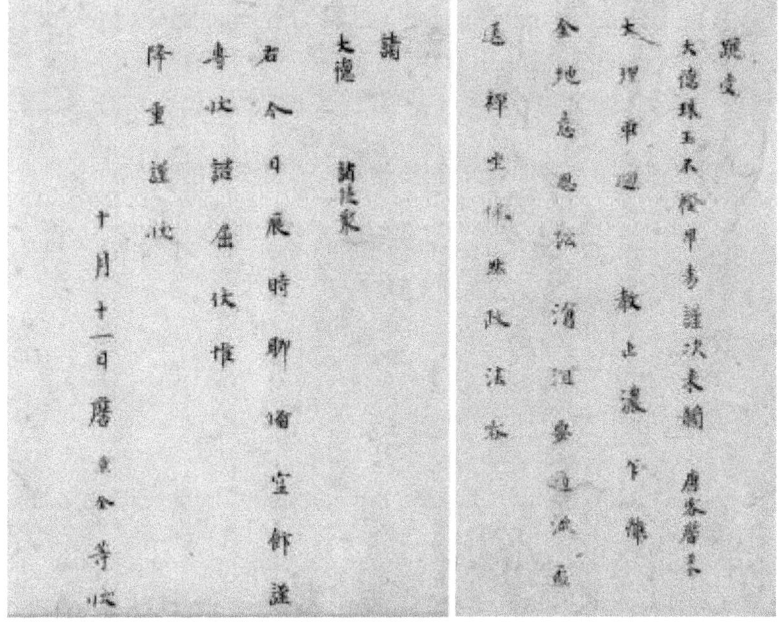

Invitation from Zhan Jingquan to Enchin

Poetic Exchange by Zhan Jingquan, Preserved at Onjō-ji Temple, Japan nearby Shiroyama Shitennō-in. Over the next few months, they interacted frequently. Enjō-ji Temple preserves an invitation card from Zhan to Enchin, dated to the eleventh day of the tenth month, which reads: "To the Greatly Virtuous Master and all your disciples: This day, at the hour of chen (7–9 a.m.), a humble meal has been prepared. This note is sent to respectfully invite you. We sincerely hope for the honor of your presence. Respectfully submitted." The term "humble meal" (kongfan, lit. "empty meal") was a conventional expression of modesty. The invitation, extended by Zhan to host Enchin and his disciples for breakfast, shows that the two groups frequently dined together, strengthening their social bonds.

Enjō-ji also holds two poems by Zhan Jingquan under the title, "Humbly Receiving the Master's Pearls of Jade, I Dare to Follow Your Rhyme." The first reads:

The great chariot of doctrine turns, its teachings profound;

Having just left the Golden Ground, my thoughts are at ease.

Across the vast ocean, you were sent by a floating cup;

In meditation, your form embodies the True Law.

Here, the "great chariot" (daliche) is a metaphor for the teachings of the Tiantai school. "Golden Ground" (jindi) again refers to Mount Tiantai. The "floating cup" alludes to the legend of the Jin dynasty monk Beidu, who could cross water in a wooden cup; the line signifies Enchin's journey across the sea to transmit the Tiantai teachings to Japan. "True Law" (zhengfa) refers to the orthodox Dharma, specifically that of the Tiantai school. The poem thus captures both Enchin's nostalgia for Mount Tiantai and his profound mission in Japan.

Zhan Jingquan's second responding poem reads:

The ultimate principle of the One Vehicle leaves no trace;

Resting in contemplation, one leans quietly by a pine.

The Three Realms are forever cleared of extraneous thought;

With single-minded sincerity, one bows to Śākyamuni's image.

The "One Vehicle" (yisheng) refers to the supreme doctrine of the Tiantai school. "Contemplation" (guanxin) is a key Tiantai term for the practice of introspection to realize the Dharma. The "Three Realms" (sanjie)—of desire, form, and formlessness—constitute the endless cycle of suffering (samsara), which Buddhism seeks to transcend. The character ji (几) refers to the Buddhist concept of genji, or one's innate spiritual capacity to receive the teachings. The poem's message is that only through devotion to the Tiantai path can one achieve the ultimate goal of liberation from the Three Realms.

Since all three poems by Li Da and Zhan Jingquan use the same rhyme words, sōng (pine) and róng (form), they were almost certainly composed at the same time in response to a single poem by Enchin. This shared rhyme scheme allows us to reconstruct the likely structure of Enchin's lost original. More importantly, these poems demonstrate their authors' profound literary skill and deep understanding of Buddhist doctrine, revealing the high level of cultural refinement among the Zhejiang merchants engaged in the Japan trade.

While in China, Enchin had visited the eminent monk Zhihuilun at Daxingshan Temple in the capital, Chang'an. After returning to Japan, he maintained his correspondence with Zhihuilun through the Zhejiang merchants. In AD 862, Zhan Jingquan served as a courier, bringing a collection of gifts from Zhihuilun to Enchin. The delivery included eight newly translated Buddhist sutras and portraits of the three great esoteric masters: Śubhakarasiṃha, Vajrabodhi, and Amoghavajra. The next year, Enchin entrusted Zhan with a letter of thanks for Zhihuilun. However, upon his next arrival in Japan in AD 864, Zhan reported that he had been unable to deliver the letter, as unrest in northern China had made the roads to Chang'an impassable.

Kaiyuan Temple in Taizhou was a renowned monastery during the Tang dynasty. Enchin not only resided there but also forged deep friendships with its monks, including Changya, Lüqiu, and Jigao. When it was time for Enchin to return to Japan, Changya personally escorted him as far as Haimen. Located at the mouth of the Jiaojiang River, Haimen was the historic maritime gateway of Taizhou and is now a subdistrict of the city. Even after returning to Japan, Enchin's correspondence with Changya and the other monks continued. One summer, he entrusted Zhan Jingquan with four catties of mercury to deliver to Changya. In his return letter, Changya noted that he had shared the mercury with Jigao and other monks but also relayed the sad news of Lüqiu's passing. He asked Zhan to carry back gifts for Enchin: local tea from Mount Tiantai and some traditional Chinese medicines. Changya expressed his great joy (xīnqìng zhī zhì, "rejoicing to the utmost") that the Japanese imperial court held Buddhism in high esteem. He ended on a poignant note, writing that due to his advanced age, he did not expect they would meet again and urged Enchin to "take the greatest care" (qiānwàn bǎozhòng). This very letter, carried by Zhan Jingquan, is still preserved today at Enjō-ji Temple.

Enchin also maintained close ties with a monk from Wenzhou named Deyuan. According to tradition, Empress Wu Zetian (r. AD 690–705) had once commissioned four hundred silk paintings depicting the Western Pure Land. One of these enormous works, measuring over seven meters long and nearly five meters wide, had somehow come into Deyuan's possession. In AD 867, Deyuan entrusted this priceless painting to Zhan Jingquan to be delivered to Enchin in Japan as a gift. Zhan himself presented Enchin with two additional Buddhist paintings, which depicted sages such as Śākyamuni, Mahākāśyapa, and Huineng.

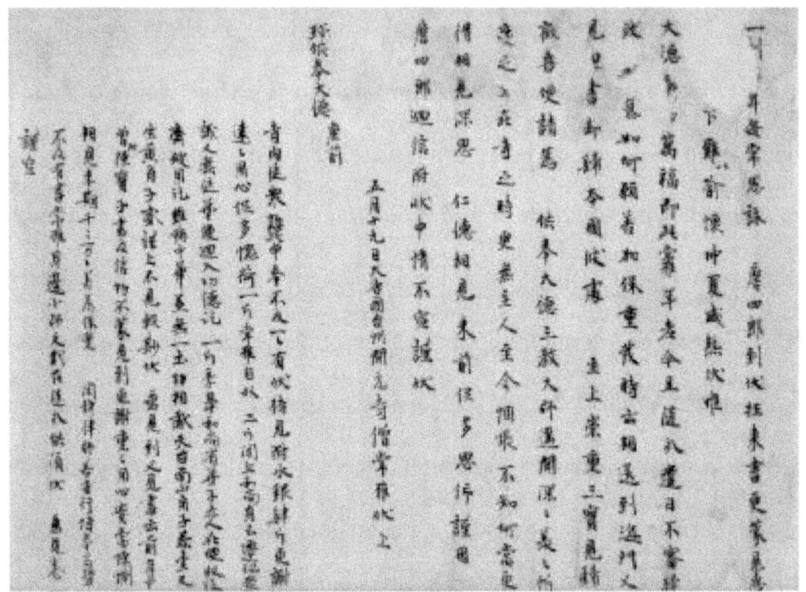

Letter from Chang Ya to Enchin

In AD 877, the merchants Li Da, Zhan Jingquan, and Li Yanxiao set sail from the Zhejiang coast for Japan. They were joined on their ship by the Japanese monks Enzai and Chison, who were returning from Tang China. Tragically, their vessel was caught in a storm, and Zhan Jingquan, Li Yanxiao, and Enzai all drowned. Li Da and Chison were among the survivors who managed to reach Japan.

Li Da, though a survivor, was not deterred from his life at sea and continued to trade between China and Japan. In AD 881, he arrived in Japan on a ship belonging to Zhang Meng, bringing with him over 120 volumes of the Buddhist Canon (Dàzàngjīng) for Enchin. When Li Da prepared for his return voyage in AD 882, Enchin entrusted him with a letter for Zhihuilun. In it,

Enchin explained that the Japanese copy of the Commentary on the Mahāvairocana Sūtra was missing sections. He recalled seeing a complete version at Daxingshan Temple in Chang'an during his time there and requested that the missing parts be transcribed and sent to him, enclosing fifty sha-kin (units) of gold dust to cover the costs. Enchin even dispatched his own disciple, Sanhui, to accompany Li Da on the mission. The letter, however, would never reach its destination; Zhihuilun had passed away in AD 876. Whether Li Da ever made it back to China remains unknown, as he vanishes from the historical records of both nations after this voyage.

2.2 The *Gangshou* of Hakata

In AD 882, the year Li Da departed Japan, the Tang Dynasty was already faltering, its authority crumbling under the violent onslaught of the Huang Chao Rebellion. Amid this era of rising warlords, Qian Liu, a native of Lin'an in Zhejiang who had once made his living in the illicit salt trade, seized the opportunity to join the military. With exceptional strategic acumen, he repeatedly vanquished rivals and rapidly consolidated his power. When the Tang finally collapsed in AD 907, China splintered into the turbulent Five Dynasties and Ten Kingdoms period. It was in this context that Qian Liu founded the Wuyue Kingdom (AD 907–978), which came to govern Zhejiang and the surrounding region.

Geographically confined to China's southeastern coast and facing a scarcity of arable land, the rulers of the Wuyue Kingdom recognized that state revenue depended on the sea. They therefore adopted a deliberate policy of promoting maritime commerce, with Japan as their most crucial trading partner. The Wuyue court actively sought official diplomatic relations, but its enthusiasm was not reciprocated. Having grown wary of continental instability, the Japanese court had already suspended its official embassies to Tang China (the kentōshi, 遣唐使) and met Wuyue's overtures with polite indifference. This diplomatic impasse left private merchants to sustain the vital economic and cultural links between the two realms. Consequently, Japanese archives preserve many accounts of Wuyue merchants making the journey to Japan, with figures like Jiang Chengxun, Jiang Gun, and Sheng Deyan being among the most prominent.

In AD 935, Jiang Chengxun journeyed to Japan to trade, presenting several sheep to officials in what is the earliest known record of a Wuyue merchant arriving on Japanese shores. He would go on to make the voyage almost annually. These merchants functioned as more than mere traders; they became operators of an essential para-diplomatic channel, carrying official correspondence between the two courts. A classic example occurred in AD 947, when Jiang Gun arrived bearing a formal letter from the King of Wuyue. The powerful Japanese statesman Fujiwara no Saneyori penned a beautiful and diplomatically nuanced reply, conveying distant admiration without political commitment: "Our lives are parted by the sea, by endless clouds and waves. / Flying south or north, the autumn goose cannot carry our greetings. / As the moon rises in the east and sets in the west, / we can only send our longing gaze with its light." Along with the letter, Fujiwara entrusted Jiang Gun with 200 taels of gold dust as a return gift for the king.

In AD 960, Zhao Kuangyin established the Song Dynasty, and by AD 978, the Wuyue Kingdom had peacefully submitted to its authority, integrating Zhejiang into the new empire. From its outset, the Song court encouraged private maritime commerce. This stood in stark contrast to the Japanese government, which maintained tight restrictions on foreign trade, inadvertently ceding a near-total monopoly over the profitable sea routes to Chinese merchants. The historical record bears this out: over the 160 years of the Northern

Song (960–1127), more than 70 merchant voyages between China and Japan can be confirmed, yet not a single one can be identified as a Japanese vessel. During this period, Taizhou was a key gateway for this trade, and its merchants were a formidable force. In AD 983, the Japanese monk Chōnen and his companions arrived in Taizhou aboard a ship belonging to the merchants Chen Renshuang and Xu Renman. Three years later, in AD 986, Chōnen's party returned to Japan from the same port on a vessel owned by Zheng Rende, a merchant from Ninghai County (now part of Ningbo), carrying with them a precious statue of Shakyamuni Buddha.

Among the Zhejiang merchants of the early Northern Song, the most renowned were Zhou Wenyu and his son, Zhou Liangshi, who hailed from Dong'ao in Ninghai County. Nestled north of the Qingxi River, Dong'ao was a strategic ancient port; ships could sail into Sanmen Bay and then across the open sea to Japan. An overland route also connected the port westward to the sacred Buddhist site of Mount Tiantai. This region was already a hub of international commerce. As early as the Five Dynasties period, merchants from the Silla Kingdom had plied the Maritime Silk Road to Sanmen Bay, leaving a lasting imprint on the local geography with place names like Xinluo'ao Mountain and Xinluofang. Inspired by the success of these Korean pioneers, local merchants from communities around Sanmen Bay began to venture into the lucrative Japan trade themselves.

The remarkable story of Zhou Wenyu and Zhou Liangshi is preserved in a rich tapestry of cross-cultural sources, from Chinese local histories and family genealogies to famed Japanese court diaries like the *Midō Kanpakuki* and *Shōyūki*. These accounts reveal that Zhou Wenyu was trading in Japan well before 1012. He journeyed frequently between Zhejiang and Japan, eventually taking a Japanese wife and fathering a son, Zhou Liangshi. This son's life epitomized the transnational identity of the merchant class: as a boy, he was sent back to his ancestral home in Dong'ao for a classical Chinese education; upon reaching adulthood, he joined his father's enterprise, plying the sea routes between his two homelands. In 1026, he attempted to leverage this unique background, presenting himself in Mingzhou (Ningbo) as a "Tribute Envoy from Dazaifu, Japan." He hoped to travel to the Song capital of Bianjing, but the Mingzhou authorities refused his request, leaving him in limbo—a man of two worlds, yet not fully an official representative of either.

Around 1027, Zhou Liangshi married Lady Shi, a woman from a prominent Ningbo family. The following year, he and his father embarked on another voyage to Japan and subsequently vanished from the historical record. After his departure, Lady Shi gave birth to their son, Zhou Bian. Widowed and devoted, she poured all her energy into the boy's upbringing, and her efforts yielded extraordinary results. Zhou Bian studied diligently and became the first person from Ninghai County to achieve the rank of jinshi (进士), the highest degree awarded in the imperial examinations. This marked the culmination of a deliberate family strategy: converting commercial wealth, earned through perilous sea voyages, into the stable and respected cultural capital of a scholar-official lineage. By successfully transitioning from the merchant class (shang) to the scholar-gentry (shi), the Zhou clan became a distinguished line of imperial officials, an object of widespread admiration.

From the Tang Dynasty to the Northern Song, generations of Zhejiang merchants braved the "perils of the whale-tossed waves" to trade with Japan. Yet their ambition was met with a stringent and restrictive policy from the Japanese government, which had several key tenets. First, Japanese subjects were forbidden from trading in China. Second, a "yearly restriction" system (nenki-sei) was enforced, permitting Chinese vessels to visit only every few years. Third, upon arrival, merchants were confined to the official guesthouse, the Kōrokan, in Dazaifu. Finally, they were required to depart Japan after concluding their business and were forbidden from taking up long-term residence. Zhou Liangshi's personal story poignantly illustrates the rigidity of these rules. Despite his Japanese mother and his repeated offerings of lavish gifts to nobles, his heartfelt pleas to remain in Japan to care for his aging mother were consistently denied.

In the decades after Zhou Liangshi's time, the economic imperatives of the Japanese state began to shift. Seeking to increase fiscal revenue, the government gradually relaxed its restrictions, permitting Chinese merchants to establish a permanent settlement in Hakata. By around 1100, a distinct Chinese quarter known as the Tōbō ("Tang Quarters") had taken shape. Archaeological surveys place this district northwest of modern JR Hakata Station, an area now occupied by landmarks such as Shōfuku-ji, Jōten-ji, and Kushida Shrine. In ancient times, this location was prime real estate, directly adjacent to the harbor. The site where Shōfuku-ji now stands, for instance, was once known as the "Hundred Halls of the Song People" (Songren Baidang), a residential zone for merchants that eventually became a burial ground after falling into disuse. In 1195, the Japanese monk Eisai founded Shōfuku-ji temple upon these ruins. Across the former Tōbō district, excavations have unearthed a wealth of Chinese ceramics. Crucially, some pieces are inscribed on their base with Chinese surnames followed by the character gāng. This is an abbreviation for gāngshǒu , the title for a merchant-captain or the leader of a trading fleet. These artifacts confirm that the goods were transported by Chinese ships under the command of men like "Zhang Gang" and "Ding Gang." While their specific regional origins are uncertain, definitive proof that Hakata's Chinese residents traded with Zhejiang comes from three remarkable stone steles discovered in Ningbo.

The discovery of these three steles is owed to the foresight of Ma Lian, a distinguished scholar from Ningbo. Known as the youngest of the "Five Mas of Peking University," Ma was a leading expert on Ming and Qing literature. Around 1930, while Ningbo was demolishing its ancient city walls to widen roads, a vast collection of inscribed bricks and stones was uncovered. Ma Lian, who was in the city at the time, immediately grasped the immense historical value of the find and personally collected over a thousand of these artifacts. Among them were the three Southern Song steles that provide a direct link to the Hakata community. In 1933, Ma Lian donated his entire collection to Ningbo's famed Tianyi Pavilion library. While most of the pieces were placed in a specially constructed gallery, the three crucial steles were mortared into the wall of an inner chamber. There they remained in obscurity for decades, their crudely carved, slanted script deterring close inspection. It was not until the 1980s that the Ningbo scholar Lin Shimin and his colleagues undertook a comprehensive study, revealing their significance and sparking intense interest from scholars worldwide. Today, these invaluable artifacts are preserved in the Ningbo Museum.

The first stele measures 36 by 38 cm. Framed by a simple border and adorned with a five-petaled lotus at its base, its inscription of roughly 66 characters in handwritten script reads: "Ding Yuan, a disciple residing in Hakata Port, Dazaifu, Japan, donates his personal funds of ten strings of cash to pave one zhàng of road. This merit is dedicated to the deities of the three realms, the enlightened sages of the ten directions, the ancestors of my house, my natal star deities, my living family, and all beings of the four dharma realms, that all may together realize the fruit of Buddhahood. Fourth month, third year of the Qiandao era (1167)."

Stele of Ding Yuan, an Overseas Chinese in Japan, Discovered in Ningbo

The second stele, similar in form and measuring 47 by 30 cm, is inscribed with 49 characters: “Zhang Ning, a disciple residing in Dazaifu, Japan, donates his personal funds to pave one zhàng of road. This merit is dedicated to the deities of the three realms, the household gods and ancestral incense, the departed ancestors of generations past, my natal star deities, and all other divinities. Fourth month, third year of the Qiandao era (1167).”

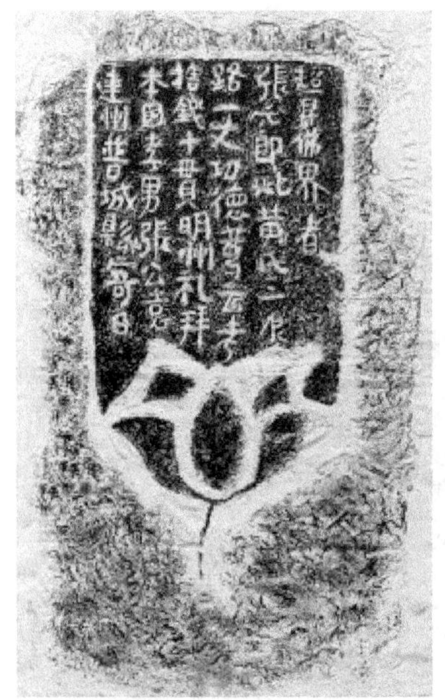

Stele of Zhang Gongyi, an Overseas Chinese in Japan, Discovered in Ningbo

Stele of Zhang Ning, an Overseas Chinese in Japan, Discovered in Ningbo

The third stele, the largest at 89 by 36 cm and similar in style, is inscribed with 43 characters: “Zhang Gongyi, a filial son from Pucheng County, Jianzhou, temporarily residing in Japan, donates ten strings of cash for one zhàng of the Worship Road in Mingzhou. This merit is dedicated to my deceased father, Zhang Liulang, and my deceased mother, Lady Huang Sanniang, that they may ascend to the realm of the Buddha."

All three steles are carved from a quartz sandstone common to the Ningbo region. Their shared style and script suggest they were crafted by the same artisan in the fourth lunar month of 1167, a time when the monsoon winds would have brought fleets of merchant ships from Japan and Goryeo to the port. The donors—Ding Yuan, Zhang Ning, and Zhang Gongyi—were clearly overseas Chinese living in Hakata. The inscriptions explicitly state they "resided" or were "temporarily staying" in Japan, and one even specifies "Hakata Port." Zhang Gongyi identifies his origin as Pucheng County, Jianzhou, indicating he and likely his companions were from Fujian. Their use of the Song Dynasty reign name further affirms their cultural identity. These steles offer a rare glimpse into the lives of non-elite members of the Hakata diaspora. The modest donations (ten strings of cash each) and a scribal error (miswriting 浦城 Pǔchéng as 普城 Pǔchéng) suggest the men were not wealthy merchant princes but ordinary sailors or traders. They came to Mingzhou for business, not to resettle.

Learning that a local temple was fundraising to repair its "Worship Road," these three Fujianese expatriates made their contributions. Their dedications reflect the syncretic folk religion of China's southeastern coast, blending appeals to Buddhist figures, Daoist deities, and ancestral spirits. The carved lotus, a potent Buddhist symbol, signifies their aspiration for the Western Paradise. These stones are thus powerful testaments that even working-class members of the community, living far from home, faithfully maintained the complex spiritual and filial traditions of their native land.

While Ding Yuan and his companions were Fujianese, it is certain that Zhejiang natives also played a pivotal role in the Hakata community. Indeed, the most prominent Chinese leader in Hakata during the 13th century was a man from Zhejiang: Xie Guoming.

About a kilometer southeast of Shōfuku-ji, near modern Hakata Station, lies a small garden dominated by a magnificent camphor tree. A multilingual sign at its entrance explains the site's significance: "The Tomb of Xie Guoming. Xie Guoming, a merchant from Song Dynasty China, lived in Hakata during the Kamakura period (1185–1333). He was a leader of the Japan-Song trade, a devout Buddhist who gene rously funded the founding of Jōten-ji temple by National Teacher Shōichi, a benefactor to the poor, and a promoter of acupuncture. Upon his death, he was buried here. The camphor tree planted by his grave is said to have grown so large that it enveloped the tomb, earning him the affectionate title, 'Lord Great Camphor' (Ōgusu-sama)."

Within the garden, beside the great tree, stands a tall stone monument inscribed with "The Epitaph of Xie Guoming." The text reads as follows:

Tomb of Xie Guoming in Hakata

This is the burial place of Xie Guoming, a native of Lin'an Prefecture of the Song Dynasty. He settled in our country, came to Hakata, and chose a residence beside the Kushida Shrine. By profession, Xie Guoming was a merchant-captain (*gangshou*), and he deeply revered the Buddhist path. Wishing to establish a Zen temple, he petitioned the Dazaifu official Fujiwara no Sukeyori for land and was granted a sacred site east of the settlement. During the Ninji era (1240–1243) of Emperor Shijō, National Teacher Shōichi returned from Song China. Overjoyed, Xie Guoming cleared the thorns and founded Jōten-ji monastery, inviting the National Teacher to be its founding abbot. It was decreed an imperial prayer hall for the peace of the nation. For more than five hundred years, its dharma lineage has flourished, all thanks to the initial efforts of Xie Guoming. He was devoted to the Way, tirelessly seeking the Teacher's guidance day and night and plumbing the profoundest depths of Zen. He was also a charitable man upon whom many of the village poor depended for sustenance. Skilled in acupuncture and medicine, he healed many from their illnesses; some of his remedies survive today. He passed away on the seventh day of the tenth month of the third year of the Kōan era (1280) and was buried east of the temple beneath a five-tiered stone stupa. A camphor sapling was planted at his side. Over the centuries, its branches grew lush and its roots coiled, enveloping the tomb until its exact location was hidden. Farmers rested in its shade, yet people who remembered his virtue still came to offer incense and flowers. It is said that prayers made here are answered. During the Kanpō era (1741–1744), the government designated a fifty-pace plot of land around the tree as Xie Guoming's grave site. Now, in the spring of the Tenpō era (1833), having petitioned the authorities, we have joined together to erect this stone monument, that his deeds may never be forgotten. We look up to his sincerity, which was dedicated to the Three Jewels above and earned the trust of the people below, protecting this sacred ground and the Great Dharma forever. His merit is worthy of being carved in stone; his virtue is worthy of this memorial.

The Eulogy Reads:

Upon a single blade of grass, a sublime temple stands. / Toppling the immortal's stove, swallowing the dragon's abyss. / Here

> and everywhere, his virtue is complete. / A merchant-captain in station, he met the National Teacher in Zen. / The crow flies, the rabbit runs; five hundred years have passed. / From a place of no-merit, the fruit of his deeds fills the great chiliocosm. In the spring of the Tenpō year of 1833, composed and inscribed with respect by Enshō Daikan, Dharma-transmitting monk of the imperially-bestowed Jōten Zen Temple in Chikuzen Province.

This epitaph was composed in the spring of 1833 by Enshō Daikan, abbot of Hakata's Jōten-ji, to memorialize Xie Guoming. It identifies him as a merchant from Lin'an (Hangzhou) of the Song Dynasty. However, the epitaph's date for his death (1280) is incorrect. A document from the Munakata Grand Shrine in Fukuoka confirms that Xie had already passed away by 1253, the year his wife took vows as a Buddhist nun. Therefore, the modern scholarly consensus is that Xie Guoming was a prominent merchant-captain (*gangshou*) from Hangzhou who was active primarily between 1233 and 1253.

The "National Teacher Shōichi" in the epitaph is the posthumous title of the Japanese monk Enni Ben'en (1202–1280). Arriving in Hakata in 1232, Enni faced persecution from rival Buddhist sects and found himself in peril. At this critical juncture, Xie Guoming extended a hand, offering Enni refuge in his own home. In 1235, Enni journeyed to China, eventually reaching Jingshan Wanshou Temple in Hangzhou. At the time, Jingshan was the most prestigious monastery of the "Five Mountains and Ten Temples" network, and its abbot, Wuzhun Shifan (1179–1249), was considered the greatest Zen master of his age. Enni studied devotedly under Wuzhun and won his master's deep esteem. In May 1241, Enni began his return journey from Ningbo, but his ship was blown off course to the Korean coast, and he did not reach Hakata until October. There, Xie Guoming again welcomed him warmly. The following year, with Xie's immense financial support, Jōten-ji temple was built, and Enni was installed as its founding abbot.

Once installed as abbot, Enni wrote to his master Wuzhun Shifan in Hangzhou, requesting calligraphic inscriptions for the new temple. Wuzhun was delighted and brushed numerous plaques, many of which survive today. In his affectionate reply, Wuzhun wrote, "I have written all the characters you asked for, but I fear your temple may be too grand and my calligraphy too small. I wonder if they will be suitable? If not, send word and I shall write them again." This letter, which reveals the deep bond between master and disciple, is now a treasured artifact in Tokyo's Hatakeyama Memorial Museum. Critically, the correspondence and the transport of these precious artworks

Portrait of Enni. Preserved in Japan

across the sea were made possible by Xie Guoming. His commercial enterprise provided the physical infrastructure for this profound cultural and religious exchange.

The partnership was tested in 1242 when a disastrous fire swept through Jingshan Temple. Upon hearing the news, Enni and Xie Guoming were deeply distressed. Xie immediately took action, financing the purchase of over a thousand planks of high-quality Japanese timber and dispatching them on several ships for the temple's reconstruction. In a 1243 letter of thanks to Enni, Wuzhun Shifan described the perilous journey: the fleet suffered heavy losses in severe storms, but one vessel with over 500 planks made it to Huating (near modern Shanghai) and another with over 300 arrived in Qingyuan (Ningbo). Wuzhun specifically asked Enni to convey his profound gratitude to "Envoy Xie" (Xie gāngshǐ), a title of respect for Xie Guoming.

This original letter from Wuzhun is now a National Treasure of Japan, housed in the Tokyo National Museum and known as the Itawatashi Bokuseki (板渡墨迹), or the "Plank-Crossing Calligraphy." It serves as powerful evi-

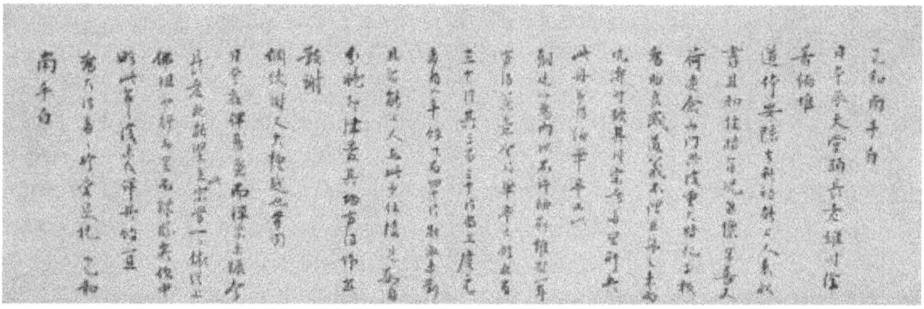

Itawatashi Bokuseki , Wuzhun

dence of Xie Guoming's immense wealth, his formidable logistical capabilities in organizing transoceanic shipping, and his enduring affection for his homeland of Zhejiang.

Deshi Bokuseki

Further evidence of this relationship exists in the Deshi Bokuseki (德敷墨迹), a letter to Enni from the monk Deshi, now also in the Tokyo National Museum. Deshi was the chief administrator (dujiansi) of Jingshan Temple, responsible for its finances. In his letter, he too refers to Xie Guoming as "Envoy Xie," thanking him for the timber donation while gently hinting at the need for more. The letter also confirms that a regular commercial trading relationship existed between Jingshan Temple and Xie's enterprise—a clear example of the symbiotic link between faith and commerce.

In Fukuoka, Xie Guoming's historical importance has evolved into legend. One popular tale recounts a year when Hakata was ravaged by famine and plague. On New Year's Eve, as the impoverished and ailing populace despaired, Xie organized a feast at Jōten-ji, serving free soba noodles so that everyone could enter the new year with a full stomach and a joyful heart. This act is said to have given rise to the tradition of eating toshikoshi soba ("year-crossing noodles") to ensure good fortune, a custom that eventually spread throughout Japan. Local folklore also credits Xie with introducing scissors from China, consequently known as "Tō-basami" ("Tang scissors"). This introduction sparked a local craft tradition, and Hakata scissors remain a designated folk craft specialty of Fukuoka to this day.

Today, the people of Fukuoka consider Xie Guoming one of the three great figures in their city's history. His legacy is immortalized in art and worship. A wooden statue of him from the Edo period (1603–1868) is enshrined in the Founder's Hall at Jōten-ji. The Fukuoka City Museum holds an Edo-period portrait, inscribed with a verse of praise:

Above Reisen Port, a great Zen forest thrives;

Built from nothing, its flourishing is the patron's merit.

I recall the jade tree born of the Xie family,

Its fragrance forever perfuming the wind in ten thousand pines.

In the poem, "Reisen Port" is another name for Hakata, and the "patron" (dānapati) refers to Xie Guoming.

While the original camphor tree at his tomb has long since passed, replaced by a successor, the memory of Xie Guoming is kept alive by more than wood and stone. For over 700 years, an unbroken tradition has honored his memory: the "Memorial Ceremony to Manifest the Virtue of Xie

Guoming," popularly known as the "Lord Great Camphor Thousand Lantern Festival" (Ōgusu-sama Sentōmyō). As Fukuoka's oldest festival, it is held annually at Jōten-ji on the evening of August 21. Participants light thousands of lanterns, chant Buddhist sutras, and offer soba noodles, expressing enduring gratitude for the merchant's benevolence. This process represents the ultimate cultural integration, transforming a foreign merchant into a revered local hero whose legacy is woven into the city's identity.

Xie Guoming, a merchant from Hangzhou, transcended his origins through acts of profound generosity, earning the lasting gratitude of the Japanese people. The seven-century-old festival held in his honor is more than a local curiosity; it is a powerful, living testament to the deep and positive contributions made by the merchants of Zhejiang's Maritime Silk Road to the culture and history of Japan.

Chapter 3. Spreading the Buddhism Across the Sea to Japan

3.1 Jianzhen and His Zhejiang Disciples

Zhejiang's Maritime Silk Road was more than a route for commerce; it was a vibrant artery of cultural exchange. A defining feature of the relationship between ancient Zhejiang and Japan was the eastward transmission of Buddhism. This transmission was a dynamic, two-way current: Japanese monks journeyed to Zhejiang seeking sacred scriptures, while Zhejiang monks crossed the sea to propagate the Dharma in Japan. It is important to clarify that the term "Zhejiang monks" encompasses not only those native to the province but also monks from across China who made their homes in Zhejiang's great monasteries, turning the region into a flourishing hub of Buddhist learning and international exchange.

The tradition of Zhejiang monks journeying to Japan to share the Dharma dates back at least to the Tang Dynasty. In AD 743, the second year of the Tianbao reign of Emperor Xuanzong, the venerable monk Jianzhen (AD 688–763) of Daming Temple in Yangzhou accepted an invitation from Japan and resolved to sail east. His first attempt failed. In early AD 744, Jianzhen embarked on a second voyage from the mouth of the Yangtze River, but a violent storm swept his vessel off course, leaving him shipwrecked on the shores of Zhoushan in Zhejiang. After his rescue, local officials provided him and his companions sanctuary at the renowned Ashoka Temple in

Ningbo. During that year, Jianzhen traveled to Hangzhou and Huzhou, delivering lectures on the Buddhist precepts. Upon his return to Ashoka Temple, he began planning a third voyage, but this attempt was foiled when fellow Chinese monks reported his intentions to the authorities. Learning from this setback, Jianzhen decided to shift his departure point to Fuzhou for his next attempt, sending his most trusted disciples ahead to procure a vessel.

In the winter of AD 744, Jianzhen and his disciples set out from Ashoka Temple for Fuzhou. Their southward path led them through Fenghua and to an overnight stay at Baiquan Temple in Ninghai. Braving heavy snows, they trekked over mountains and through valleys to reach Guoqing Temple on the sacred Mount Tiantai. From there, they passed through Linhai and took shelter at Chanlin Temple in Huangyan. Their plan was to enter Fujian by way of Wenzhou, but officials intercepted them at Chanlin Temple and escorted Jianzhen back to Yangzhou, crushing his fourth attempt to reach Japan. Undeterred, Jianzhen embarked on his fifth voyage from Yangzhou in AD 748. This time, fierce gales and towering waves assailed his ship, forcing it to shelter along the Zhejiang coast for more than two months before it was finally driven far south, drifting helplessly to Hainan Island. It was during this harrowing ordeal that an infection tragically claimed his sight.

In late AD 753, the now-blind Jianzhen embarked on his sixth and final voyage from Huangsipu, near the mouth of the Yangtze River (in modern-day Zhangjiagang, Suzhou). After more than two months at sea, he at last set foot in Dazaifu, Japan. Although his ultimate departure was not from Zhejiang, the province had been the crucible for his perseverance. His second and fifth voyages forced him to take refuge on its shores, while his third and fourth attempts were planned entirely within its borders. Jianzhen's profound connection with Zhejiang underscores the province's pivotal role on the Maritime Silk Road.

Upon his arrival, Jianzhen was greeted with overwhelming enthusiasm by all echelons of Japanese society, from the common people to the imperial court. The emperor bestowed upon him the honorific title Dentō Daishi ("Grand Master of the Dharma Light"), and he is venerated to this day as the founder of Japan's Ritsu (Vinaya) school of Buddhism. His influence was a holistic cultural transmission, profoundly shaping Japanese architecture, medicine, pharmacology, literature, calligraphy, and cuisine. The magnificent Tōshōdai-ji Temple in Nara, now a UNESCO World Heritage site, was his own design. Jianzhen also carried to Japan a trove of Buddhist scriptures, statues, and precious artifacts, a significant portion of which had direct ties to Zhejiang. Three examples stand out:

1. The Southern Edition of the Nirvana Sutra. In AD 417, after returning from his pilgrimage to India, the Eastern Jin monk Faxian translated a portion of a Sanskrit scripture, creating a six-volume work. In AD 421, the Indian monk Dharmakṣema, who lived in the Northern Liang kingdom, produced a

complete 40-volume translation. Then, in AD 431 in Jiankang (modern Nanjing), a team led by the monk Huiyan and the scholar Xie Lingyun used Dharmakṣema's text as a base, referencing Faxian's earlier work, to create a polished and refined 36-volume version. This text became known as the Southern Edition of the Nirvana Sutra. Xie Lingyun (AD 385–433), a pivotal figure in this great literary and religious undertaking, was a celebrated writer, traveler, and Buddhist intellectual from Shangyu in Zhejiang.

2. The Works of Zhiyi, Founder of the Tiantai School. Jianzhen's collection included foundational texts by the great master Zhiyi, such as the Commentary on the Bodhisattva Precepts, The Methods of Tiantai Calming and Contemplation, The Profound Meaning of the Lotus Sutra, Words and Phrases of the Lotus Sutra, Outline of the Four Teachings, The Minor Treatise on Calming and Contemplation, and The Six Wondrous Dharma Gates. This demonstrates that Jianzhen, though a master of the Nanshan lineage of the Ritsu school, was also instrumental in introducing the influential Tiantai school to Japan.

3. Masterpieces of Calligraphy by Wang Xizhi and Wang Xianzhi. Jianzhen carried with him an original work in running script by the "Sage of Calligraphy," Wang Xizhi (AD 303–361), and three original works by his equally brilliant son, Wang Xianzhi (AD 344–386). Both masters hailed from Shaoxing in Zhejiang. These priceless scrolls were presented to the Japanese imperial court. Some scholars have speculated that the Wang Xizhi piece was

the famed Sangluan Tie (Letter on Bereavement), now a treasure of Japan's Imperial Household Agency, but compelling evidence for this claim has yet to emerge. The precise identity of these four masterpieces remains one of history's tantalizing mysteries.

On his final, successful voyage in AD 753, Jianzhen was accompanied by fourteen disciples. Two of them, Situo and Fazai, came from the great monasteries of Zhejiang.

In Japan, Situo authored the *Enryaku Sōroku*, the nation's first compilation of biographies of eminent monks. Though the original work is now lost, surviving fragments state: "Situo was a native of Yizhou who resided at Kaiyuan Temple and later entered Mount Tiantai. His lay surname was Wang, a descendant of the immortal Wang Qiao of the Langya Wang clan." This passage indicates that Situo was born in Yizhou (modern Linyi, Shandong) and belonged to the illustrious Langya Wang clan. While the "Kaiyuan Temple" mentioned could be the one in his native Yizhou, it is far more likely to be the Kaiyuan Temple of Taizhou in Zhejiang (today's Longxing Temple in Linhai). This conclusion is strongly supported by The Record of the Great Tang Monk's Eastward Journey, a biography of Jianzhen based on Situo's own writings, which explicitly identifies him as a "monk from Kaiyuan Temple in Taizhou."

The *Enryaku Sōroku* further records that Situo was ordained by imperial decree of Emperor Xuanzong and "received the precepts and studied under the master Jianzhen of Yangzhou. He spent nineteen years in Tang China, assisting his master in Buddhist works; he endured twelve years of hardship crossing the sea, building boats for four attempts and setting out to sea five times." This timeline indicates that by the time of the final, successful voyage in AD 753, Situo had been Jianzhen's disciple for nineteen years, placing his ordination in Yangzhou around AD 734. While the exact sequence of his early life is uncertain, the evidence strongly suggests he first studied at Kaiyuan Temple and Mount Tiantai before traveling to Yangzhou. Once he became Jianzhen's disciple, he remained by his master's side for nineteen years, constantly "assisting his teacher in Buddhist works" without separation, a period of devotion that would have precluded any return to his former temples in Zhejiang.

Situo was Jianzhen's most faithful disciple. He remained at his master's side through every one of the six perilous attempts to cross the sea—an ordeal captured in the poetic phrase from the *Enryaku Sōroku*: "building boats for four attempts and setting out to sea five times." Jianzhen's biography, *The Record of the Great Tang Monk's Eastward Journey*, starkly illustrates this loyalty. It notes that while more than two hundred followers abandoned the quest over the years, only two—the scholar-monk Puzhao and the "Tiantai monk" Situo—remained steadfast. They faced every danger without flinching, persevering "through all six crossings over twelve years," and at last arrived in Japan with their master.

Upon arriving in Japan, Situo first lived with Jianzhen at the Ordination Hall of Tōdai-ji Temple. The emperor granted them two parcels of land for a new monastery, one of which was the estate of a former prince. It was on the advice of Situo and Puzhao that Jianzhen chose this princely estate to design and build Tōshōdai-ji Temple. Situo's expertise in this field is well documented. The *Enryaku Sōroku* records that the emperor once commanded him to "create a model for an octagonal pagoda at Saidai-ji Temple," confirming his status as an architectural specialist and leaving little doubt that he participated in the design and construction of Tōshōdai-ji. Japanese historical sources also praise his mastery of sculpture, stating he "attained the wondrous art of creating Buddhist images." The magnificent statues of the Vairocana Buddha and the Medicine Buddha still enshrined in the Golden Hall of Tōshōdai-ji are attributed to his hand. Legend also tells that Situo, longing for his homeland, built a Chinese-style temple in Nara named Jitsuen-ji, which was later renamed Denkō-ji. Today, the temple is dedicated to the Kṣitigarbha Bodhisattva, and its camellias are among the most celebrated flowers in Nara.

Years before Jianzhen's arrival, a monk named Dōsen from Fuxian Temple in Luoyang had been invited to Japan in AD 736 to teach the Dharma, taking up residence at the Western Tang Hall of Daian-ji Temple in Nara. After Jianzhen's party arrived, Dōsen came to recognize Situo's profound learning and solid foundation in the scriptures. Deeply impressed, he invited Situo to Daian-ji to lecture on seminal texts such as *the Commentary on the*

Four-Part Vinaya. Situo remained at Daian-ji for four or five years, where he mentored a new generation of distinguished monks. In addition to his teaching, he was also summoned to the imperial court to perform sacred rites, including the sprinkling of fragrant water.

In his final years, Jianzhen confided in Situo, saying, "I wish to pass away in a seated posture. After I die, display my portrait in a hall." This request reveals the profound trust the master placed in his disciple. On the sixth day of the fifth month in AD 763, Jianzhen passed away peacefully, seated in meditation at Tōshōdai-ji. To fulfill his master's wish, Situo created a stunning seated portrait statue using the traditional hollow dry-lacquer technique (dakkatsu kanshitsu). Now enshrined in the Mieidō (Portrait Hall) of Tōshōdai-ji, it is Japan's oldest portrait sculpture and is designated a National Treasure. In 1978, Deng Xiaoping paid his respects to the statue during a visit to Japan. This act catalyzed a joint Sino-Japanese effort to arrange a symbolic "homecoming" tour. In April 1980, Emperor Hirohito of Japan met with Senior Monk Morimoto Kōshun, head priest of Tōshōdai-ji Temple, who was to escort the statue of Jian Zhen to China for an exhibition. On April 13, Morimoto Kōshun and his delegation arrived in Shanghai aboard a special flight with the statue. The statue was exhibited in Shanghai, Yangzhou, and Beijing, during which time Deng Xiaoping personally met with the Japanese representatives.

The statue of Jianzhen was crafted using the traditional Chinese technique of hollow dry-lacquer with a ramie cloth core. The process began with a wooden armature wrapped in straw, which was then sculpted over with clay to create a model. Next, layers of ramie cloth saturated with raw lacquer were meticulously applied over the clay form. After the lacquer hardened, the internal armature and clay were removed through an opening in the back, leaving a lightweight, hollow shell—a feature that made it easier to rescue from the temple in the event of a fire. The statue's hands, however, were carved from wood. The final stage involved painting the surface with lifelike colors. This sophisticated technique is attributed to the Eastern Jin artist Dai Kui (AD 326–396). Although a native of Anhui, Dai Kui fled the turmoil of the Wei, Jin, and Northern and Southern Dynasties period, settling in Shan County (modern Shengzhou) in the northern foothills of Mount Tiantai. In the Tiantai region, the art of hollow dry-lacquer sculpture has been passed down for centuries and was inscribed on China's first list of National Intangible Cultural Heritage in 2006. In essence, Situo transmitted this distinctive sculptural tradition of the Mount Tiantai area directly to Japan.

Situo's life-sized statue stands 80.1 cm tall. It depicts Jianzhen robed in his kasaya, seated in the full-lotus posture (kekka-fuza). His hands are held in his lap in the meditation mudra (dhyāna mudra): right hand resting on the left, palms upward, with the tips of the thumbs gently touching. The master's eyes are closed, a faint, serene smile plays upon his lips, and his facial muscles are relaxed, conveying a countenance that is at once full, peaceful, compassionate, and dignified. In his expression, one can almost feel the depth of his wisdom and his boundless care for all beings. The kasaya drapes over his body in soft, flowing lines, its generous folds enhancing the statue's profound sense of stillness and stability. The work is a testament to Situo's sublime artistry and extraordinary talent.

Jianzhen

After the passing of Jianzhen, the monk Sitou composed a five-character poem titled "*In Mourning for the Great Monk Who Carried the Lamp to Japan*." The poem reads as follows:

A sage of highest virtue, you sailed across the sea,

The golden light of Dharma had journeyed to the East.

The fragrance of your teachings, a lingering sweet scent,

The torch of wisdom kindled, a new flame in the breeze.

The moon now sets behind the Vulture's sacred peak,

A pearl returned to realms of Brahma's holy keep.

Your spirit soars beyond the bounds of life and death,

Your teachings live, a timeless legacy bequeathed.

In the poem, "a sage of highest virtue" refers to Jianzhen, and "the golden light" alludes to the Buddha's teachings. These opening lines praise Jianzhen for bringing the wisdom of Buddhism to the shores of Japan. "The fragrance of your teachings" and "the torch of wisdom" are both metaphors for the flourishing of Buddhism that followed in his wake. "The Vulture's sacred peak," a hallowed site in Buddhist lore, and "Brahma's holy keep," the celestial palace of a Hindu deity adopted into the Buddhist tradition, are poignant allusions to Jianzhen's passing. The final couplet conveys a timeless truth: though the master has departed, his teachings, the enduring Dharma, will forever illuminate the path for those who follow. This poem is a poignant expression of deep affection for Jianzhen and simultaneously serves as a testament to his own profound literary talent.

Although Jianzhen received support from many nobles and even the emperor, he also endured slander from conservative factions. To defend his master's reputation, Situo wrote a three-volume biography, A Record of the Great Tang Master Who Transmitted the Precepts: *The Biography of the Great*

Monk Jianzhen (abbreviated as *The Great Monk's Biography*). In a savvy act of cultural translation, Situo entrusted his work to the Japanese literary giant Ōmi no Mifune (AD 722–785, also known as Mabito Genkai), a scholar of imperial descent hailed as the "foremost man of letters" of his day. He asked Mifune to revise the text to suit a Japanese audience. In AD 779, Mifune completed his adaptation, the *Tō Daiwajō Tōseiden* (*Record of the Great Tang Monk's Eastward Journey*), which survives in full and is now a vital source for studying Jianzhen and Sino-Japanese exchange.

Although Situo's original manuscript is lost, his authorial fingerprints are all over Mifune's text. For example, the Tōseiden uses Tang Dynasty era names (like "the twelfth year of Tianbao") and specifies "Japan" before titles like "Japanese king," "Japanese envoy," and "Japanese fellow monks." A Japanese author like Mifune would have no need to use foreign era names or to clarify that his own countrymen were "Japanese." These are the clear marks of a Chinese author writing for a Chinese audience. Another clue lies in the lists of Jianzhen's companions, where Situo's name almost invariably appears last—a gesture of humility from the original author. Thus, Mifune's Tōseiden is deeply infused with Situo's work. In recognition of this, a manuscript of the text preserved at Kanchi-in Temple in Kyoto explicitly names its authors as "The Tiantai monk Situo and Mabito Genkai."

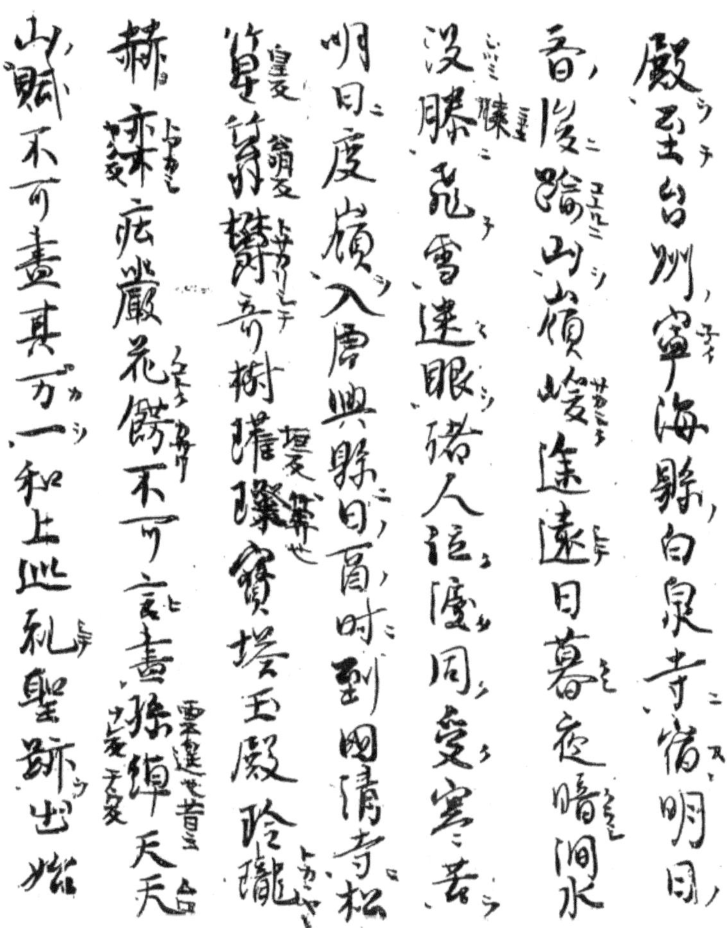
嚴至台州寧海縣白泉寺宿明日
齋後踰山嶺峻途遠日暮夜暗澗水
没膝飛雪迷眼諸人泣涙同受寒苦
明日度嶺入唐興縣日暮時到國清寺松
篁蓊鬱奇樹璀璨寶塔玉殿玲瓏
赫奕荘嚴花餝不可言盡孫綽天台
山賦不可盡其万一和上巡礼聖跡出始

The record of Jianzhen's journey from Ninghai County to Guoqing Temple as described in a Japanese manuscript of *Record of the Great Tang Monk's Eastward Journey*

The other Zhejiang monk who accompanied Jianzhen was Fazai. The *Tōseiden* clearly identifies him as a "monk from Lingyao Temple in Quzhou." While no records of him survive in Zhejiang, and his birthplace remains unknown, Japanese sources describe him as "intelligent and highly ambitious." They state that he "studied under Master Jianzhen, perfected his understanding of the precepts, and deeply penetrated the Tiantai teachings. In Tang

China, he propagated the Dharma at Lingyao Temple in Quzhou, and his fame was known throughout the land." Before his death, Jianzhen personally appointed Fazai as the jōza (head monk) of Tōshōdai-ji, making him the temple's second patriarch. As Jianzhen's successor, Fazai continued the construction of the monastery, completing several of the monks' quarters. Regrettably, little else is known about this important figure.

3.2 Song Dynasty Monks: The Journey East

Situo and Fazai both hailed from temples in Zhejiang and are the earliest known Zhejiang monks to have crossed to Japan, serving as pioneers in spreading Buddhism from Zhejiang to Japan. However, during the subsequent Five Dynasties and Northern Song periods, few Zhejiang monks traveled to Japan. It was not until the late Southern Song Dynasty that a small wave of Zhejiang monks made the eastward journeys to Japan. Among the earliest monks was Jiyuan (1207-1299).

Jiyuan, originally from Luoyang in Henan, entered the monastic life at a young age at Tiantong Temple in Ningbo. He became a disciple of Rujing (1163–1228), the thirteenth patriarch of the Caodong (Sōtō) Zen school. In 1223, the Japanese monk Dōgen (1200-1253) sailed to Song China, visiting famous Zhejiang temples such as Tiantong Temple, King Ashoka Temple, and Jingci Temple, and eventually became a disciple of Rujing. Thus,

Dōgen and Jiyuan became fellow disciples. In 1227, Dōgen left Zhejiang and returned to Japan. Jiyuan had originally intended to go to Japan with Dōgen. However, due to Rujing's serious illness, Jiyuan remained in China. After Rujing's death, Jiyuan departed for Japan in 1228 and, following Dōgen, studied Buddhism at Kōshō-ji Temple in Uji, Kyoto, and Eihei-ji Temple in Fukui Prefecture. In 1261, Jiyuan founded Hōkyō-ji Temple in Ōno City, Fukui Prefecture—today recognized as the second principal center of the Japanese Sōtō Zen school. Hōkyō-ji Temple still preserves a portrait of Jiyuan.

The statue of Lanxi Daolong preserved in Japan

Following Jiyuan, another influential monk from Zhejiang, Lanxi Daolong (1213–1278), made his way to Japan. Born in Fujiang, Xishu (modern-day Fuling, Chongqing), Daolong entered the monastic life as a youth and studied under Wuzhun Shifan at Jingshan Temple, later continuing his training at Tiantong Temple in Ningbo. At Tiantong Temple, Daolong met Myōkan Chikyō, a Japanese monk from Sennyū-ji Temple in Kyoto, who informed him that while Buddhism was thriving in Japan, Zen Buddhism had yet to take root. This inspired Daolong to devote himself to spreading Zen in Japan. In 1246, Daolong, accompanied by his disciple Giyō Shōnin and others, set sail from Ningbo to Japan. He visited various temples, including Enkaku-ji in Fukuoka, Sennyū-ji in Kyoto, and Jufuku-ji in Kamakura. By this time, Japan had entered the Kamakura Shogunate period (1192–1333). Hōjō Tokiyori (1227–1263), the ruling regent, greatly esteemed Daolong and appointed him abbot of Jōraku-ji Temple in Kamakura. In 1253, Hōjō Tokiyori founded Kenchō-ji Temple in Kamakura and invited Daolong to become its founding abbot. After Tokiyori's death, Daolong briefly served as founding abbot of Zenkō-ji Temple, also in Kamakura, before returning to Kenchō-ji, where he spent his final years. Upon his death, the Japanese emperor honored him with the posthumous title "Daikaku Zenji" (Great Enlightenment Zen Master). Before Daolong's arrival, Japanese monks typically practiced a syncretic form of Buddhism, combining Tiantai, Shingon, and Zen traditions. One of Daolong's most significant contributions was to shift Japanese monastic practice toward a "pure Zen" tradition, both through doctrinal exposition and concrete institutional reform. Many artifacts related to Daolong are still preserved in Japan. Kenchō-ji Temple in Kamakura houses a portrait of Daolong (with his autograph inscription), a bronze bell (with an inscription penned by Daolong), Daolong's written monastic rules and discourses (Hōgo (Dharma Sayings) and Kisoku (Monastic Rules)), and a wooden seated statue of Daolong. Other artifacts related to Daolong are also preserved elsewhere in Japan, such as his calligraphy work "Fūran" (Wind Orchid) at the Gotoh Museum in Tokyo, signed "Written by Kenchō Bhikkhu Lanxi Daolong."

The wooden statue of Lanxi Daolong preserved in Japan

Another notable monk connected to Daolong was Wuan Puning (1197–1276). Born in Chengdu, Sichuan, Puning entered the monastic life at an early age. He studied under Wuzhun Shifan in Zhejiang and visited several important temples, including King Ashoka Temple in Ningbo and Jingshan Temple in Hangzhou. He came to be known as one of the "Four Eminent Disciples" of Wuzhun. Puning spent time at many major temples in Zhejiang, such as Lingyin Temple in Hangzhou, Tiantong Temple in Ningbo, and

Lingyan Temple in Xiangshan. In 1260, Puning accepted an invitation from Lanxi Daolong and Ennin to travel to Japan He first resided at Shōfuku-ji Temple in Hakata before Ennin invited him to Tōfuku-ji Temple. Hōjō Tokiyori greatly admired Puning, even claiming to have visited him in a dream. After repeated requests from Tokiyori, Puning agreed in 1262 to become the second abbot of Kenchō-ji Temple in Kamakura. However, in late 1263, Hōjō Tokiyori passed away, and Puning lost his chief supporter at court.. Contemplating his return to China, he composed a poignant verse in 1265 before departing:

Mindless, I roamed this land;

My heart longed for Song.

In mind and no-mind,

The path to Heaven lives.

After returning to China, Puning lived at Shuanglin Temple in Wuzhou (Yiwu) and at Longxiang Temple on Jiangxin Islet in Wenzhou. Despite residing in Southern Song China, Puning continued to maintain correspondence with Japanese monks. The Kitamura Museum in Kyoto houses a handwritten letter by Puning addressed to the Japanese monk Tōgan Ean, titled "Words to Tōgan Ean", dated 1268. The Nara National Museum preserves another letter by Puning to the same monk, titled "Letter to Tōgan Ean", written in 1270. Both letters were written on specially treated paper decorated with lotus pond motifs. As such, these documents not only stand as important witnesses to the Buddhist exchanges between Zhejiang and Japan, but also provide rare physical evidence for the study of papermaking practices in Song Dynasty Zhejiang. In addition, the MIHO Museum in Shiga Prefecture holds a piece of Puning's calligraphy titled "Qianshen". The extant *Sayings of Zen Master Wuan Puning* compiles his principal writings and teachings.

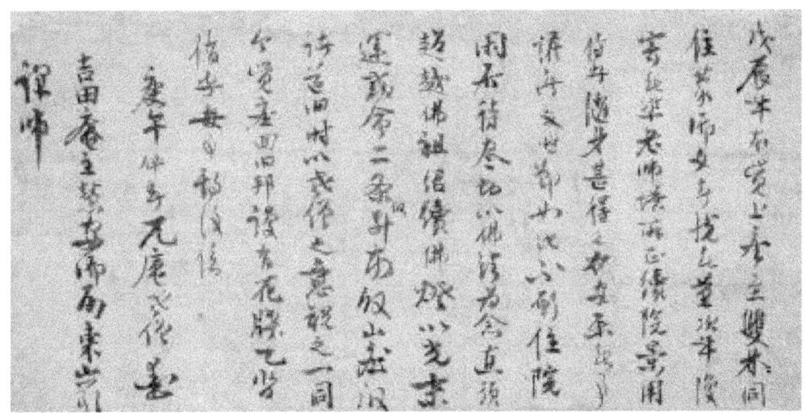

Letter to Tōgan Ean by Pu Ning

The Buddhist lineage that Puning established in Japan became known as the Wu'an School or the Sōgaku School .

While the monks mentioned above lived in Zhejiang monasteries for extended periods, they were not originally from Zhejiang. However, during the Southern Song period, a growing number of monks native to Zhejiang began traveling to Japan. Among them, two figures stand out as particularly significant:

1.Daxiu Zhengnian (1215–1289)

Born in Yongjia, Wenzhou, Daxiu Zhengnian traveled through Zhejiang and Jiangsu to study with eminent monks before joining Hangzhou's Jingshan Temple in 1250, where he studied under Abbot Shixi Xinyue (?-1256). At Jingshan, he formed a bond with Musō Jōshō (1234–1306), a Japanese monk, and their four-year companionship deepened Zhengnian's understanding of Japan. After Xinyue's death, he resided at Xinchang's Great Buddha Temple and Ningbo's Tiantong Temple. In 1269, at age 54, he sailed from Tiantong to Japan, where he was warmly received by Lanxi Daolong at Kamakura's Kenchō-ji Temple. Daolong generously yielded leadership of Zenkō-ji Temple to Zhengnian. Later, Zhengnian served as abbot of Kenchō-ji and Jufuku-ji Temples in Kamakura. In 1279, while at Jufuku-ji, news of the Southern Song's fall stirred deep sorrow, expressed in his lament: "Tidings from the west bring unbearable news of my homeland" and "The Way

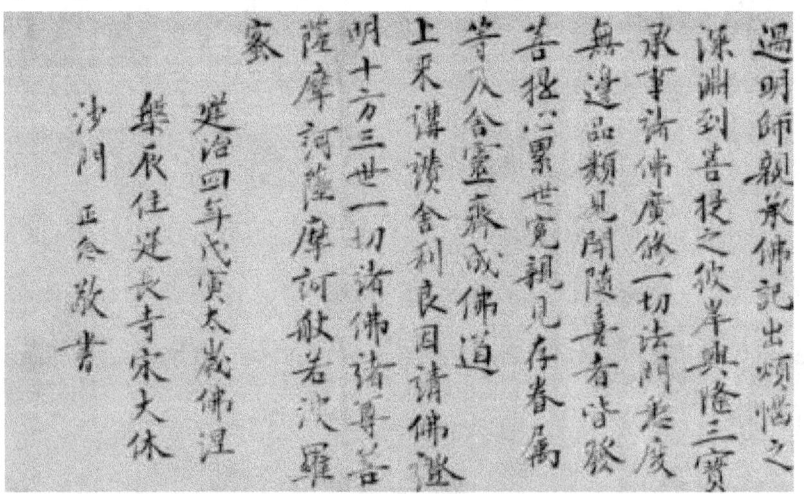
遇明師親承佛記出煩惱之
深淵到菩提之彼岸興隆三寶
承事諸佛廣修一切法門究度
無邊品類見聞隨喜者皆發
菩提心累世冤親見存眷屬
等入合靈乘成佛道
上來諷讚舍利良因請佛證
明十方三世一切諸佛諸尊菩
薩摩訶薩摩訶般若波羅
蜜
建治四年戊寅太歲佛涅
槃辰住建長寺宋大休
沙門 正念 敬書

Autograph Letter by Daxiu Zhengnian (Partial), Preserved in Japan

follows time's course, yet tears of grief stain my robes." In 1284, he became abbot of Engaku-ji Temple. He passed away at Shōkan-ji Temple in 1289. His teachings are preserved in The Analects of Master Daxiu. The Zen lineage he founded is known as the Daxiu or Butsugen School.

Among Daxiu Zhengnian's surviving artifacts, the most renowned is the Preface to the Tiantai Stone Bridge Eulogy Scroll. The Tiantai Stone Bridge, a natural wonder on Mount Tiantai, was believed during the Song Dynasty to house five hundred Arhats, with Fangguang Temple nearby as their sacred abode. This drew pilgrims from far and wide, including Japanese monks like Jōjin (1011–1081) and Eisai (1141–1215). In 1262, Musō Jōshō, a former fellow student of Zhengnian under Shixi Xinyue at Jingshan Temple, visited the bridge. Offering tea to the Arhats, he heard their voices in a dream, inspiring two poems.

The first poem reads:

Through rugged paths I trekked to offer tea,

Five hundred Arhats glow in evening's light.

Three bows, then waking, my dream-eyes clear:

All dharmas are but fleeting, empty blooms.

The second poem reads:

Twin gorges roar with cascading falls,

Clouds part to show peaks and golden halls.

Such is the way of the Venerable Ones—

Why call me from the seas of the far east?

Jōshō shared these poems with eminent monks across China, who responded with 82 verses—two each from 41 Southern Song monks. Confirmed Zhejiang monks include Wuchu Daguan of Aiyuwang Temple, Xuzhou Pudu of Hangzhou's Zhongtianzhu and Lingyin Temples, Dongzhou Weijun of Xinchang's Yunju Temple, and Miaohong of Tiantai's Wannian Bao'en Guangxiao Zen Temple. Others, such as Taiqiao Banyun De'ang, Xiacheng Deyong, Tiantai Delian, Tiantai Zongyi, Tiantai Zhiyue, Qiantang Jingtan, and Siming Ruji, are likely Zhejiang monks, though their lives remain obscure. Of these 82 poems, 74 are not found in Chinese records like *The Complete Collection of Song Poetry*, making them a precious resource for studying Song-era Zhejiang

At Xinchang's Great Buddha Temple, Musō Jōshō met his senior monastic brother, Daxiu Zhengnian, then serving as abbot. Sharing his two poems, Jōshō inspired Zhengnian to respond with two poems.

The first poem reads:

I pour a cup of pre-rain tea, rich and fine,

The room aglow with dawn's ethereal light.

If dreams unveil a wondrous sight,

New blooms arise before your enlightened gaze.

The second poem reads:

The bridge spans waterfalls and rugged cliffs,

Venerable Ones greet with radiant smiles.

In one moment, all illusions fade away,

Descending with the mist down mountain paths.

The "bridge spans waterfalls" refers to the Tiantai Stone Bridge. "New blooms arise" alludes to the Tiantai custom of offering tea to Arhats. Unlike today's tea brewing, Song-era tea involved whisking finely ground tea powder with a dash of boiling water using a bamboo chaxian into a thick paste. At Tiantai, this paste was offered to Arhats, and flower-like patterns seen in

Eulogy to the Tiantai Stone Bridge Scroll Preface, Daxiu Zhengnian

it were deemed miraculous, symbolizing divine favor. Thus, "new blooms" implies that Jōshō's tea offering at the Stone Bridge yielded sacred patterns, reflecting his profound Buddhist attainment.

In 1265, Jōshō returned to Japan with a scroll of 84 poems—his own and those of 41 Southern Song monks—titled Tiantai Stone Bridge Eulogy Scroll (or Musō Jōshō's Dream Journey to Tiantai Stone Bridge Scroll or Gatha). In early summer 1274, Jōshō visited Zenkō-ji Temple in Kamakura, reuniting with Zhengnian, its abbot. Their reunion, decades after studying together at Jingshan, was a heartwarming surprise. Presenting the scroll, Jōshō requested a preface. Deeply moved by this memento from over two decades past, Zhengnian, nostalgic for his Chinese teachers and friends, held it tenderly before writing a poignant preface. He reflected, "Your days in Tang China echo my life now in Japan." He concluded that through the Dharma, monks could transcend time and space, "drumming in Tang and dancing in Japan." This preface, a treasured artifact, is preserved at Tokyo's Gotoh Museum.

2. Wuxue Sogen (1226–1286)

Born Xu in Yin County (modern Ningbo), Wuxue Sogen took monastic vows at Hangzhou's Jingci Temple in his youth and studied under Wuzhun Shifan at Jingshan Temple. After Wuzhun's passing, Sogen journeyed through Zhejiang, visiting renowned monasteries like King Ashoka Temple, Lingyin Temple, and Tiantong Temple in Ningbo. He later served as abbot of Ningbo's Baiyun Nunnery and Taizhou's Zhenru Temple. In 1275, as Yuan armies swept south, sowing chaos, Sogen sought refuge at Wenzhou's Nengren Temple. Legend recounts that in 1276, when Yuan troops entered the temple, all fled save Sogen, who remained composed in the main hall. As a sword was held to his neck, he calmly recited a poem:

No place in heaven or earth holds my lone staff steady,

Yet joy, for self and all things are but void.

Prize the Great Yuan's three-foot blade,

It cuts the spring breeze in a lightning's fleeting shade.

The "staff" represents Sogen, a solitary monk. The opening lines convey: "The universe offers no refuge for me, yet self and phenomena are empty." This suggests that death at the Yuan's hands is meaningless, embodying Sogen's fearless embrace of mortality. The final lines urge the soldiers to avoid futile killing, likening it to slashing the spring breeze in a lightning's shadow. Struck by his words, the soldiers withdrew in awe, offering respectful bows. This celebrated poem, known as *Ode to Facing the Sword*, remains iconic.

In 1279, at the behest of Hōjō Tokimune (1251–1284), regent of the Kamakura Shogunate, Wuxue Sogen left Ningbo's Tiantong Temple for Japan, taking up the abbacy of Kamakura's Kenchō-ji Temple. In 1282, with Tokimune's substantial support, Sogen founded Engaku-ji Temple in Kamakura. Two years later, he returned to Kenchō-ji, where he lived until his passing. His remains, first interred at Kenchō-ji, were relocated to Engaku-ji in 1335. Engaku-ji preserves his legacy with artifacts like a wooden statue carved soon after his death, a 1284 portrait, his "Wuxue" seal, and personal letters. A cypress tree, reportedly planted by Sogen in the abbot's garden, endures. Legend holds that upon Sogen's arrival in Kamakura, a divine heron from Tsurugaoka Hachimangū Shrine guided him, inspiring the name "White Heron Pond" at Engaku-ji. Kyoto's Shōtenkaku Museum holds his 1279 "Gatha to Chōraku-ji Ichio," and Tokyo's Nezu Museum displays his 1280 calligraphy. After his death, the emperor bestowed the titles "Butsukō Kokushi" (Buddha Light National Teacher) and "Enman Jōshō Kokushi" (Perfect Ever-Shining National Teacher). Sogen's writings appear in *The Analects of Butsukō Kokushi.*

His profound influence in Japan is evident in the enduring fame of *Ode to Facing the Sword.* Legend credits this poem with saving him from Yuan

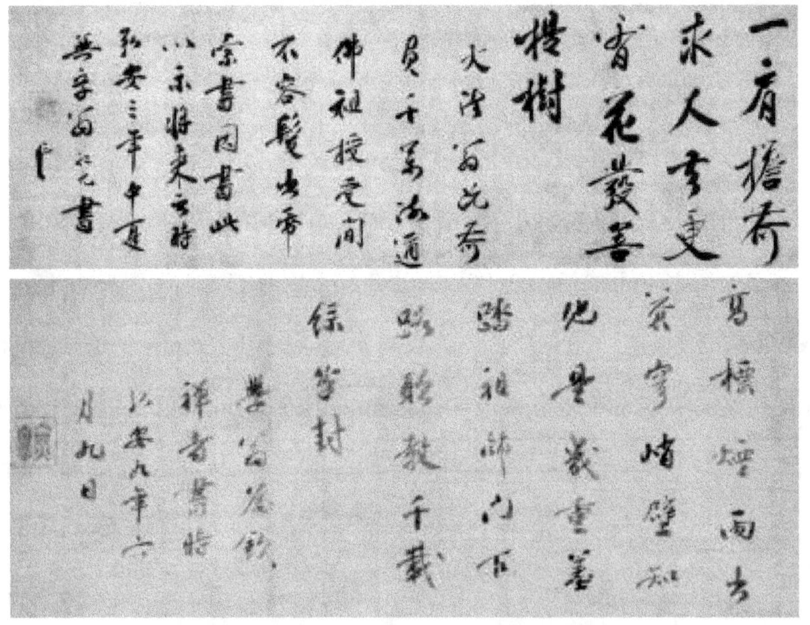

Calligraphic Work by Wuxue Sogen, Preserved in Japan

soldiers. In Japan, the story grew increasingly embellished. Remarkably, Setsuson Yūbai (1290–1355), a Japanese monk, brought the poem back to China.

Setsuson Yūbai, a monk at Kenchō-ji and Engaku-ji under Wuxue Sogen's guidance, knew his mentor's legacy well. In 1307, he traveled to China, visiting Yuan Dadu (modern Beijing) and Mount Song. Around 1309, he reached Wanshou Temple in Huzhou, earning the admiration of Abbot Shuping Long. By 1310, Huzhou officials, suspecting him of spying for Japan, arrested and tortured him, sentencing him to death. Legend holds that in 1313, facing execution, Yūbai boldly recited Sogen's *Ode to Facing the Sword*. His fearless composure stunned the officials, who spared his life. Exiled to Sichuan, Yūbai survived, but Shuping Long, his devoted protector, died in prison.

It remains unclear whether Yūbai's recitation of *Ode to Facing the Sword* truly saved him, but the tale spread widely in China, with many mistakenly attributing the poem to him. In 1325, Japanese monk Chūgan Engetsu (1300–1375) visited Benjue Temple in Jiaxing, meeting Abbot Lingzhi Ruzhi from Taizhou. Lingzhi said, "Your compatriot Setsuson Yūbai, with a sword at his throat in China, fearlessly chanted: 'No ground in heaven or earth to plant my staff alone, / Yet joy, for self and Dharma are but void. / Cherish the Yuan's three-foot blade, / It cleaves the spring breeze in a flash of light.' Awestruck, the officials spared him and left in remorse." Chūgan Engetsu explained that Wuxue Sogen, a Zhejiang native, authored the poem, not Yūbai. Skeptical, Lingzhi Ruzhi retorted, "Everyone here credits Yūbai. Yet you and other Japanese deny it. Are you all intent on tarnishing your compatriot's name?" Chūgan likely felt wronged by the accusation. Over time, mounting evidence from Japanese monks convinced Lingzhi, who recorded Sogen's authorship in Biography of Zen Master Wuxue.

In 1325, as Lingzhi Ruzhi and Chūgan Engetsu debated whether Setsuson Yūbai authored *Ode to Facing the Sword*, Yūbai, exiled in Sichuan, was pardoned and freed. He spent several years in Sichuan, Hunan, and Jiangsu, returning to Japan in 1329. There, he thrived as a Buddhist leader and literary figure. His Min'e Collection gathers writings from his time in China, while his Japanese poems and essays appear in Discourses of Zen Master Hōkaku Shinkū. Through these works, Wuxue Sogen's legacy spread widely in Japan.

Wuxue Sogen's *Ode to Facing the Sword* has endured in Japanese culture. Natsume Sōseki (1867–1916) quoted it in his novel I Am a Cat. Its celebrated line, "It cleaves the spring breeze in a flash of light," became a popular phrase, used in ads for swords and video games to evoke sharpness or speed, diverging from Sogen's original intent. This shift underscores Sogen's lasting impact on Japanese culture.

Chapter 4.The Divine Ships of the Song Dynasty Sailing from Mingzhou

4.1 The Embassy of An Tao to Goryeo

In an age before flight, the ocean was the only highway to foreign lands, and for the diplomatic envoys of China's imperial dynasties, the sailing ship was their sole conveyance. Zhejiang, situated at the midpoint of China's coastline, was a natural gateway to the seas. From its ports, sea lanes stretched east to Japan, north to the Korean Peninsula, and south to the distant shores of Southeast Asia. Consequently, the Zhejiang Maritime Silk Road became a vital artery for countless diplomatic missions. Among the envoys who sailed north, none is more famous than Xu Jing of the Northern Song Dynasty.

The dawn of the 10th century ushered in an era of profound transformation across East Asia. In AD 916, Yelü Abaoji founded the Khitan state, which would become the Liao Dynasty. Just two years later, in AD 918, Wang Geon established the Goryeo Dynasty, setting in motion the unification of the Korean Peninsula. Then, in AD 960, Zhao Kuangyin founded the Song Dynasty. The century and a half that followed was a theater of treacherous intrigue and shifting alliances. In this volatile world, Zhejiang, separated from the Korean Peninsula by just a narrow strait of water, assumed an indispensable role in the official relationship between the Song and Goryeo courts.

The Song and Goryeo realms were bound by a shared heritage, a world shaped by the brushstrokes of Chinese characters and the teachings of Confucius. This common culture provided a solid foundation for friendship. In AD 943, Goryeo's founding monarch, Wang Geon, laid down ten injunctions for his descendants. The fourth was a powerful directive to follow the traditions of the Han people of the Central Plains and reject the ways of the Khitans: "The Khitans are a nation of beasts; their customs are different, and their language is foreign. Be wary of adopting their style of dress and institutions." Yet, noble aspirations often bend to harsh realities. Faced with the formidable Liao Dynasty on its border, Goryeo was forced to forge a foreign policy born of necessity and aimed at survival. Between 1009 and 1019, Liao armies launched massive invasions of Goryeo. Goryeo pleaded with the Song for assistance, but the Song court, concerned with its own security, remained aloof and offered no aid. As a result, Goryeo tilted toward the Liao, and its diplomatic ties with the Song withered. For more than forty years after 1031, all official contact between the two courts ceased.

The ascension of Emperor Shenzong to the Song throne in 1067 marked a turning point. He championed a new strategy: an alliance with Goryeo to contain the Liao. Goryeo, for its part, was keen to restore diplomatic relations, and thus began a golden age of exchange between the two states. In 1071, the Goryeo envoy Kim Je led a grand delegation of over one hundred people to the Song court, making landfall at Dengzhou in Shandong after their sea crossing. Emperor Shenzong, recognizing the mission's importance, ordered a magnificent reception, and the envoys eventually returned home from the same port.

The success of this visit ignited a mutual desire in both capitals to cultivate a deeper relationship. However, Goryeo could not ignore the watchful eyes of the Khitans next door. To avoid provoking their powerful neighbor, Goryeo requested a change in the tribute route, asking to land at Mingzhou (modern-day Ningbo) instead of Dengzhou. The request was strategically astute. Dengzhou was perilously close to Khitan-controlled territory, whereas Mingzhou was safely distant. The Song court had already, for political and military reasons, forbidden its merchants from trading in the Dengzhou area to prevent collusion with the enemy via the sea. At the same time, the Song government actively channeled maritime trade with Goryeo through Mingzhou, eventually decreeing that any commercial vessel not using the Mingzhou route was operating illegally. Mingzhou thus became the sole official port for Goryeo traffic. The Song court immediately granted Goryeo's request, even though the overland journey from Mingzhou to the Song capital of Bianjing (modern-day Kaifeng) was far longer and more expensive than the route from Dengzhou.

In 1073, Goryeo dispatched a tribute mission to the Song emperor led by Kim Yang-gam, the Grand Minister of the Royal Stud. The delegation arrived in Mingzhou that autumn, and local officials immediately relayed the news to the imperial court. Emperor Shenzong took personal command of the reception arrangements, issuing a series of meticulous orders: first, experienced navigators were to be sent to guide the envoys' ships into port; second, the relevant authorities were to prepare a grand welcoming ceremony; third, all expenses were to be covered by the state treasury to avoid burdening the common people; fourth, private trade between the local populace and the Goryeo envoys was strictly forbidden; and fifth, the delegation was to be secretly investigated for any Liao spies in its midst. In the first month of the new year, 1074, Kim Yang-gam's mission traveled north from Mingzhou along the Grand Canal to Bianjing, where Emperor Shenzong formally received them in the Chuigong Hall.

To solidify the relationship with Goryeo, Emperor Shenzong dispatched a diplomatic mission from Mingzhou in the spring of 1078, led by An Tao. It was the first official Song delegation sent to Goryeo since the restoration of ties, and the emperor attached extraordinary importance to it, hosting a magnificent farewell banquet and personally selecting its members. Shenzong was so meticulous that he even judged the envoys on their physical appearance. The chief envoy, An Tao (1034–1108), a native of Kaifeng in Henan, had been famous for his intellect since childhood and had risen rapidly through the official ranks thanks to a recommendation from the great scholar Ouyang Xiu (1007–1072). An Tao was a man of striking features and commanding presence. Emperor Shenzong was greatly impressed upon meeting him and kept him as a trusted official at court. Indeed, An Tao's dignified bearing was a key reason for his appointment. In stark contrast was the unfortunate Lin Xi (1035–1101) of Fujian. The court had designated Lin as deputy envoy, but on the eve of departure, the emperor abruptly dismissed him. Shenzong found Lin's appearance disagreeable, deeming him a man of melancholic and somber bearing, utterly devoid of spirit. "The people of Goryeo have awaited our envoys for a long time," the emperor explained. "The purpose of our mission is to convey the court's warmth and goodwill. If the Goryeo people were to see Lin Xi's face, they would be sorely disappointed and could never grasp our true intentions." Perhaps sensing this was not the most stately of reasons, Shenzong insisted that Lin Xi had been secretly unwilling to undertake the mission, having only accepted under pressure. To prove his judgment correct, the emperor demoted Lin and reassigned him to Hangzhou to oversee the Loudianwu, an office that managed government-owned properties.

The deputy envoy chosen by Emperor Shenzong himself was Chen Mu, another native of Fujian. Chen was a poet who had achieved the rank of bangyan, or second-place laureate, in the imperial examinations of 1061. To have caught the emperor's eye, he must have possessed not only great talent but also an impressive demeanor. At least two other principal members of the mission had ties to Zhejiang. One was Feng Ji (1033–1107), a native of Yin County, who was a respected writer and calligrapher. He was an ancestor of Feng Fang (1492–1563), a famous calligrapher from Ming-dynasty Ningbo.

The other was Zheng Xihan, who had previously served as the county magistrate of Kaihua in Quzhou.

To guarantee the mission's success, Emperor Shenzong issued a special edict in the first month of 1078, ordering Mingzhou to construct ships exclusively for the embassy. In the third month, the emperor personally bestowed names upon the two great vessels. One he christened Lingxu Zhiyuan Anji Shenzhou (Divine Ship that Soars Through the Void to Travel Afar in Safety and Peace), and the other Lingfei Shunji Shenzhou (Divine Ship that Flies with Spirit for a Smooth and Favorable Voyage). Because of their immense size, they were popularly known as "wanhu ships." A hu was an ancient unit of volume, and "wanhu," or "ten thousand hu," was a term used to express a vessel's vastness. The Tang poet Du Fu once captured this sense of scale in a line describing the bustling trade on the Yangtze River: "Sichuan hemp and Wu salt have flowed since ancient times, on ten-thousand-hu ships that sail like the wind." These two magnificent sailing ships were likely built at the mouth of the Yong River in what is now Zhenhai District, Ningbo, the site of a major Song-dynasty shipbuilding center. In 2008, a replica "wanhu divine ship" was constructed in Zhenhai as a monument to the ancient Maritime Silk Road.

Of course, the mission's success also depended on cooperation from Goryeo. To that end, in the fourth month of 1078, the Song court dispatched Gu Yungong, the Naval Commissioner of Mingzhou, to travel to Goryeo aboard a merchant vessel. He carried a diplomatic dispatch announcing the imminent arrival of the Song embassy. King Munjong of Goryeo was overjoyed at the news and ordered his court to make meticulous preparations for the reception, declaring that the performance of his officials in this task would be a basis for rewards and punishments.

In the sixth month of 1078, An Tao's embassy, sailing aboard the Lingxu Zhiyuan Anji Shenzhou and the Lingfei Shunji Shenzhou, departed from Dinghai (modern Zhenhai) in Mingzhou. They arrived in Goryeo to a rapturous welcome. The Korean chronicle Goryeosa ("History of Goryeo") states that "the king and the people of the nation rejoiced with delight" , while the Chinese Songshi ("History of the Song") records that Goryeo's "people of the nation cheered as they came out to greet them". King Munjong assembled a high-level reception committee, which included two officials who had previously visited the Song: Kim Je, now promoted to Minister of Punishments, and Kim Yang-gam, now Minister of Revenue. The king specially lodged the Song delegation in the state guesthouse, named the Sunchon-gwan. The name "Sunchon" meant "Obedience to the Celestial Dynasty"—that is, the Song court. The depth of the Goryeo king's esteem for the Song mission was thus made plain.

Two days later, King Munjong sent the crown prince to the Sunchon-gwan to escort the Song embassy to the royal palace. Though ailing, the king had himself supported by attendants so he could personally greet the delegation in the great hall. The central ceremony of the reception was Munjong's acceptance of the Song emperor's imperial edict. Deeply moved, the king declared, "That the Great Song Emperor has specially dispatched envoys to my small country brings me incomparable honor, and at the same time, I am struck with a sense of profound humility." He then issued a decree ordering all Goryeo officials to treat the Song delegation with the utmost hospitality.

Before the Song embassy departed, King Munjong submitted a memorial to the Song emperor. In it, he expressed his gratitude and made a personal plea for the emperor to send physicians to treat his illness, as well as a gift of medicines. In the ninth month of 1078, An Tao's delegation sailed back to Mingzhou by the same route they had come. Emperor Shenzong immediately summoned them to the capital, Bianjing. He was exceptionally pleased with the outcome of the mission, and every member of the delegation, including Feng Ji and Zheng Xihan, received a promotion.

A key reason for the promotion of the chief envoy, An Tao, was Emperor Shenzong's belief that he had demonstrated impeccable diplomatic etiquette—that he "knew the rites." In truth, An Tao's behavior in Goryeo had been anything but proper. *The Goryeosa* records that before the delegation's departure, King Munjong presented them not only with the customary official gifts of robes, belts, saddles, and horses, but also with an immense additional bounty of gold, silver, treasures, grain, and other goods. The quantity was so great that it could not fit aboard their two "wanhu ships." An Tao and his men then demanded that these gifts be exchanged for silver currency, a request King Munjong felt compelled to grant. The people of Goryeo were dismayed. "It has been long since we have seen an envoy from the Central Kingdom!" they lamented. "We never imagined they would behave in such a manner." An Tao's conduct undoubtedly damaged the Song's prestige. When officials at the Song court learned of the incident, they submitted memorials to Emperor Shenzong, accusing An Tao and his men of having "betrayed righteousness, disgraced their commission, and invited the contempt of foreigners," demanding that they be punished for their crimes. But the emperor, basking in the diplomatic achievement of An Tao's successful mission, completely ignored the accusations. He even had the written charges forwarded to An Tao and Chen Mu, a clear signal of his backing. His actions reveal the depth of his desire to forge a close diplomatic bond with Goryeo, an objective that overshadowed any concern for his envoy's personal misconduct.

An Tao's successful mission, based out of Mingzhou, significantly raised the city's political profile. The Song court subsequently took a series of measures to solidify Mingzhou's function as the primary diplomatic window to Goryeo. In 1079, Emperor Shenzong personally named two new facilities in Zhenhai for receiving Goryeo envoys: a state guesthouse called the Lebinguan (Hall for Delighting Guests) and a banquet hall named the Hangjiting (Pavilion of Safe Passage). He also increased the special budget allocated to Mingzhou for hosting Goryeo missions to 2,600 strings of cash to ensure their lavish reception.

When An Tao returned from Goryeo, he brought back the ailing King Munjong's request for renowned physicians and effective medicines. Emperor Shenzong treated the matter with extreme urgency. An Tao's mission had returned to Mingzhou in the ninth month of 1078. By the tenth month, the Song court had already selected a team of court physicians—including Xing Zao, Shao Huaji, and Qin Jie—and appointed Wang Shunfeng, a Palace Attendant, to lead the medical delegation. In the seventh month of 1079, Wang Shunfeng's mission of over 80 people arrived in Goryeo to treat the king. The entire process, from receiving the request to the medical team's arrival, took less than a year—a testament to remarkable efficiency, driven by the emperor's high regard for Goryeo. The delegation also brought a vast quantity of medicinal herbs from across China, including wuyao (lindera root) from Zhejiang's Taizhou region. This transfer of physicians and pharmaceuticals demonstrates that the Zhejiang Maritime Silk Road was also a conduit for medical exchange.

Emperor Shenzong anticipated that King Munjong, upon receiving the medicines, would likely dispatch a mission to express his thanks, and that it would surely land at Mingzhou. In the sixth month of 1079, he sent officials to Mingzhou to prepare a welcome, instructing that if the Goryeo delegation was led by a prince, Hu Yuan, the Vice Prefect of Quzhou, should be placed in charge of the reception. As it happened, the mission Goryeo sent was led by Minister of Revenue Ryu Hong and Vice Minister of Rites Pak In-ryang. They set sail late in 1079, but a typhoon struck their fleet off the Zhejiang coast, damaging their ships so severely they could not continue. They put into Mingzhou, hoping to purchase new vessels. Emperor Shenzong, ever intent on cultivating the relationship with Goryeo, made an extraordinary gesture: he decided to lend them one of the great Divine Ships used by the Song embassy, the Lingfei Shunji Shenzhou.

After the Goryeo delegation's ships were battered off the coast of Zhejiang, their tribute goods, including bolts of Goryeo cloth, were lost to the sea. The items washed ashore in various places, where they were collected by coastal residents in areas like Wenzhou. Emperor Shenzong issued a decree that all recovered tribute items must be surrendered to the authorities on pain of punishment. To ensure compliance, he added a powerful incentive: if anyone who found and hid the goods was reported by an informant, that informant would receive thirty percent of the items' value as a reward. This measure encouraging denunciation proved to be highly effective.

Pak In-ryang, a leader of this Goryeo delegation, was a celebrated man of letters in his own country. He had previously accompanied Kim Je on the 1071 tribute mission, during which he composed a poem in classical Chinese that was highly praised by Song scholars: "Before the temple gate, guest oars challenge the surging torrent; Beneath the bamboo, monks play chess in the leisurely daylight." Because local chronicles in Zhejiang, such as the Yin County Gazetteer, transcribed accounts of this poem, it was later mistaken as having been written in Mingzhou. In fact, its title is "Composed While Passing Guishan Temple in Sizhou on a Mission to the Song," and it has no connection to Ningbo. Nevertheless, after his harrowing experience in the storm off the Zhejiang coast, Pak In-ryang was indeed rescued by men from Ningbo. The rescue party was led by Zhang Zhong, the County Defender of Xiangshan. Pak was a master of Chinese poetry, and it is likely that Zhang was also a poetry lover. The scene of the Goryeo tribute envoys, having sailed across the sea only to face a tempest and narrowly escape death, may well have inspired the host and his guest to exchange verses. What Zhang could never have anticipated was that this act of cultural communion would lead to his downfall. An official at court impeached him, arguing: "Zhang Zhong, the County Defender of Xiangshan in Mingzhou, has dared to compose poetry with the Goryeo tribute envoys, which suggests possible collusion with a foreign power." The emperor, far away in Kaifeng and unaware of the circumstances, ordered Zhang to be demoted.

In the first month of 1080, Pak In-ryang and the other Goryeo envoys reached Bianjing and were granted an audience with Emperor Shenzong. Having lost their tribute in the shipwreck off the coast of eastern Zhejiang, they arrived empty-handed and could only beg the emperor's forgiveness. Shenzong was not concerned, attributing the loss to "an unforeseen storm" and declaring that the envoys were not at fault. Pak and his delegation also recounted to Song officials the story of how Zhang Zhong, the County Defender of Xiangshan, had rescued them from the sea. After investigating the facts, Emperor Shenzong recognized Zhang for his meritorious service in saving the Goryeo envoys and rescinded his punishment. Furthermore, before the Goryeo mission returned home, the emperor had a letter sent to the king of Goryeo, clarifying that the loss of the tribute was due to a maritime disaster and that Pak In-ryang and his men should not be blamed.

In 1083, King Munjong (Wang Hwi) of Goryeo passed away. Emperor Shenzong not only dispatched a mission led by Wang Shunfeng from Mingzhou to offer condolences but also ordered the government of Mingzhou to select prominent Buddhist temples and assemble 37 monks to conduct a full month of memorial services for the Goryeo king. This month-long Buddhist mourning ceremony for a foreign monarch is likely the only one of its kind in Zhejiang's history. It underscores the profound importance the Song emperor placed on the relationship with Goryeo and reflects Mingzhou's central role in the diplomacy between the two states.

In 1085, Emperor Shenzong also died and was succeeded by Emperor Zhezong (Zhao Xu, 1077–1100). The relationship between the two nations was not affected by the successive deaths of their monarchs, although the Song court became less proactive than it had been in Shenzong's time. Goryeo sent several missions to the Song, but the Song did not dispatch any formal embassies in return. In 1096, Wang Ong ascended the Goryeo throne as King Sukjong. Eager to maintain good relations with the Song, he decided to send envoys to inform the Song emperor of his accession. In 1098, King Sukjong dispatched a mission led by Yun Gwan to the Song court. In his memorial, Yun referred to himself as a "subject" (chen) and to the Song as the "Imperial Dynasty." Upon receiving the news, Emperor Zhezong sent officials to Mingzhou to await their arrival. Yun Gwan's party reached Mingzhou in the eleventh month of that year. When they had an audience with Emperor Zhezong in Bianjing, they requested copies of books such as the Taiping Yulan (Imperial Readings of the Taiping Era) and the Shenyi Pujiufang (Formulary of the Holy Physicians for Universal Relief). The emperor replied that the books would be given to them on their next visit.

In the sixth month of 1099, Yun Gwan and his delegation returned to Goryeo from Mingzhou. He would never see Emperor Zhezong again. In the first month of 1100, the emperor died at the young age of 23. He was succeeded by Emperor Huizong (Zhao Ji, 1082–1135). In the fifth month of that year, the Song court informed Goryeo of this great affair of state via Mingzhou. The king of Goryeo dispatched a mission in the sixth month to offer condolences for the passing of Emperor Zhezong, and another in the seventh month to congratulate Emperor Huizong on his accession. With this, the relationship between the Song and Goryeo entered a new phase.

4.2 Xu Jing's Illustrated Maritime Record

Since the founding of the Northern Song, its primary adversary had been the Khitan-led Liao Dynasty. By the reign of Emperor Huizong, however, the Liao was in decline, while the Jin Dynasty (1115–1234), founded by the Jurchen people, was rising with astonishing speed. Emperor Huizong saw an opportunity to achieve what his ancestors could not: to ally with Goryeo and destroy the Liao once and for all. If the strategy of earlier Song emperors was to "ally with Goryeo to contain the Liao," Huizong's policy became "ally with Goryeo to annihilate the Liao." Driven by this grand ambition, he moved urgently to strengthen diplomatic ties. In 1103, Emperor Huizong dispatched Liu Kui, the Vice Minister of Revenue, and Wu Shi, a Supervising Secretary, on a mission to Goryeo, bearing exceptionally lavish gifts of silk, weaponry, and artifacts of gold and jade. The delegation, which also included four physicians such as Mou Jie and Fan Zhicai, departed from Mingzhou in the fifth month and returned in the seventh. A remarkable feature of this embassy was that several of its members authored books about Goryeo. These included Wu Shi's 20-volume *Jilin Ji* (*Record of Jilin*), a 30-volume *Jilin Zhi* (*Gazetteer of Jilin*) by an attendant named Wang Yun, and a three-volume *Jilin Leishi* (*Classified Account of Jilin*) by another attendant, Sun Mu. "Jilin" was a literary name for the Korean Peninsula. Regrettably, Wu Shi's work is lost, only eight fragments of Wang Yun's survive, and Sun Mu's book is severely damaged. Even so, these remnants are of irreplaceable value for studying Goryeo's politics, products, customs, and language. For example, Sun Mu's Jilin Leishi notes that although Goryeo's land was poor, it was rich in products like ginseng and pine nuts, and that it minted its own currency, such as the Haedong Tongbo and Samhan Tongbo, in imitation of the Song. Wang Yun's Jilin Zhi describes a yellow lacquer tree on Goryeo's islands, whose sap, harvested in June, had the color of gold and was dried in the sun. In Zhejiang, this product was known as "Silla Lacquer."

The constant flow of Song and Goryeo envoys through Mingzhou led Emperor Huizong to conclude that a high-level diplomatic institution should be established there. In 1117, the Song court founded the Goryeo Embassy in Mingzhou, an office dedicated to receiving delegations from Goryeo and the only one of its kind in the entire Jiangnan region. Emperor Huizong personally brushed the calligraphy for its name plaque. According to historical records, the embassy was located at the western end of Baokui Alley, beside Moon Lake in modern-day Ningbo. In 1999, archaeologists excavating the site discovered a trove of artifacts, including "Zhenghe Tongbao" coins minted in 1111, porcelain from the Yue kilns, and Goryeo celadon. Today, the Museum of Mingzhou-Goryeo Exchange History stands on this historic ground.

After the establishment of the Goryeo Embassy, Mingzhou played an even more pivotal role in Song diplomacy. The king of Goryeo, communicating through officials in Mingzhou, requested that the Song emperor dispatch medical experts skilled in fields such as "internal medicine" (*dafangmai* 大方脉) and the surgery of "sores and swellings" (*chuangzhongke* 疮肿科). In response, Emperor Huizong sent a team of imperial physicians, who arrived in Goryeo in the seventh month of 1118. In 1123, the Song dispatched another embassy to Goryeo. This mission, led by Lu Yundi, would later be remembered as one of the most famous in the history of Song-Goryeo relations.

In the spring of 1122, Emperor Huizong was preparing to send Lu Yundi to lead an embassy to Goryeo. Before the mission could depart, however, news arrived in the ninth month that the king of Goryeo, Yejong, had died. Lu Yundi's mission was thus expanded to include offering official condolences. The delegation set out in 1123. Its chief envoy was Lu Yundi, a native of Shangqiu in Henan, who held the title of Grand Master of Remonstrance (jishizhong). The deputy envoy was Fu Moqing from Shaoxing in Zhejiang, a Secretariat Drafter (zhongshu sheren). A key member of their retinue was Xu Jing (1091–1153), a native of Hexian in Anhui. Xu Jing had little interest in the civil service examinations but was a man of great accomplishment in calligraphy, poetry, painting, and music. It is said that King Yejong of Goryeo had once requested that the Song court include a skilled calligrapher in a future embassy. It was likely for this reason that Emperor Huizong, himself a passionate devotee of calligraphy, selected Xu Jing, whose work he admired. Upon his return from Goryeo, Xu Jing compiled a 40-volume work based on his experiences, which he completed in the autumn of 1124 and presented to the emperor.

This book, the Xuanhe Fengshi Gaoli Tujing (Illustrated Account of the

Embassy to Goryeo in the Xuanhe Era) , contains a detailed record of the round-trip voyage from Ningbo to Goryeo. It is a priceless document for the study of the Zhejiang Maritime Silk Road, its value being twofold.

First, it provides an invaluable foundation for the study of ancient ocean-going ships.

Xu Jing explains that according to Song government regulations, when the court dispatched an overseas mission, the authorities in Fujian and Zhejiang were to hire private ships. These chartered vessels, known as "guest ships" (kezhou), were brought to the shipyards of Mingzhou to be lavishly decorated and outfitted. Each guest ship was over ten zhang long, three zhang deep, and two-and-a-half zhang wide, with a capacity of two thousand hu of grain. The interior was divided into separate compartments for storing fresh water, for cooking, and for quartering soldiers. On the aft deck, a "bridge house" was constructed for the members of the embassy, complete with windows on all four sides and luxurious appointments. Each ship was manned by a crew of over 60 sailors. Xu Jing described the hull of a guest ship in a memorable line: "Its top is as flat as a scale-beam, its bottom as sharp as a blade; it is prized for its ability to cleave through the waves." This confirms that the ocean-going vessels plying the Zhejiang Maritime Silk Road had V-shaped hulls. Of particular importance are several key technologies that Xu Jing documents aboard these ships.

The first is the bamboo stabilizer. On the tumultuous open sea, a ship over ten zhang long and two-and-a-half zhang wide would pitch forward and back, but its side-to-side roll would be far more violent. To dampen this rolling motion, sailors bundled together large bamboo poles and fastened them to the sides of the ship's hull to increase hydrodynamic resistance. Xu Jing, unfamiliar with the concept of resistance, simply wrote: "On both flanks of the ship's belly, large bamboos are bound into bundles to fend off the waves." We can call this device a jianyao zhutuo, or "anti-rolling bamboo bundle." These bundles were a temporary measure, later evolving into fixed bilge keels permanently attached to the hull. A Northern Song wooden ship unearthed in Ningbo in 1978–1979 was equipped with bilge keels made of half-rounded timbers, a feature still common on modern marine vessels. Maritime historians believe the bilge keel first appeared in the West in the first quarter of the 19th century. The Ningbo discovery thus suggests that China was using this technology approximately 700 years earlier. The bamboo stabilizer, the direct precursor to the bilge keel, represents a major contribution of ancient China to world shipbuilding history.

The second is the stone anchor and pulley system. When a modern ship needs to anchor at sea, it drops an iron anchor from its bow. The anchor's sharp flukes dig deep into the seabed, holding the vessel fast. From Xu Jing's Xuanhe Fengshi Gaoli Tujing, we learn that in the Song era, before the widespread use of iron anchors, sailors used stone anchors. These were constructed by clamping a large, rectangular stone between two sturdy wooden hooks. The weight of the stone would sink the device, allowing the wooden hooks to dig into the seabed mud. A thick rattan cable was tied to the end of the anchor. Because the anchor was extremely heavy, it was difficult to raise by hand. Sailors therefore ran the rattan cable through a pulley mounted on the ship's bow, which made lowering and raising the anchor much easier. The discovery of Song and Yuan dynasty stone anchors in Quanzhou and along the coast of Japan has confirmed the accuracy of Xu Jing's account. In especially rough seas, additional stone anchors could be deployed from the sides of the ship to hold it steady.

Third, Sails and Wind Vanes. Xu Jing tells us that a guest ship was equipped with ten sculling oars, but these were used mainly for maneuvering in and out of port. On the open sea, the vessel relied on wind power. Each ship had at least two masts: a mainmast ten zhang high and a foremast eight zhang high. There were two types of sails: cloth sails (bufan) and mat-and-batten sails (lipeng). As the name suggests, the cloth sails were likely made of hemp or a similar fabric; a single ship carried at least fifty of them. The lipeng were woven from bamboo strips and could be angled to catch the wind. When the wind was favorable (blowing from behind), the crew would hoist all fifty cloth sails. When sailing with a crosswind, they used the adjustable lipeng. Since favorable winds were rare, the lipeng were used more frequently. At the top of the mainmast were ten small sails known as "wild fox sails," which were used when the air was calm. To determine the wind's direction, a pole was erected on the ship, topped with a device made of feathers called a wuliang (literally, "five ounces"). Because the feathers were so light, they would pivot with even the slightest breeze, functioning much like a modern weather vane.

The fourth is the sounding lead. As someone who had personally experienced an ocean voyage, Xu Jing wrote with authority: on the high seas, the sailor's fear is not of deep water, but of shallows where a ship might run aground. He added that because the ships had V-shaped hulls, if one became stranded and the tide receded, it would be unable to rest upright on the seabed and would capsize—a sailor's greatest worry. To prevent this, the crew used a sounding lead. This was a lead weight tied to a rope, which was lowered to the seabed to measure the water's depth. To date, underwater archaeologists in China have found two such artifacts: one from the Ming-dynasty "Nanao No. 1" shipwreck in Guangdong, and another from the Qing-dynasty "Xiaobaijiao No. 1" shipwreck in Xiangshan, Zhejiang. The latter, cast from a lead-tin alloy, is 9.3 cm high, conical in shape, and has a hole at the top for the rope. Xu Jing's account shows that by the Song Dynasty, the sounding lead was already in common use on ships sailing the Zhejiang Maritime Silk Road.

The fifth is the night communication and compass. Xu Jing recounts that when the fleet was sailing in dangerous waters, the command ship would periodically raise a torch, and the other ships would raise torches in response. In an age without radio, this was how a fleet communicated at night to ensure maximum safety. Of particular significance is a passage in the Xuanhe Fengshi Gaoli Tujing that reads: "At night, it is impossible to stop in the middle of the ocean; one can only navigate by the stars and constellations. If the sky is dark and overcast, then one uses the floating magnetic needle to determine north and south." This is a clear description of celestial navigation supplemented by a magnetic compass. The passage provides powerful evidence that by the Northern Song Dynasty, the compass was in use on ships sailing the Zhejiang Maritime Silk Road. Some scholars have even called Xu Jing's work "the earliest book to record a successful round-trip, long-distance ocean voyage from China navigated by compass."

Xu Jing records that the Song embassy's fleet consisted of eight sailing ships: six guest ships and two "Divine Ships" (shenzhou). As mentioned earlier, for An Tao's 1078 mission, Emperor Shenzong had ordered the construction in Ningbo of two enormous "wanhu ships" with long, auspicious names. Emperor Huizong, believing his own mission to be of even greater importance, commissioned two even larger ships and gave them even longer names: the Dingxin Lishe Huaiyuan Kangji Shenzhou (Divine Ship of Innovation for Favorable Crossings, Cherishing Those Afar in Health and Peace) and the Xunliu Anyi Tongji Shenzhou (Divine Ship that Follows the Currents in Ease and Comfort for Universal Passage). These two Divine Ships were also built at the shipyards at the mouth of the Yong River in Zhenhai. Although Xu Jing provides a relatively detailed account of the size and features of the guest ships, he says little about the two Divine Ships, noting only that in their dimensions, equipment, cargo, and crew, they were three times the size of a guest ship. He describes them as "towering like mountains" and "without peer in any age." We are left to imagine their mountain-like grandeur based on his description of the smaller vessels.

Second, it provides a firsthand account of the sea route from Zhejiang to Goryeo.

Xu Jing's Xuanhe Fengshi Gaoli Tujing reads like a ship's log, vividly documenting the sea route and the journey from Mingzhou to Goryeo:

On the 14th day of the fifth month, in the fifth year of the Xuanhe reign (1123), officials hosted a farewell banquet for the embassy inside the walls of Mingzhou (in what is now Haishu District, Ningbo).

On the 16th day, the fleet weighed anchor at the Sanjiang Estuary in modern-day Ningbo and sailed east down the Yong River.

On the 19th day, the fleet reached the mouth of the Yong River at modern-day Zhenhai. The men went to the Dragon King Temple at the foot of nearby Zhaobao Mountain to burn incense and pray for a safe voyage. During the ceremony, a lizard-like creature appeared, which everyone took to be an incarnation of the Dragon King of the Eastern Sea. It was seen as a highly auspicious omen, a sign that the Dragon King would protect them on their journey and that they could set sail in safety.

On the 24th day, the sky was clear. Some officials climbed to the summit of Zhaobao Mountain, where they burned incense and prayed toward the vast sea. The eight ships of the embassy then departed from the mouth of the Yong River. With gongs and drums sounding and banners flying, the fleet sailed past Zhaobao Mountain and out into the open ocean. They navigated past Hutou Mountain (later called Hudun Mountain, now connected to the mainland by land reclamation), Qili Mountain (modern Qilishi), Jiaomen (modern Zhongzhumen), and the two Xie Islands (modern Daxie and Xiaoxie). In the afternoon, they anchored at Lupu (in the area of Chuanshan Village in today's Beilun District, Ningbo). This means that after leaving the Yong River, the fleet did not sail directly northeast. Instead, it followed the coastline of what is now Beilun District to the southeast, before turning toward Shenjiamen in the Zhoushan archipelago.

On the morning of the 25th day, the fleet sailed into Shenjiamen. At the time, it was a small settlement of a few families who made their living by fishing and cutting firewood. That afternoon, a storm suddenly blew in with wind and rain. In response, the crew of each ship launched a small wooden model boat into the sea. Inside the model were Buddhist sutras, food, and a slip of paper with the names of everyone on board. This ritual was an offering to the spirits of the sea, a plea for their protection and a safe passage for the fleet.

On the 26th day, the fleet arrived at Meicen Island (modern-day Mount Putuo). The members of the embassy and the soldiers on board all went ashore to pay homage to the bodhisattva Guanyin, joining the island's monks in an all-night prayer vigil.

On the 28th day, the weather was clear. At dawn, all eight ships of the embassy set sail together. As they were about to leave the land behind and enter the open ocean, Chief Envoy Lu Yundi and Deputy Envoy Fu Moqing donned their formal court robes and bowed in the direction of the capital, Bianjing, in a gesture of farewell. They then cast thirteen Taoist talismans into the sea, including the "Placard for the Master of Winds and the Dragon King" and the "Talisman of the Celestial Officials," to pray for calm seas and a safe journey. Here, the water turned a deep turquoise. The fleet entered the waters of the Shengsi Islands, passing Hailü Reef (later known by names such as Hailuo Reef or Haijiao), Penglai Mountain (modern Daishan, known in antiquity as the "Immortal Isle of Penglai"), and Banyang Reef (in the area of the modern East and West Banyang Reefs).

On the 29th day, the fleet gradually left the waters of Zhejiang, entering first the Baishuiyang (White Water Ocean, the sea between the mouths of the Qiantang and Yangtze Rivers) and then the Huangshuiyang (Yellow Water Ocean, the sea north of the Yangtze to Haizhou Bay in Jiangsu). People in Xu Jing's time already understood that this area was near the mouth of the Yellow River, which carried immense quantities of silt into the sea, making the water "turbid and muddy." Thus, it was known as the Yellow Water Ocean. The heavy silt deposits made the sea shallow, and many sailors had lost their lives when their ships ran aground. As the fleet crossed this treacherous sea, the crew made sacrifices of chickens and millet to the spirits of the dead. More importantly, they constantly used sounding leads to measure the depth, ensuring their ships would not meet the same fate.

The Song fleet sailed north from the mouth of the Yong River, hugging the coasts of Zhejiang and Jiangsu. After crossing the Yellow Water Ocean, however, at approximately 34 degrees north latitude off the coast of Jiangsu, the ships made a sharp turn to the east, heading for the southwestern tip of the Korean Peninsula. The water here was very deep and the visibility poor. In Xu Jing's words, it was "as dark as ink," and so this sea was called the Heishuiyang (Black Water Ocean). Xu Jing wrote that in this ocean, "the furious waves surged and broke, standing tall as a thousand mountains." The ships were tossed up and down so violently that the passengers "felt their stomachs churn and could barely catch their breath."

After a difficult eastward crossing of the Black Water Ocean, the fleet sighted Jiajie Mountain (modern Xiaoheishan Island) on the second day of the sixth month. Xu Jing noted that this island marked "the boundary between the Chinese and the barbarians." The fleet had now entered Goryeo's waters. They sailed north along the western coast of the Korean Peninsula, passing a series of islands: Baishan (modern Hongdo), Heishan (modern Daeheuksando), Yueyu (modern Jeonhujeungdo), Kushanshan (modern Wido), the Qunshan Islands (modern Gunsan Archipelago), Heshang Island (modern Daemuui-do), Niuxinyu (modern Yongyu-do), and Ziyan Island (modern Yeongjong-do). On the tenth day of the month, they rode the tide into the mouth of the Yeseong River. After anchoring for a time, they finally went ashore at Yeseong Port on the twelfth day. On the thirteenth, they completed the final leg of their journey overland, arriving at the Goryeo capital, Kaesong.

After the Song fleet anchored, Goryeo officials in brightly colored boats came out to welcome the members of the embassy ashore and escort them to the guesthouse. The following day, a grand ceremony was held to mark the embassy's entry into the capital. A procession was led by a color guard holding bright banners, followed by cavalry and a musical troupe that sang and danced. The Song emperor's edict was carried on a specially made, ornate carriage. The Song envoys, dressed in splendid court attire, rode on horseback, flanked on both sides of the road by fully armed soldiers. In the Goryeo royal palace, Chief Envoy Lu Yundi and Deputy Envoy Fu Moqing stood facing south, with the other members of the embassy ranked behind them according to their status. The king of Goryeo stood facing north to receive the edict from Emperor Huizong. The entire ceremony was one of extreme solemnity, fully reflecting Goryeo's vassal relationship to the Song court. The Song embassy also held a special memorial service for the late King Yejong, a ceremony that was likewise conducted with an air of stately superiority.

The Song embassy began its sea voyage from the mouth of the Yong

River on the 24th day of the fifth month, precisely when the southerly monsoon winds were blowing strong. As a result, their journey was relatively smooth, and they reached Goryeo's Yeseong Port on the twelfth day of the sixth month, a voyage of less than a month. After completing their diplomatic duties, the envoys boarded their ships on the fifteenth day of the seventh month to return by the same route. This time, however, they faced contrary winds, and they did not reach Zhenhai until the 27th day of the eighth month. The return journey had taken over a month. This clearly illustrates the degree to which the ancient Zhejiang Maritime Silk Road, in the age of the wooden sailing ship, was subject to the whims of nature.

The triumphant return of Xu Jing's mission to Mingzhou solidified the relationship between the two nations and further elevated Mingzhou's status in the Song's foreign relations. This, in turn, created a favorable political environment for the continued prosperity of the Zhejiang Maritime Silk Road.

Chapter 5: The First Communities of Zhejiang Emigrants in Western Europe

5.1 Shuangyu Port on the Zhejiang Coast

Before the 16th century, when merchants, monks, and diplomats from Zhejiang traveled the Maritime Silk Road, their destinations were primarily Japan and the Korean Peninsula. A few made their way to Southeast Asia, the most famous being Zhou Daguan (c. 1266–1346) of Wenzhou. In 1295, serving as an interpreter for a Yuan Dynasty mission, he sailed from Wenzhou to the kingdom of Zhenla (modern Cambodia). He returned to Ningbo in 1297 and wrote A Record of Cambodia about his experiences. Until 1500, however, the world of Zhejiang's seafarers was confined to Asia; no records suggest any had traveled beyond the continent. But as the 16th century began, a rising tide of globalization propelled some to cross the oceans and journey to Europe.

The close of the 15th century marked the beginning of Europe's Age of Discovery, which raised the curtain on the first era of globalization. Spain and Portugal spearheaded this movement. For the Portuguese, the primary goal was to find a sea route to Asia by sailing around Africa. In early 1488, a fleet commanded by Bartolomeu Dias reached the Cape of Good Hope. Late in 1497, Vasco da Gama's expedition successfully rounded the Cape, and in May 1498, it arrived in Calicut, a commercial hub on India's west coast. This voyage blazed a new trail from the Atlantic directly to India. In the years that followed, wave after wave of Portuguese explorers followed this route, pushing ever eastward.

In 1511, the Portuguese captured Malacca, throwing open the maritime gates to China. By 1513, if not earlier, they had arrived on the coast of Guangdong. The Chinese, knowing nothing of these newcomers, called them Folangji, a name derived from Franj, the Arabic term for Europeans. The Portuguese sailed up and down the Guangdong coast, frequently engaging in piracy. In 1522, after Ming forces defeated them at Xicaowan, they were guided by Chinese merchants north along the coasts of Fujian and Zhejiang. Around 1524, they established a trading base in Zhejiang they called Liampo. Scholars have confirmed that Liampo was a transliteration of "Ningbo" and referred to what the Chinese called Shuangyu Port, located on modern-day Liuheng Island in the Zhoushan archipelago. Unfortunately, despite extensive searching, archaeologists have yet to pinpoint its exact location.

From their base at Shuangyu Port, the Portuguese engaged in smuggling on a massive scale. The port soon became a magnet for Chinese smugglers from provinces like Jiangsu, Zhejiang, and Fujian, as well as their counterparts from Southeast Asia, Japan, and even the coast of East Africa. Shuangyu transformed into a den of international armed smugglers. Led by the Portuguese, these gangs colluded with powerful families in Zhejiang and Fujian for illegal trade while simultaneously raiding coastal communities near Ningbo, burning homes, and brazenly kidnapping Ming soldiers to hold them for ransom.

The escalating smuggling and violence at Shuangyu Port eventually captured the attention of the imperial court. In the autumn of 1547, the Jiajing Emperor dispatched Zhu Wan (1494–1550) to oversee a unified anti-smuggling campaign along the Zhejiang and Fujian coasts. In 1548, Zhu Wan assembled troops and launched an attack on Shuangyu. Before dawn on the seventh day of the fourth lunar month, the smugglers made a desperate attempt to break the blockade, bursting from the harbor in their ships. While in pursuit, Ming forces entered and searched the port, discovering 27 abandoned vessels, over twenty thatched huts, and a temple to the sea goddess Tianfei. They burned everything to the ground. In what became known as the Battle of Shuangyu, Ming forces not only seized advanced Portuguese weaponry but also captured three Africans. This battle marked the first military clash between Chinese and Europeans in Zhejiang's history and the first recorded Chinese victory over an armed European force.

Portrait of Zhu Wan

After destroying the smugglers'den, Zhu Wan initially intended to garrison troops at Shuangyu, but his soldiers refused to be stationed there. After personally inspecting the site, Zhu Wan decided the only way to prevent smugglers from reoccupying the harbor was to fill it in. His men drove wooden stakes into the harbor entrance and then packed the space with stones. Since then, Shuangyu Port has lain buried under silt, its location lost to history.

Though active for less than three decades (1524–1548), the Portuguese presence at Shuangyu had a profound and lasting impact. First, as the earliest European trading post in East Asia, it placed the Ningbo region at the forefront of globalization's arrival in China. Second, it forged a direct maritime link—from Shuangyu to Malacca, Goa, and Lisbon—integrating Ningbo into a global trade network for the first time. Third, its trade ties with Japan made Shuangyu a pivotal hub connecting the East and South China Sea routes, which also facilitated the first direct cultural transmission from Europe to Japan. Fourth, Shuangyu became China's first base for direct exports to Europe, with porcelain being the primary commodity. A blue-and-white porcelain cup in the Beja Regional Museum in Portuga stands as evidence. It bears a Portuguese inscription: "EM TEMPO DE PERO DE FARIA DE 1514", indicating that this piece was commissioned in 1541 by a man named Pero de Faria. This individual was a Portuguese colonizer who served twice as the Governor of Portuguese Malacca, from 1526 to 1529 and again from 1539 to 1543. A report by Zhu Wan from 1548 confirms that smugglers were trading silk and porcelain with "Bieru Fuli" (a transliteration of Faria) in Malacca via Shuangyu. Fifth, the battle of Shuangyu led the Ming government to shift its policy from suppression to accommodation, which resulted in the decision to allow the Portuguese to settle in Macau. Finally, the sea route from Shuangyu to Europe carried the first natives of Zhejiang to Western Europe, making them the earliest overseas Chinese from the region.

5.2 The Men from Ningbo in a Spanish Court

Deep within the judicial records of the Archivo General de Indias in Seville, Spain, lay a collection of documents concerning the first overseas Chinese from Zhejiang. They remained unknown for centuries until their discovery in the 21st century by Spanish scholar Juan Gil. To understand the significance of these records, one must first understand the context of Spanish colonial rule in the Americas.

While the Portuguese sought a route to Asia around Africa, the Spanish pursued a westward passage across the Atlantic. In October 1492, funded by the Spanish crown, Christopher Columbus crossed the Atlantic and landed in the Bahamas. Convinced he had reached the Indies, he called the native people Indios ("Indians"). Later, in 1519, Ferdinand Magellan set out on his historic circumnavigation of the globe, entering the Pacific in 1520 and landing in the Philippines in March 1521. By the latter half of the 16th century, Spain had established colonial rule in the Philippines and began referring to the native Filipinos as Indios as well. To distinguish the two groups in translation, we will refer to the Filipinos under Spanish rule as Indios, while using "Indigenous Americans" for the native peoples of the Americas.

From the beginning of their overseas expansion, both Spanish and Portuguese colonizers enslaved Indigenous peoples, often trafficking them back to Europe. As early as 1500, the Queen of Spain banned the importation of enslaved Indigenous Americans into Spain, a decree the government reaffirmed multiple times since 1511. However, while Spanish law explicitly forbade the enslavement of Indios from its own colonies, it contained critical loopholes. A slaveholder could legally keep an enslaved person if they could prove the person came from a Portuguese colony. Furthermore, if Indigenous people refused to convert to Christianity or submit to the Spanish king, the Spanish could wage a so-called "just war" against them, and anyone captured in such a war was denied the right to freedom. These laws triggered a flood of lawsuits in Spain. Many enslaved people claimed to be Indios from Spanish colonies and demanded their freedom, while their owners tried every means possible to prove their slaves were from Portuguese territories or were legitimate prisoners of a "just war." These cases were primarily heard by two bodies: the House of Trade (Casa de la Contratación) in Seville and the Council of the Indies (Consejo de Indias) in Madrid.

One of these lawsuits was brought by a plaintiff identified as a Chino (Chinese), whose Spanish name was Diego Indio, or Diego for short. The defendant was a Portuguese monk named Juan de Morales. In July 1572, Diego filed a complaint with a religious court in Seville, claiming that he was an Indio who had been illegally enslaved by Morales and demanding his freedom. Fearing the religious court might be biased in favor of a monk, Diego filed a second complaint in October with the secular House of Trade. The case would take three full years to resolve.

According to the court records, Diego testified that he was "from China" and that his hometown was a place called "Liampo"—clearly a transliteration of Ningbo. The records state, "Because he was a child when he left his homeland, Diego has few memories of it. He remembers only that his home was near the sea," but he could not say whether it was on an island or the mainland. "He does not even know who his parents were." Diego recalled that in his hometown, "there were cows, sheep, goats, and chickens... and a fruit called longuen (longan) and another called lachi (lychee)." He claimed there were Spanish people there but no Portuguese, and that the area produced gold, silver, linen, cotton, velvet, and satin. When Diego was six or seven, he was taken from his home by a Spanish official named Francisco de Castañeda. In a church named for the Virgin Mary, a priest baptized Diego, and one of Castañeda's servants acted as his godfather. The court record continues: "When Castañeda left Liampo by ship, he took Diego and 14 or 15 other Indios (whose names Diego had forgotten) with him, and they set out for the city of Lima." This suggests their first stop after crossing the Pacific was Lima, Peru. Later, Castañeda arranged for a ship to take Diego and the others to Spain. During the Atlantic crossing, however, they were attacked by French pirates. By the time Diego and the other survivors reached Lisbon, they were "destitute, sick, and starving." The authorities in Lisbon placed Diego in the service of a Portuguese shoemaker named Juan Fernandes, who taught him the trade.

The record states that after Diego had lived in Lisbon for about ten years, the monk Morales passed by the shoemaker's shop and was struck by Diego's unusual appearance. He asked Diego where he was from, and Diego replied that he was Chinese. Morales told him that while there were no other Chinese in Lisbon, there were many in Seville who could help him return to his homeland. Trusting the monk, Diego went with him to Seville around 1565. There, Morales employed him as a shoemaker for five reales a week, plus food. Diego worked diligently, saving money for his return journey. The court records note, "Diego still remembers the dialect of his homeland but rarely speaks it," because although there were a few other Indios in Seville who spoke a Chinese language, none could understand his specific dialect. In 1572, Morales decided to seek his fortune in the Americas and sold Diego to another man for 92 ducados. This prompted Diego to sue, arguing that as an Indio, he was a free man under Spanish law and could not be sold. He declared to the court: "I am not a slave. I came to Seville from Lisbon voluntarily because Morales promised to help me return to China... I am a free man with my own trade. I gave Morales the money I earned to buy food and clothing for my journey back to China."

Several witnesses testified on Diego's behalf, most importantly a married couple living in Seville: Esteban de Cabrera and Juana de Castañeda. The court record describes Esteban as an 84-year-old "Indio from China" and a "native of Limpoa" (Ningbo). Esteban told the judge that Ningbo was "in China, on the other side of New Spain, which is under the rule of His Majesty the King of Spain." He stated that "Ningbo is on the sea, but it is not an island. Because it is on the mainland, one can travel from there to all parts of the interior." He added, "Diego was born and raised in Ningbo, as was I," and "I knew him when he was a little boy of six or seven." The record continues: "About 26 years ago, Governor Castañeda arrived in that part of China with two or three ships, and because Ningbo is a seaport, he entered it."

Esteban testified in 1572, which would place Castañeda's arrival in Ningbo around 1546. When asked if he knew Diego's family, Esteban replied, "I do not know his parents. I first met Diego in Castañeda's house in Ningbo." He recalled that a few days later, Castañeda left Ningbo and sailed for Mexico, taking both Esteban and Diego with him. After three months in Mexico, they traveled to Nicaragua. Esteban stated, "Governor Castañeda sent a ship of Indios from China and Peru back to Spain, and Diego and I were on it." He then recounted the pirate attack and how he and Diego were separated in Lisbon. When they met again in Seville, Diego told him that he had come to the city with Morales, who had promised to help him get back to China.

The court clerk described Esteban's wife, Juana, as being "dark-skinned" and 40 years old. Juana testified that she was a "native of the city of Lima," meaning she was an Indigenous American. "I first met Diego in Lima when he was a small child," she said, "but I do not remember anyone mentioning where he was born." She continued, "When Governor Castañeda sent a group of Indios from China and Peru back to Spain, Diego was among them. I was a young girl at the time, a servant in the governor's household, and by his order, I returned to Spain with them." She also recounted the pirate attack during the voyage. Juana concluded her testimony by telling the judge, "Diego is a free man, just like my husband and I." Given her age, it is likely she was a teenage orphan whom Castañeda had taken into his household.

Diego had three other key witnesses who testified in 1575: Isabel Garcia, Francisco Diaz, and Rodrigo de Cabrera. Isabel Garcia, a 55-year-old Indigenous American from Panama, stated that she had known Diego for five years. She believed he was from China because "China is very close to Panama, and the Indios from both places are really of the same people and speak the same language." She added, "They also look the same."

Francisco Diaz, a tailor of about 45 living in Seville, told the judge, "I myself grew up in Ningbo," and therefore, "I can converse with Diego in the Ningbo dialect." He testified that Diego not only looked and acted like a native of Ningbo in his appearance, complexion, and temperament, but could also accurately describe unique aspects of the region, proving he was undoubtedly from there. Francisco added, "I came here from China 30 years ago. I have heard that all Indios who come from China are free people."

Rodrigo de Cabrera, a 47-year-old oil-presser, also claimed to be from Ningbo. His testimony stated: "About 27 years ago, Governor Castañeda came to Ningbo in China... The plaintiff, Diego, who was about eight years old then, came to Castañeda's residence to be his servant. After a few days, Castañeda left for Lima, taking both me and Diego with him." The testimonies of Francisco (left 1545), Rodrigo (left c. 1548), and Esteban (left 1546) all point to a departure around 1546, which would make Diego about 35 when he filed his lawsuit.

The records present a narrative where Diego, Esteban, Francisco, and Rodrigo, all natives of the Ningbo area, were taken by Castañeda around 1546. Their journey took them east across the Pacific to Peru, through Central America, and finally across the Atlantic to Seville. This eastward route from Spain to China via the Americas corresponds to what the Italian missionary Giulio Aleni (1582–1649) called the "Eastern Route." Aleni also described a "Western Route," from Portugal around Africa. Diego and his witnesses claimed they had taken the Eastern Route, while the defendant, Morales, insisted Diego had come via the Western Route.

5.3 Diego's Victory

Morales introduced himself to the court as an educated monk from Portugal and told a completely different story. "About ten years ago," he testified, "I purchased Diego in Goa. He was a prisoner of war. Because he was a war captive, I took him to an island in Mozambique, where he served me as a slave for several years. I later brought him to Portugal, and then to Seville.

During this whole time, I have owned him as a slave, and he has never objected. Although he is a skilled shoemaker, he has always acknowledged that he is my personal slave." Morales claimed Diego had learned his trade from a shoemaker in Goa named Diego Ramos. Morales had purchased him from Ramos in exchange for another young slave plus 47 gold coins (pardaos), and had then taught Diego how to pray.

Morales claimed that upon arriving in Seville, Diego was coached by Esteban and other Indios to fabricate his story. He reminded the court that "parts of Asia are under the rule of the Portuguese, not the Spanish." Therefore, even if Diego were an Indio, he came from a Portuguese territory, not a Spanish one, and thus was not entitled to freedom under Spanish law.

Morales produced his own witnesses, including three enslaved people from Mozambique: Hernando (20), Diego (22), and Felipa (23). Hernando testified that he had known Morales for 15 years and Diego for 10, and that he had been present when Morales purchased Diego in Goa, even remembering the price. According to Hernando, Diego was originally a Muslim who had converted to Christianity. The other two witnesses, Diego and Felipa, both stated they had met Morales and the plaintiff in Mozambique. The witness Diego added that in Goa and Mozambique there were many Indios like the plaintiff from "the part of China belonging to the Portuguese." Several other enslaved people also testified to having seen the plaintiff in Mozambique.

Thus, the two sides presented completely contradictory stories. According to Morales, Diego had been purchased as a slave in Portuguese Goa and brought to Europe via the Western Route around Africa. According to Diego, he was a free man from a Spanish territory who had come to Europe via the Eastern Route across the Americas. These conflicting accounts made for a long and complex trial.

After Diego filed his complaint in October 1572, the court appointed an attorney, Francisco Sarmiento, as his legal guardian. Meanwhile, Morales left for the Americas, leaving an agent in Seville to handle his affairs and writing letters to the court to defend himself. In 1573, Alonso petitioned the House of Trade for the imprisonment of Diego. Meanwhile, the lawyer Sarmiento requested that a judge order the arrest of Morales in the Americas and have him returned for imprisonment. In July 1573, the court ruled in favor of Morales. Sarmiento immediately appealed to the Council of the Indies in Madrid, which agreed to hear the case. After more testimony and fierce debate, in July 1575, the Council finally ruled that Diego was a free man and was entitled to compensation.

Although the Diego case concluded after three years of trial, the full truth did not emerge. This is because Professor Hill also discovered Esteban's will, signed on March 15, 1599. The 1572 court record stated Esteban was 84 years old, which was clearly a clerical error; otherwise, he would have been 110 when drafting his will. When Esteban testified for Diego in 1572, his wife, Juana, was only 40, suggesting he was likely no more than 50 at the time. He testified in 1572 that he had left China 26 years earlier (in 1546). If this is credible, he would have been in his twenties when he left China, and in his seventies or eighties when he made his will in 1599. More importantly, in this will, Esteban claimed he was born in Canton (Guangdong), not Ningbo. He stated that he went from Canton to the Portuguese-held Macau and then departed from Macau, eventually reaching Europe. This indicates he traveled to Europe via the western route of the global maritime circuit, not the eastern route as he had previously testified during Diego's trial. Since Esteban likely never passed through the Americas, we do not know where he met the American Indian Juana, nor when they married. In his will, Esteban bequeathed his estate to his daughter, Francisca de Altamirano. Her husband, Miguel de la Cruz, was a tailor and was also likely Chinese. The will also instructed that some property be donated to a local church in Seville. Esteban listed several debtors, including Francisco, who had testified for Diego, and two "Japanese" (japón) individuals named Paulo and Manuel. While scholars had previously believed the first Japanese arrived in Seville in 1614, the discovery of this will shows they were present there as early as 1599. Esteban appointed his son-in-law, Miguel, as the executor of his will and authorized him to collect the debts.

Esteban's 1572 testimony that "Ningbo... is not an island" supports the claim in his will that he was from Guangdong, not Ningbo. The "Ningbo" of that era, Liampo, was in fact the island port of Shuangyu. Esteban's ignorance of this basic geography suggests he was not a native of the area.

The claim that Francisco de Castañeda brought the men from "Ningbo" around 1546 is also problematic. While there was a real Spanish official of that name who served as interim governor of Nicaragua (1531–1535), he gained a poor reputation and fled to Panama and Peru to escape punishment. He did later transport enslaved Indigenous people from Peru to Spain. However, he was never the governor of Peru, as Juana testified. Most importantly, the real Castañeda returned to Madrid in 1541 and died in May 1542, years before he supposedly sailed to China and long before Diego's trial began.

The entire story of a Spanish ship sailing from China to the Americas around 1546 is chronologically impossible. The Spanish did not establish a foothold in the Philippines until 1565, which is when they discovered the round-trip route across the Pacific. No historical sources, Chinese or foreign, place Spanish ships at Shuangyu Port during that period; the only Europeans active on the China coast at that time were the Portuguese. Diego's claim that there were "no Portuguese, but some Spaniards" at Shuangyu is a clear contradiction of the historical facts. It is far more likely that Diego and the others were brought to Europe on Portuguese ships via the Western Route, just as Esteban described in his will.

Why, then, did Diego and his witnesses insist on this fabricated story? The answer lies in Spanish law. To win his freedom, Diego had to prove he was an Indio from a Spanish territory, not a Portuguese one. The most plausible explanation is that the small Chinese community in Seville, likely led by the older and more established Esteban, conspired to win their countryman's freedom. Using what little they knew of Spanish law and global geography, they crafted a narrative designed to place Diego's origins firmly within the Spanish sphere of influence. That they succeeded also reveals the Spanish court's profound ignorance of the geography and politics of East Asia—an ignorance that also fueled the grandiose and unrealistic plans for the conquest of China that were popular among Spanish colonists at the time.

To secure his countryman's freedom, Esteban was willing to perjure himself, claiming to be from Ningbo. Diego himself, however, was likely telling the truth about his origins in or near Shuangyu. If the story were a complete fabrication, it would have been far simpler to claim he was from a place indisputably under Spanish rule, like the Philippines. Choosing a contested location lent his story a degree of credibility. Whether Francisco and Rodrigo were truly from Ningbo is impossible to say; they may have claimed to be natives simply to bolster Diego's case.

According to the testimony, Diego was only seven or eight when he was taken from his home around 1546. Francisco and Rodrigo were not yet 20, and Esteban was in his early twenties. Having left as a small child, Diego had few memories of his homeland. He knew it was by the sea but could not say if it was an island. His claim that his home produced longans and lychees was undoubtedly an error, as neither fruit grows in the Ningbo region. They are, however, common in Guangdong, suggesting that Esteban, a native of Guangdong, likely fed Diego this incorrect detail. Morales's side was also guilty of fabrication; the claim by his witness Hernando that Diego was originally a Muslim was pure invention, as Islam had no following among the Han Chinese of 16th-century Zhejiang.

As soon as the Portuguese arrived on the coast of China in the early 16th century, officials began to condemn them for abducting children. In 1549, Zhu Wan reported that the Portuguese "abduct, cook, and eat boys and girls." This claim that the Portuguese were cannibals who feasted on children became a common trope, even finding its way into the official History of the Ming Dynasty. While these stories were born of fear and imagination, not fact, the case of Diego proves that the Portuguese did indeed abduct children from China's coast and sell them into slavery. Diego, Francisco, and Rodrigo were all kidnapped as children or teenagers. The most likely scenario is that Diego was first abducted by Portuguese slavers, passed through several hands, was eventually sold to Morales in Goa, and from there was brought to Western Europe.

The case of Diego reveals the existence of a small but tight-knit Chinese community in mid-16th-century Seville. Though they occupied the lowest rungs of society, they supported themselves and their families with their skills as shoemakers, tailors, and oil-pressers. Having arrived in Europe as enslaved people with nothing to their names, through hard work and frugal living they managed to accumulate some small property of their own. Diego saved money for his return to China; Esteban's will included a donation to a local church. The case also shows that despite having left China as a child with almost no memory of his home or even his parents, Diego's longing to return never faded. From the very beginning of globalization, the Chinese who set foot on European soil demonstrated the traits that would come to define overseas Chinese communities everywhere: honest work, diligence, frugality, and a deep and abiding love for their homeland. These are the genes that have allowed these communities to not only survive but thrive, no matter the hardships they faced.

The history of Chinese overseas migration dates back at least to the late Tang dynasty in the 10th century. By the Song dynasty, large numbers of Chinese were settling in Southeast Asia. As the 12th-century writer Zhu Yu noted, Chinese who went overseas and did not return within the year were said to be "living among the barbarians." These overseas Chinese were often referred to with the respectful title of Tang Ren ("people of Tang"), and the Yuan-dynasty traveler Wang Dayuan recorded that the people of Brunei "especially respected and loved the Tang Ren." For centuries, the primary destination for Chinese emigrants was Southeast Asia. But around 1500, when Europeans began their great voyages of exploration and seized the reins of globalization, the rulers of the Ming dynasty turned a blind eye to the changing world. They closed China's doors and refused to face the challenges of this new era. As a result, not only were the interests of overseas Chinese left unprotected, but residents of China's coastal regions became prey for Western colonial slavers. Early Chinese migrants to Europe, like Diego, arrived on the Iberian Peninsula against this historical backdrop. They were like fallen leaves caught in the tide of globalization, tossed about by the whims of fate until they washed up on a distant shore. This process can be called their "westward drift." For the Chinese who "drifted west" to the Iberian Peninsula in the 16th century, the journey was one of profound physical and mental suffering. Though Ming rulers, viewing China as the world's only civilized center, dismissed the Europeans as "barbarians," the first Chinese to set foot in Iberia were mostly enslaved. As a result, in 16th-century Spain, the word Chino became synonymous with "lowly slave," while the term Indio signified freedom. This is precisely why the Chinese man Diego fought so tenaciously for three years to prove he was an Indio from a Spanish territory. His victory teaches us that the tide of globalization, once risen, is unstoppable. Attempting to resist it by closing one's doors is an exercise in futility. Only by actively embracing and engaging with the process of globalization can the word "Chinese" command respect on the world stage, and only then can Chinese people live with dignity anywhere in the world.

Part II. Foreign Sojourners in Zhejiang

Countless merchants, monks, and envoys journeyed from Zhejiang to distant shores along the Maritime Silk Road. In turn, their counterparts from across the globe arrived by the same sea routes, each helping in their own way to connect Zhejiang with the wider world.

Chapter 6. Mount Tiantai and Monks from the Korean Peninsula

6.1 Early Buddhist Exchanges between Zhejiang and the Korean Peninsula

Zhejiang's Mount Tiantai is both a place of breathtaking natural beauty and a world-renowned sanctuary of Buddhist devotion. In the latter half of the 6th century, Zhiyi (AD 538–597), a native of Jingzhou in Hubei province, traveled to Mount Tiantai and established the Tiantai School, the first fully realized school of Buddhism indigenous to China. Because its teachings are rooted in the Lotus Sutra (Miàofǎ Liánhuá Jīng), the school is also known as the Fahua or "Lotus" School. Zhiyi himself came to be revered as the "Great Master of Wisdom" (Zhìzhě Dàshī) and the "Great Master of Tiantai" (Tiāntái Dàshī).

As Zhiyi was establishing the Tiantai School, the Korean Peninsula was embroiled in its turbulent Three Kingdoms period. The rival kingdoms of Goguryeo (37 BC–AD 668), Baekje (18 BC–AD 660), and Silla (57 BC–AD 935) were locked in a fierce struggle for supremacy. In these chaotic, war-torn times, people from all walks of life, from royalty to commoners, desperately sought a spiritual sanctuary. Buddhism offered that much-needed harbor for the soul. Against this backdrop, beginning in the late 4th century, monks from the peninsula undertook perilous journeys to China to study the Dharma. At least two of them, Prajna and Yeongwang, made their way to Mount

Tiantai to study directly under Zhiyi.

Prajna, a monk from Goguryeo, began his Buddhist studies in Jinling (modern Nanjing) under the Chen Dynasty (AD 557–589). When the Sui Dynasty conquered the Chen in AD 589, Prajna left Jinling and wandered throughout China. In AD 596, he arrived at Fulong Temple on Mount Tiantai and became a disciple of Zhiyi. Recognizing Prajna's great potential, Zhiyi told him, "You have a deep karmic connection to the Tiantai School. You should find a quiet place to cultivate alone, and you will surely achieve enlightenment. About three kilometers from here is Huading Peak, the highest point on Mount Tiantai, where I myself once engaged in ascetic practice. Go there and do the same, and you are certain to attain profound insight." Prajna followed this advice and spent the next sixteen years in solitary practice on Huading Peak. Throughout this time, he never left the summit and continued his devotions even through the night. In 613, sensing his life was nearing its end, he descended to bid farewell to the monks at Fulong Temple and Guoqing Temple. A few days later, he passed away peacefully, seated in meditation at Guoqing Temple. Prajna is the first monk from the Korean Peninsula known to be buried on Mount Tiantai.

Yeongwang was born into a noble family in Silla. A gifted child, he converted to Buddhism at a young age but grew dissatisfied with the superficial nature of the teachings then common on the peninsula. He traveled to the Jiangnan region of China, where he met Zhiyi, who was lecturing on Tiantai doctrine in Jinling. Yeongwang became his disciple and, after several years of study, gained a profound understanding of the Tiantai School. At Zhiyi's arrangement, he once lectured on the Lotus Sutra, earning the admiration of all who heard him. Yeongwang later deepened his studies on Mount Tiantai. According to legend, several celestial beings appeared to him one day and invited him to preach the Tiantai doctrine in the heavens. Yeongwang silently consented. His breath stopped, and his spirit ascended, only to return to his body ten days later.

After years of devoted study, Yeongwang felt he had mastered the core teachings of the Tiantai School and resolved to return to Silla by sea. As he was leaving from Mount Tiantai, his port of departure was likely in Zhejiang's Taizhou or Ningbo. Legend holds that after Yeongwang and dozens of companions were far out at sea, their vessel came to a sudden halt. A horseman appeared, galloping across the waves toward them. "The Sea God invites you to his palace beneath the waves to preach the Dharma," he announced. Yeongwang replied, "I will go, for the sake of spreading the Dharma. But what is to become of my companions and this ship?" The horseman answered, "They will all descend with you. Do not worry about the ship." At that, Yeongwang and the others stepped off the boat onto a straight, flower-strewn path that had appeared in the sea. Hundreds of attendants from the Sea God's court welcomed them into a magnificent undersea palace, where Yeongwang preached the Lotus Sutra. In gratitude, the Sea God gifted him many treasures and returned the entire party safely to their ship.

After returning to Silla, Yeongwang dedicated himself to propagating the Tiantai teachings until his death at the age of eighty. According to Silla legend, after his cremation, his tongue remained miraculously preserved, as if still alive. His two sisters enshrined it, and it was said that the tongue would sometimes recite passages from the Lotus Sutra. When his sisters encountered difficult passages in their own study of the sutra, the tongue would reportedly provide explanations. While these marvelous stories were undoubtedly embellished to promote the Tiantai School, they reveal the profound reverence the people of the Korean Peninsula held for its teachings.

During the Tang Dynasty, monks from the Korean Peninsula continued to travel to Zhejiang to study Tiantai teachings, though only scant, fragmented records of a few individuals survive. The Southern Song monk Zhipan of Ningbo, in his Comprehensive Chronicle of the Buddha and the Patriarchs (Fózǔ Tǒngjì), notes that the seventh Tiantai patriarch, Xuanlang (AD 673–754), had three disciples from Silla—Farong, Liying, and Chunying—who returned to their homeland from Mount Tiantai in AD 730. Local chronicles from Taizhou mention a "Silla Garden" in front of Guoqing Temple, said to have been built by a Silla monk named Wukong during the Tang, but nothing more is known of his life.

In AD 892, a Silla monk named Daoyu arrived on Mount Tiantai and took up residence at Pingtian Temple (now Wannian Temple). Daoyu was known for his profound compassion and relentless, unwavering asceticism.

He wore the same heavy, patchwork robe year-round and sustained himself on leftover food he collected. When building a fire to boil water or tea, he would cast aside any piece of firewood that contained insects, unable to bear the thought of them being burned. In the summer and autumn, he would bare his chest, back, and legs, offering his own blood to feed mosquitoes and other insects until he was bleeding profusely. It is said that he once encountered a tiger, which simply sniffed him and walked away. Yet, Daoyu never learned to speak Chinese. In AD 935, the Buddhist scholar Zanning (919–1001), a native of Deqing in Zhejiang, stayed in the same room as Daoyu while visiting Shiliang on Mount Tiantai. He found they could not communicate, as Daoyu could only make unintelligible sounds. Nonetheless, Zanning praised Daoyu's profound empathy in his work, the Biographies of Eminent Song Monks. After living at Pingtian Temple for over forty years, Daoyu passed away in AD 938.

Before Daoyu arrived on Mount Tiantai, two momentous events had reshaped China. The first was the An Lushan Rebellion (AD 755–763), which left the Tang Dynasty severely weakened. The second was the large-scale persecution of Buddhism under Emperor Wuzong (r. AD 840–846), a devastating blow from which Guoqing Temple on Mount Tiantai did not escape; its buildings were demolished, and its monks were forced to return to lay life. The period of Daoyu's residency on the mountain was one of even greater turmoil. In AD 907, the Tang Dynasty fell, plunging China into the fractious and chaotic Five Dynasties and Ten Kingdoms period (AD 907–979). That same year, Qian Liu (AD 852–932), a native of Lin'an in Hangzhou, founded the Wuyue Kingdom (AD 907–978), which ruled over Zhejiang and the surrounding areas.

Amid this colossal upheaval, the Tiantai School, battered by successive blows, had fallen into severe decline and was on the verge of collapse. Its scriptures were almost entirely lost, leaving no textual basis for transmitting the teachings. At the time of the Wuyue Kingdom's founding, the abbot of Guoqing Temple was Qingsong, a native of Taizhou. Although respected as the fourteenth Tiantai patriarch, he lacked access to written texts and could only lecture from memory, earning him the moniker "Venerable of Lofty Discourse." After his death, his disciple Yiji (AD 919–987), from Yongjia in Wenzhou, became the fifteenth patriarch. He established his own monastery by Luoxi Stream on Mount Tiantai, at the foot of today's Xiangyun Peak. Desperate to remedy the dearth of scriptures, Yiji searched far and wide but, after years of effort, managed to find only a single copy of Zhiyi's Commentary on the Vimalakirti Sutra in Jinhua. In stark contrast, the distant kingdom of Goryeo (918–1392)—a dynasty founded by Wang Geon (AD 877–943) that unified the Korean Peninsula in AD 936—had preserved a rich collection of Tiantai texts. It was in this context that Yiji appealed to the master Deshao (AD 891–971) for help in retrieving these scriptures from Goryeo.

Deshao, a native of Longquan (or perhaps Jinyun) in Zhejiang, became a monk in his youth. He sought out famous masters, eventually settling on

Mount Tiantai, where he taught the Dharma for many years and founded several temples. Qian Hongchu (AD 929–988), a grandson of Qian Liu, was a devout Buddhist who had served as the prefect of Taizhou and deeply revered Deshao. Upon becoming king of Wuyue at the end of AD 947, he appointed Deshao as the "National Preceptor" (Guóshī). Although Deshao himself was a second-generation patriarch of the Fayan school, a branch of Chan Buddhism, he had strong ties to the Tiantai tradition. He used his influential position to persuade King Qian Hongchu to dispatch an official mission to Goryeo to request the Tiantai scriptures. The king agreed, sending envoys with a letter from Deshao and valuable gifts.

King Gwangjong of Goryeo (AD 925–975) took the request from Wuyue very seriously. In 960, he dispatched a Goryeo monk named Chegwan to escort a collection of Buddhist scriptures to Wuyue and engage in doctrinal discussions with Chinese monks. The king specifically instructed Chegwan: "These are restricted texts. When you arrive in China, you may question the monks on the difficult points within them. If they cannot answer, do not hand over the scriptures and return home at once." Chegwan departed Goryeo in AD 960 and arrived at Luoxi Stream on Mount Tiantai the following year to meet Yiji. Contrary to the king's expectations, Chegwan was so impressed by Yiji's profound scholarship that he not only presented all the scriptures with deep admiration but also became Yiji's disciple. He remained at Luoxi to study the Tiantai teachings until his death around AD 970. After he died, a manuscript titled Essentials of the Tiantai Fourfold Teachings (Tiāntái

Sìjiàoyí) was found among his belongings. In this work, Chegwan had provided a clear and accessible explanation of Tiantai doctrine, and it subsequently became a fundamental introductory text for students of the school. The book, written during his time on Mount Tiantai, became widely circulated; the Comprehensive Chronicle states it was "popular in all regions," even reaching the Korean Peninsula and Japan. Over one hundred scholars throughout history have written commentaries on it.

6.2 Baoyun Yitong

Chegwan's act of bringing a trove of Tiantai scriptures from Goryeo to China laid a firm foundation for the school's revival. Later Tiantai scholars would declare, "The restoration of our school truly began here." Yet another monk from the Korean Peninsula, a contemporary of Chegwan, would make an even greater contribution. Upon arriving in Zhejiang, he would become the sixteenth patriarch of the Tiantai School and a central figure in its renaissance. This monk was Yitong (AD 927–988).

The story of Yitong's life is primarily recorded in the Comprehensive Chronicle of the Buddha and the Patriarchs, compiled by the Southern Song monk Zhipan. According to this work, Yitong was born into a royal family of Goryeo with the surname Yun and the courtesy name Weiyuan; his mother's surname was Shu. Marked by unusual signs at birth, he was sent as a child to study Buddhism at a Goryeo monastery called Guishan Temple. As a young man, he developed a deep understanding of the Avatamsaka Sutra and the

Treatise on the Awakening of Faith. Around the year AD 950, he traveled to China. Unfortunately, Korean records contain no mention of his family or Guishan Temple, leaving his life before arriving in China a mystery.

Upon arriving in China, Yitong first went to Yunju Temple on Mount Tiantai to study Chan Buddhism under Master Deshao. Yunju was a flourishing temple at the time, home to some 500 monks. In contrast, the monastery at Luoxi, where the fifteenth Tiantai patriarch Yiji resided, was desolate and in decline. In the words of the Southern Song monk Zongxiao of Ningbo, the Tiantai School, ravaged by the chaos of the Five Dynasties, was hanging on by "a single thread." For reasons that remain unknown, Yitong, after achieving some success in his Chan studies under Deshao, made the decision to go to Luoxi to study the Tiantai tradition under Yiji.

Under Yiji's guidance, Yitong dedicated himself to his studies, and his mastery of Buddhist doctrine grew daily. He became Yiji's most brilliant disciple and earned a wide reputation for his scholarship. After living at Luoxi for nearly twenty years, Yitong decided to leave Mount Tiantai and return to Goryeo to spread the teachings of the school. He traveled to the port of Ningbo to wait for a merchant ship. At the time, Ningbo's highest official, Prefect Qian Weizhi (949–1014)—the great-grandson of King Qian Liu and adopted son of King Qian Hongchu—heard of Yitong's arrival. He went to pay his respects with great ceremony and asked Yitong to administer the Buddhist precepts for him. Other officials and monks in Ningbo also flocked to seek his guidance. Qian Weizhi earnestly implored Yitong to stay and teach in Ningbo. Yitong replied, "My plan is to return to Goryeo to spread the Dharma, not to remain here." The prefect countered, "The goal of spreading the Dharma is to bring salvation to all sentient beings. If that is so, why must you return to Goryeo? Can you not also save all beings by staying here?" Persuaded by Qian Weizhi's insistence, Yitong agreed to remain in Ningbo.

At that time in Ningbo, there was a powerful official named Gu Chenghui, a former transport commissioner of Fuzhou. The area around Moon Lake (Yuehu) in old Ningbo was an exclusive district for wealthy aristocrats, and Gu owned a residence on the lake's eastern shore. Having heard Yitong lecture on the sutras many times and developing a deep admiration for him, Gu donated his lakeside estate in AD 968 to be converted into a temple for Yitong's use. Under Yitong's leadership, the monastery grew rapidly; within a decade, it had over 100 rooms, 70 Buddhist statues, and a community of more than 50 monks. In late AD 981, Yitong's disciple Yande traveled to the capital, Bianjing, to petition Emperor Taizong for an imperial name plaque for the temple. The following year, the emperor bestowed upon it the name "Baoyun Chan Temple." From then on, the monastery was known as Baoyun Temple, and Yitong himself became known as Baoyun Yitong or Master Baoyun Tong.

The imperial plaque greatly enhanced Baoyun Temple's prestige and spurred its growth, while Yitong's own fame "shook China," earning him widespread reverence. Qian Hongchu, the former king of Wuyue who had by then peacefully submitted his territory to the Song, corresponded with Yitong and composed several poems in his honor, three of which survive today. One is titled Eulogy for the Dharma Master Baoyun Tong: "In this triple world, our great master is born; An auspicious white curl, a face like the full moon. The pearl of his precepts illuminates all, the sea of his wisdom is boundless; A blessing for heavens and earth, we gaze upon him in admiration." In his Comprehensive Chronicle, Zhipan notes that Yitong had an uṣṇīṣa (the protuberance on the Buddha's head) and eyebrows that measured five or six inches long when straightened. Qian Hongchu's poem vividly evokes Yitong's majestic appearance and long white eyebrows. Another of his poems, Sent to the Dharma Master Baoyun Tong of Siming, reveals his deep admiration: "Though a thousand miles separate us, distance cannot impede our shared feeling for the Way. Since we parted, it feels as if a lifetime has passed. You have grasped the profound mystery, free from any desire for fame or fortune. On this autumn night in the monastery garden, who accompanies the sound of your sutra chanting?"

In his time at Baoyun Temple, Yitong trained numerous disciples, the two most important being Zunshi (964–1032) and Zhili (960–1028). Zunshi, a native of Ninghai, was later granted the title "Master of Compassionate Clouds" (Cíyún Dàshī) by the Song emperor. He praised his master Yitong, saying: "After Zhang'an had gone and Jingxi had passed, this master of men was born to carry on their brilliant light." "Zhang'an" was the style name of the fifth Tiantai patriarch, Guanding (AD 561–632), and "Jingxi" that of the ninth, Zhanran (AD 711–782). Zhili, a native of Yin County, inherited Yitong's mantle and was later granted the title "Master of Dharma Wisdom" (Fǎzhì Dàshī).

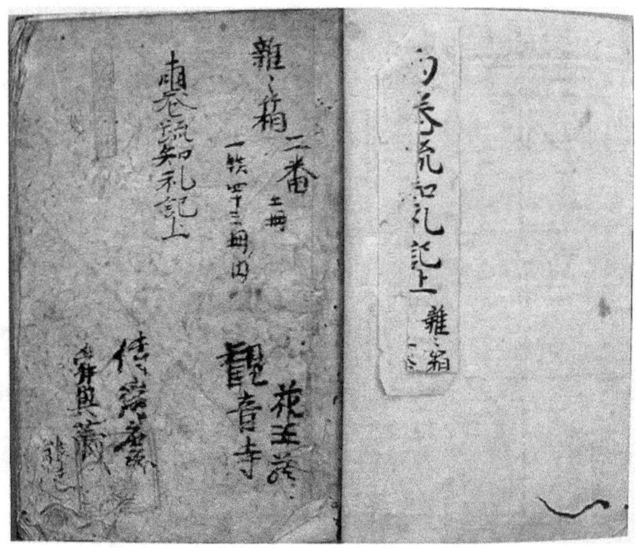

Japanese Collection of Zhili's Works: Commentary in Two Scrolls

The Tiantai School, which originated on Mount Tiantai and flourished during the Sui and Tang dynasties, had declined after the fall of the Tang to the point where it was "hanging on by a single thread." Yitong's arrival in Ningbo, his dedicated teaching, and his nurturing of brilliant young disciples like Zunshi and Zhili sparked a gradual revival, earning him the title "Founding Father of the Tiantai Renaissance." The center of the school also shifted from Mount Tiantai to Ningbo. The Ming Dynasty monk Wujin (1554–1628), who restored the patriarchal seat on Mount Tiantai, lamented in his Annals of the Tiantai Mountains: "The orthodox teaching of the Tiantai, from Master

Zhiyi down twelve generations to Luoxi, was always propagated from this mountain. But after Baoyun (Yitong) taught in Siming and Fazhi (Zhili) led the revival, the Way spread throughout the land, flourishing especially in Siming and the Wu region, while Mount Tiantai itself faded, just as Buddhism in India faded after it reached its zenith in China." The Republican-era Gazetteer of Yin County summarized it thus: "After the Five Dynasties, the Tiantai school waned at Tiantai but flourished in Mingzhou (Ningbo)."

Yitong's presence in Ningbo not only revived the Tiantai School but also sparked a flourishing of the city's broader Buddhist and cultural life. Baoyun Temple quickly became a major center within the city, and both the master and his temple became a source of pride for generations of Ningbo residents. The Southern Song statesman Shi Hao (1106–1194), a native of Ningbo, wrote a poem praising Yitong after a visit to the temple: "The doctrine of cessation and contemplation peaked in the Sui. In this final age of the Dharma, it was fading into obscurity. Then Master Tong arose from the shores of the Three Hans. With sails full for ten thousand miles, he left his raft to follow his teacher. Having attained the Way, he planned his return. But the patrons of Siming, the Gu family, donated their home to be a temple and invited him with all propriety. It was named Baoyun, a towering golden sanctuary. Once the master took up residence, disciples flocked like shadows. The shoes piled up outside his door; his fame reached the ends of the earth. He reconnected the broken thread of Tiantai, reviving the school from its decline." These lines vividly summarize Yitong's contribution. Quan Zuwang (1705–1755), a leading scholar of the Qing Dynasty, wrote of Moon Lake: "The lakeside mansions tower, their green tiles and red eaves too numerous to count... The former residence of the transport commissioner later became a sacred monastery... This land is a realm of immortals and Buddhists... By the lake stands the Baoyun memorial stone, where Yitong taught the Dharma." Quan himself noted that the "transport commissioner's residence" that "became a sacred monastery" was indeed Baoyun Temple, originally donated by Gu Chenghui.

According to historical records, the original Baoyun Temple, founded on Gu Chenghui's donated estate, was located just east of the present-day Ningbo First People's Hospital in Haishu District. In 1220, during the Southern Song, local officials established the Yin County Academy to the west of the temple. By the early Ming Dynasty, the academy had expanded and was now adjacent to the temple. The academy's scholars and students complained that the sounds of chanting from Baoyun Temple disrupted their study of the Confucian classics and demanded that the local government relocate the monastery. The monks, for their part, also found the proximity to the academy inconvenient and were amenable to moving. In 1500, the monks of Baoyun Temple found a vacant plot in the Zhuhu neighborhood by Moon Lake and moved the temple there. The original temple grounds were then absorbed by the Yin County Academy.

The new Baoyun Temple in the Zhuhu neighborhood continued to thrive during the Ming and Qing dynasties. The Map of the Ningbo Prefecture drawn in the latter half of the 19th century clearly depicts Baoyun Temple with its red outer walls. After the fall of the Qing Dynasty, as Ningbo began to establish a modern education system, the temple remained. A 1914 map of Ningbo shows a higher primary school (the predecessor of today's Zhenming

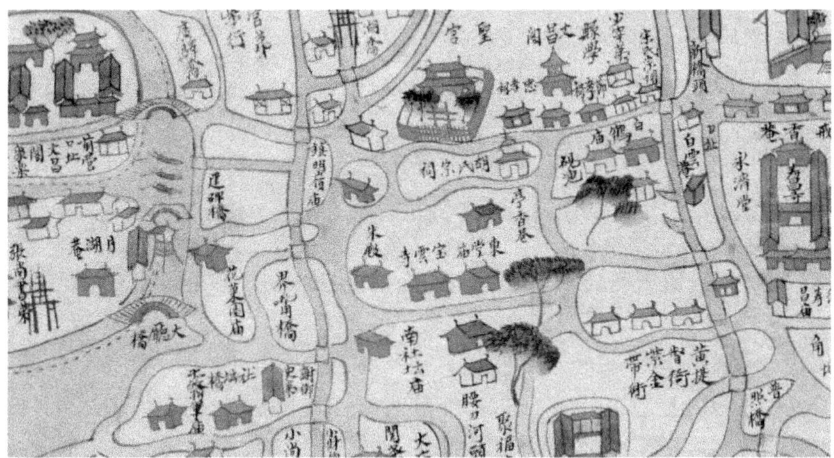

Baoyun Temple as Depicted on the *Map of Ningbo Prefecture* from the Late Qing Dynasty

Central Primary School) located just north of the temple. By the founding of the People's Republic in 1949, Baoyun Temple had fallen into ruin, with only the main Mahavira Hall still standing. The temple was later demolished entirely, and its site was successively occupied by a local textile mill and a battery factory. Today, it is a residential area.

After living in Ningbo for two decades, Yitong passed away in 988. Following his cremation, his remains were interred in the northwest corner of the grounds of Ayuwang Temple, where he had often been invited to lecture.

Over sixty years later, however, his tomb had become neglected and overgrown. Around the year 1125, monks from Baoyun Temple and Ayuwang Temple jointly relocated his remains to Wushi'ao, a site across from Ayuwang Temple. Thus, this great Tiantai patriarch from the Korean Peninsula was laid to rest in the soil of Zhejiang, a lasting symbol of the cultural exchange between the two regions.

6.3 A Goryeo Prince

Yitong, born on the Korean Peninsula, crossed the sea to China's Jiangnan region and, at a critical moment when the Tiantai School was "hanging on by a single thread," inherited its lineage and shouldered the mission of its revival. He made an indelible contribution to the development of the school and the flourishing of Buddhism in Zhejiang, and was honored by posterity as the sixteenth Tiantai patriarch. Nearly a century after his death, another Goryeo monk would carry the Tiantai teachings from Zhejiang back to his homeland. This monk was Yitian (1055–1101).

Yitian was the fourth son of King Munjong of Goryeo. His birth name was Wang Xu, and his courtesy name was Yitian. To avoid the naming taboo of the Song emperor Zhezong (r. 1077–1100), whose personal name was Zhao Xu, the Goryeo prince later adopted Yitian as his primary name. At the age of eleven, his parents sent him to a monastery to study Buddhism. He was a dedicated and tireless student, quickly rising to the position of Monastic Supervisor (sengtong) and receiving the royal title "Protector of the World"

(Youshi). After his death, the king of Goryeo granted him the posthumous title "Great Awakening" (Dajue) and named him National Preceptor (Guoshi). He is thus also known as the Monastic Supervisor Yitian and the National Preceptor Dajue.

When Yitian was studying Buddhism, the dominant schools in Goryeo were the Huayan and Faxiang schools. Although Tiantai teachings had been introduced, they had not been systematized and lacked official state recognition. Yitian primarily studied the Huayan school but held a deep interest in other traditions. He particularly lamented that the Tiantai School had not yet taken root in Goryeo and resolved to travel to Song China to seek out a master. Through the merchant ships that sailed between Goryeo and the Song, he established close contact with eminent Chinese monks.

Among the Song monks with whom Yitian corresponded was Jingyuan (1011–1088), a native of Jinjiang in Quanzhou, whose lay surname was Yang. In his youth, Jingyuan sought out masters in northern China, including the capital Dongjing (Kaifeng) and Mount Wutai, before moving to the south. He is honored as the seventh (or tenth) patriarch of the Huayan school, and some of his writings had already reached Goryeo during his lifetime. The king of Goryeo greatly admired him and once entrusted merchants traveling to Mingzhou (Ningbo) with letters and gifts of gold for Jingyuan. When Mingzhou officials reported this to the court, the Song emperor Shenzong gave special permission for Jingyuan to accept them. Yitian also admired

Jingyuan and sent a personal letter expressing his respect. Realizing Yitian was no ordinary monk, Jingyuan invited him to China. This invitation only strengthened Yitian's desire to study in the Song. He formally petitioned the king of Goryeo for permission to travel, but because the Song and the neighboring Liao dynasty were in a state of confrontation, the Goryeo court feared that a visit by a prince of Yitian's status might offend the Liao. Permission was denied. Undeterred, on the seventh night of the fourth lunar month of 1085, Yitian and a few disciples disguised themselves, secretly boarded the ship of a Song merchant named Lin Ning, and set sail from Goryeo. They arrived in Banqiao, Mizhou (modern Jiaozhou, Shandong), on the second day of the fifth month.

From Banqiao, Yitian traveled overland to the Song capital, Bianjing, arriving on the sixth day of the seventh month. On the twenty-first day, Emperor Zhezong granted him an audience. At the end of the eighth month, accompanied by Song officials, Yitian left Bianjing and journeyed south along the Grand Canal, reaching Hangzhou by the end of the year. Jingyuan was then serving as the abbot of Dazhong Xiangfu Temple in the city, and Yitian went there to meet him at last. The two, who had long corresponded, felt they had known each other for years and deeply cherished their meeting. Around this time, the prefect of Hangzhou, Pu Zongmeng, invited Jingyuan to become the abbot of Huiyin Temple, located northwest of Mount Yucen, just outside the city. Yitian followed his master to Huiyin Temple and donated silver for its reconstruction.

While Yitian was studying in Hangzhou, his mother in Goryeo, missing her son, persuaded the king to write to the Song emperor and ask for Yitian's prompt return. Upon receiving the request, Emperor Zhezong summoned Yitian back to the capital. Accompanied by Jingyuan, Yitian departed Hangzhou for Bianjing, the master and disciple discussing Buddhist philosophy the entire way. Yitian arrived back in the capital on the thirteenth day of the second month of 1086 and, a few days later, took his formal leave of the emperor. On the second day of the third month, he and Jingyuan left Bianjing and traveled south. Along the way, they made a special visit to Zhenru Temple in Xiuzhou, where Jingyuan's own master, Changshui, had passed away. Finding that Master Changshui's commemorative stupa had fallen into ruin, Yitian donated money to the temple monks for its repair.

In the fourth month of 1086, Yitian and Jingyuan returned to Huiyin Temple in Hangzhou. Jingyuan conducted a formal ceremony to transmit the Dharma to Yitian, charging him with the mission of propagating Buddhism upon his return to Goryeo. He presented Yitian with three personal treasures he had kept for fifty years—a sutra, an incense burner, and a fly whisk—as tokens of their master-disciple lineage. Jingyuan composed two poems to mark the occasion. The first reads: "This green censer and black whisk have aided my talks, as I climbed the lotus dais for fifty years. Today I pass them to the Kingdom of the Eastern Sea, to burn incense, wield the whisk, and teach the Dharma to gods and men." The second reads: "You left your country, anxious amidst the ocean dust, and returned to Zhejiang in the spring. Do not say that many sages have sought the Dharma, for since ancient times, from a royal palace there has been only one." The "Kingdom of the Eastern Sea" refers to Goryeo, and "from a royal palace there has been only one" refers to Yitian, showing Jingyuan's high hopes for his royal disciple. Yitian responded with his own poem of thanks: "Our karmic bond must span countless eons; I have been privileged to study your words for many years. Now receiving these tokens of faith, what more could I wish for? In the light of wisdom's sun, one beholds Yitian (Righteous Heaven)." In his poem, Yitian expressed both his gratitude to Jingyuan and his resolve to spread the Dharma in Goryeo.

After leaving Hangzhou, Yitian did not immediately sail for home but instead embarked on a pilgrimage to Mount Tiantai. At Fulong Temple, standing before the stupa containing the remains of the school's founder, Master Zhiyi, he vowed to transmit the Tiantai teachings back to Goryeo, the "Land to the East." He also climbed to Shiliang (Stone Beam Bridge) to view the waterfall and pay respects to the arhats. From Mount Tiantai, Yitian traveled to Mingzhou (modern Ningbo) and stayed at Yanqing Temple in the city. There, he was hosted by the monk Mingzhi, a native of Yin County, whom Yitian took as a teacher, and Mingzhi's disciple Falin, who became a good friend. While in Mingzhou, Yitian also visited Ayuwang Temple to meet its abbot, Huailian (1009–1090). A native of Fujian, Huailian was a highly accomplished master. Goryeo records preserve a poem he wrote for Yitian, titled "A Short Verse for the Monastic Supervisor from Gyerim," which praises the prince for "spurning the great throne of the eastern sun, to shave his head and don the kasaya robe."

On the twelfth day of the fifth month, Yitian boarded a Goryeo diplomatic vessel and departed from Ningbo, reaching his homeland on the twenty-ninth. He then dedicated himself to spreading the Tiantai teachings in Goryeo, becoming the founder of the Goryeo Tiantai School. In the fifth month of 1097, he completed the construction of a new national temple in Goryeo, modeled after and named for Guoqing Temple on Mount Tiantai, and served as its first abbot. After returning home, Yitian maintained a frequent correspondence with monks in Zhejiang. He once invited the Ningbo monk Falin to come lecture at his new Guoqing Temple for three years. Falin wrote back accepting the invitation with pleasure, but for unknown reasons, it appears he never made the journey.

Yitian's connection with Jingyuan and Huiyin Temple in Hangzhou was especially strong. In 1088, he sent 180 scrolls of scriptures to the temple via sea merchants, a collection that included a translation of the Avatamsaka Sutra that had been lost in China. That November, Jingyuan passed away at Huiyin Temple. When Yitian heard the news, he sent a special envoy by merchant ship to Hangzhou to pay his respects. He also petitioned the Song government for permission to bring some of Jingyuan's sacred relics back to Goryeo for veneration, a request Emperor Zhezong granted over the objections of his ministers. In 1099, Yitian donated 2,000 taels of gold for the construction of a scripture pavilion at Huiyin Temple to house the Avatamsaka Sutra and other precious texts. Jingyuan's disciple Xizhong oversaw the project, which was completed in early 1101. Xizhong even sent a drawing of the finished pavilion to Yitian in Goryeo. Tragically, shortly after its completion, Yitian died in Goryeo on the fifth day of the tenth month, 1101, at the young age of 47. Nevertheless, the Goryeo Tiantai School he founded was passed down through generations, becoming a major Buddhist tradition on the Korean Peninsula, and the mark he left on Huiyin Temple did not vanish with his death.

Huiyin Temple was originally founded by the Wuyue king Qian Liu in 927 but had fallen into disrepair by the Song Dynasty. It was under Jingyuan's leadership that the temple began to flourish again. Yitian's donation of priceless scriptures and funds for the scripture pavilion brought great fame to the temple, which became known as the "Foremost Sanctuary of the Huayan School." Because of his generous patronage, Huiyin Temple also acquired the popular nickname "Goryeo Temple." From the end of the Song Dynasty until the 1911 Revolution, the temple endured countless natural and man-made disasters, experiencing cycles of revival and decline. It was completely destroyed between 1860 and 1864 during the fierce fighting between Qing and Taiping forces in Hangzhou. After 1949, the site was used as a flower nursery and a lumber yard. In 2004, the city of Hangzhou began reconstructing Huiyin Temple. After more than two years of work, it was officially opened to the public in 2007. Today, it stands as a unique tourist attraction that uses temple architecture as a vessel for religious and cultural heritage, drawing large numbers of visitors each year.

As the stories above show, though separated by vast distances, Zhejiang's Mount Tiantai and the Korean Peninsula share a deep karmic bond. During the Tang Dynasty, Korean monks came to Mount Tiantai to study the Dharma. During the Five Dynasties and Northern Song, lost Tiantai scriptures flowed back to Zhejiang from the peninsula. Yitong shouldered the task of reviving the school when it was on the brink of extinction, while Yitian planted the seeds of Tiantai in his homeland and brought them to flower. Why did such a profound connection exist? One explanation emerged in the Song Dynasty: Master Zhiyi, the founder of the Tiantai School, was once on the coast of Taizhou when he saw fishermen taking their catch. Filled with compassion, he bought the struggling fish, administered Buddhist precepts to them, and released them back into the ocean. These fish, now imbued with the power of the Dharma, swam across the East China Sea to the Korean Peninsula, causing the Tiantai School to flourish there. Later, when the school's scriptures were lost in China, monks from the peninsula returned them and helped revive the school, repaying Master Zhiyi's act of mercy. This mystical tale, obviously crafted to illustrate the Buddhist principle of karma and promote compassionate action, nonetheless reflects an underlying historical reality: the fish reached the peninsula via the East China Sea. The legend thus indirectly attests to the vital role of the Maritime Silk Road in connecting Zhejiang and the Korean Peninsula.

Chapter 7 Medieval European Travelers and the Quest for the Celestial City

7.1 Marco Polo's Portrait of Hangzhou

The ancient Maritime Silk Road did more than just connect Zhejiang province with other Asian nations; its sprawling network extended all the way to Europe. Of the many Europeans who journeyed to and from Zhejiang along this sea route, the most celebrated is unquestionably the Venetian merchant Marco Polo (1254–1324).

Marco Polo was born into a Venetian merchant family; Polo was his surname, Marco his given name. His grandfather had three sons: Marco the Elder, Niccolò, and Maffeo. Marco was the son of Niccolò. The Polo family's ancestral home still stands today, nestled against a canal less than a five-minute walk from Venice's famed Rialto Bridge. The original house, however, was destroyed in a fire in 1597. The building seen today is a reconstruction that has since passed through many hands and no longer belongs to the Polo family. A plaque affixed to the house reads: "This was the house of Marco Polo, who traveled to the farthest parts of Asia and described them. By order of the City Council, 1881."

Marco Polo's Former Residence

In that era, Venice was a prosperous and powerful mercantile republic. In April 1204, the armies of the Fourth Crusade captured Constantinople, the capital of the Byzantine Empire. For its decisive naval support, Venice was rewarded with vast territories and control over three-eighths of the city itself. This led to the rise of a Venetian quarter where many citizens, including the Polos, lived and conducted business. To expand the family enterprise, Niccolò and Maffeo Polo relocated from Venice to Constantinople. Scholars disagree on the year of their departure, with some arguing for 1253, before Marco's birth, and others for 1260. To this day, there is no consensus.

Around the first half of 1261, Niccolò and Maffeo journeyed from Constantinople to the port of Soldaia (present-day Sudak) on the Crimean Peninsula, the site of another family trading post. From there, they ventured into the territory of the Golden Horde to trade. When war cut off their route home, the brothers were forced to press eastward. Their journey took them across Central Asia to the city of Shangdu (a UNESCO World Heritage site since

2012, located in modern-day Inner Mongolia), where they were granted an audience with the Yuan emperor, Kublai Khan. The Khan tasked the brothers with acting as his envoys to Rome, with a plea for the Pope to send missionaries to China. The Polos began their long journey home from Shangdu in early 1266 and finally arrived in Venice in 1269, where they found that Niccolò's wife had passed away and his son, Marco, had grown into a fine young man.

In 1271, Marco Polo set out from Venice for Asia with his father, Niccolò, and his uncle, Maffeo. After a grueling four-year trek, they reached Shangdu in the summer of 1275. Shortly thereafter, Kublai Khan received the three Polos in Dadu (modern-day Beijing), the Great Capital of the Yuan Dynasty. According to Marco's own account, he earned the Khan's great favor and was dispatched on imperial inspections throughout China and on missions to foreign lands, including Burma. In early 1291, the Polos joined a diplomatic mission sent by Kublai Khan, which set sail from the port of Quanzhou. They traveled the Maritime Silk Road to the Ilkhanate in Western Asia, and from there continued by land and sea, finally reaching their native Venice in 1295. Surviving documents show that upon his return, Marco Polo resumed his life as a merchant.

Medieval Italy was not a unified country but a land divided among powerful, independent city-states, such as Genoa, Florence, and Pisa, in addition to Venice. At some point after his return, Marco Polo was thrown into a Genoese prison. The reasons for his incarceration are debated. One theory holds that he was captured during a naval battle between Venice and Genoa in 1294; another points to a similar clash in 1298. Some modern scholars, however, find it improbable that a man in his forties, having survived two decades of adventure abroad, would willingly join a dangerous sea battle. They propose he may have been captured by pirates operating on behalf of Genoa. Regardless of the reason, it is certain that Marco Polo found himself in a Genoese prison cell.

In that Genoese prison, Polo's cellmate was a man from Pisa named Rustichello. It is widely believed that Rustichello was taken prisoner after Pisa's navy suffered a disastrous defeat by Genoa in the 1284 Battle of Meloria, and that he remained imprisoned until 1299. Others suggest he was captured in later conflicts in 1296 or 1298. Rustichello was a writer of popular romances; a fragment of his work on Arthurian legend, titled *Meliadus*, survives today. During their confinement, Polo recounted his adventures in the East to Rustichello, who transcribed the stories in a mix of French and Italian. The resulting book was likely titled *Le Devisement du Monde* (*The Description of the World*), but is now known simply as *The Travels of Marco Polo*. Scholars have found that the book's introduction bears a remarkable resemblance in its phrasing and structure to Rustichello's *Meliadus*, a testament to the literary talent that was instrumental in transforming Polo's spoken tales into a work that achieved global renown.

Although the original manuscript of The Travels of Marco Polo is long lost, the book was an instant sensation. It was translated into many languages and widely circulated through handwritten copies, which gave rise to numerous versions with different titles. Manuscripts continued to be discovered as late as 2007. A 2015 survey by French scholar Christine Gadrat-Querfelli identified 141 known manuscripts, including the F text (Franco-Italian), FG (French), TA (Tuscan), VA (Venetian), and Z (Latin). The F text is considered the closest to the original, but the precise lineage connecting these versions remains a matter of scholarly debate. In addition to these manuscripts, a pivotal early printed version is the R text, an Italian translation edited by the scholar Giovanni Battista Ramusio (1485–1557) and published in 1559. In the Chinese-speaking world, Marco Polo was first mentioned in 1837 in the missionary journal Dong-Xi Yang Kao Mei Yue Tong Ji Zhuan. Today, the most popular Chinese version remains Feng Chengjun's translation, first published by the Commercial Press in 1936.

In The Travels, northern China is called "Cathay," after the Khitan people whose Liao Dynasty (907–1125) once ruled the vast region. The Yuan capital Dadu is called "Khanbaliq," its Mongolian name. Southern China is referred to as "Mangi" or "Manzi," a transliteration of the Chinese pejorative manzi (蛮子), a derogatory term used by northerners for the people of the Southern Song. Hangzhou is called "Quinsai," a rendering of the Chinese Xingzai. After the Southern Song court established its capital there in 1138, it named the city Xingzai, meaning "temporary imperial residence," to signal its resolve to one day reconquer its ancestral lands in the north. Inspired by the Chinese proverb "Heaven above, Suzhou and Hangzhou below," Marco Polo also famously called the city the "Celestial City" (celli ciuitas).

According to the narrative, Marco Polo entered Zhejiang from the north, traveling south through cities like Huai'an, Yangzhou, Nanjing, Zhenjiang, and Suzhou. He eventually reached Wuxing (part of modern-day Huzhou), praising it as a "great and wealthy city." From Wuxing, he came to a city he calls Cianga (spelled variously as Caiugan, Ciangan, or Cangan in different manuscripts). This city, he wrote, "is very large and rich. The people are idolaters, subject to the Great Khan, and use paper money. They live by trade and crafts, and they weave many kinds of fine taffeta." From this city, he claimed, it was a three-day horseback ride to Hangzhou.

From the 19th through the early 20th century, scholars debated the original Chinese name for "Cianga." Some argued it was Chang'an, now a town in Haining, Zhejiang. During the Song and Yuan dynasties, Chang'an was a major transport hub on the Grand Canal. Its importance is noted in the Yongle Encyclopedia, which records that the Chang'an station maintained 30 boats and hundreds of households to support the courier system. However, Chang'an is only about 50 kilometers from Hangzhou—a single day's ride on horseback, not three. As the scholar Feng Chengjun noted, "Yuan-dynasty Chang'an was only a few hours from Hangzhou by canal boat, which contradicts the three-day journey mentioned in the book." Other suggestions, like

Songjiang, Jiaxing, or Changxing, were also unconvincing. The mystery was finally solved in 1932 with the discovery of a Latin manuscript of The Travels in Toledo, Spain. This version, known as the Z text, had been donated by a Bishop Zelada (1717–1801). It states the journey from "Cianga" to Hangzhou was a one-day ride, confirming that Cianga was indeed Chang'an. The "three days" mentioned in other manuscripts was likely a copyist's error.

After leaving the town of Chang'an, Marco Polo reached Hangzhou. His description of this city is one of the most brilliant and essential parts of his Travels, accounting for nearly a fifteenth of the entire book. However, the details about Hangzhou vary significantly across different manuscripts. The scholars A. C. Moule and Paul Pelliot identified 60 distinct thematic sections on Hangzhou, but their presence and length differ by version: the F text contains 31, the Z text 24, and the R text 57. As a result, material found in one manuscript may be absent in another. Even when topics overlap, the word count can diverge dramatically; the description of the imperial palace, for instance, is nearly 700 words in the R text but only one or two hundred in others. These discrepancies reflect the complexity of the book's manuscript tradition and suggest that the Hangzhou chapters are a crucial key to untangling its history.

The Travels refers to Hangzhou as "Quinsai" and describes its location as having "on one side a lake of fresh and very clear water, and on the other a very large river." The clear lake is undoubtedly West Lake, and the large river is the Qiantang. The book's account of the city focuses on five main aspects.

First, its sheer scale: The city "is a hundred miles in circumference, and has twelve thousand bridges of stone." The bridge arches were "so high that a ship could pass under them without lowering its mast, while carts and horses could still cross overhead." Polo adds that the city had "160 main streets, each with 10,000 houses," for a total of "1.6 million homes, among which were interspersed magnificent palaces." The streets were "paved with stone," and the city contained "3,000 baths, supplied by springs, which the people take great delight in frequenting; and some are large enough to accommodate a hundred people at once."

Second, the beauty of West Lake: "Within the city is a lake, which has a compass of thirty miles. Along its shores are built most beautiful palaces and mansions, of the richest and most powerful nobles of the city. There are also a great number of temples of the idolaters. In the middle of the lake are two islands, on each of which stands a palace of wonderful size and splendor, built in the manner of an imperial court." The lake was filled with "a great number of boats and barges of all sizes for the purpose of pleasure," which could hold "ten, fifteen, or twenty or more people." He concluded that "truly for the delectation of the senses, nothing in the world can be more gratifying than a boat ride on this lake. For from the boat, one can behold a panoramic view of the whole city, with its numberless palaces, temples, monasteries, gardens, and trees."

Third, the magnificent imperial palace: "The city was also home to the palace of the exiled king of Mangi, the largest in the world. It was ten miles in circumference, surrounded by high, crenelated walls, and contained the most beautiful and delightful gardens imaginable, full of the world's finest fruits. There were also fountains and lakes teeming with fish. In the center stood a palace of the most splendid design." The palace itself "was divided into three parts... One entered through a great central gate, with the other two parts on either side. There was a platform supporting a great pavilion with a roof held up by columns painted in gold and azure. The main hall, directly opposite the gate, was similarly painted, with golden columns, a gilded ceiling, and walls painted with scenes from the lives of past kings." The grounds contained "groves, springs, orchards, and animal parks," as well as an ornate covered gallery "six paces wide" that "ran all the way to the lake." Along this gallery were "ten courtyards on each side, each rectangular with a cloister, and each having fifty chambers with gardens, where the king's one thousand concubines resided."

Fourth, its bustling commerce: "The city has ten great marketplaces, in addition to a countless number of small ones along the streets." Around the major markets were "lofty houses, the lower stories of which are shops where all sorts of merchandise is sold, including spices, precious stones, and pearls." There were also "large stone warehouses for merchants from India and other countries to store their goods." Three days a week, he noted, "forty to fifty thousand people come to the market, bringing all the necessities of life to sell."

Fifth, its sophisticated fire-prevention system: "In the city is a hill, upon which stands a tower with a wooden plank. Whenever there is a fire or other alarm, a watchman strikes this plank with a mallet, producing a great sound that can be heard from afar, letting the people know of the danger." Additionally, "stone towers were built in every district, where residents could store their belongings in case of fire." When a fire did break out, "a wooden clapper would be struck as a warning, and the watchmen from the other bridges would rush to help extinguish the blaze and move the merchants' and other victims' property to the safety of the stone towers or the islands in the lake."

The Travels also makes special mention of Ganpu (in modern Haiyan County, Zhejiang), a trading port on Hangzhou Bay. Polo writes: "The sea is twenty-five miles from the city of Hangzhou, near a port called Ganfu. A great number of ships are found there, which carry all sorts of merchandise to and from India and other foreign parts, adding greatly to the city's value. A great river flows from the city of Quinsai to this seaport, by which ships can come and go with their cargo. Many cities stand along the course of this river."

7.2 The Celestial City on Parchment

Marco Polo's description of Hangzhou as "the finest and noblest city in the world" ignited the European imagination. As his book was copied and passed from hand to hand, scribes began to add exquisite illustrations inspired by the text. Among the most famous of these early illustrated versions is the Livre des merveilles (Book of Marvels), now held in the Bibliothèque Nationale de France.

The version of the Livre des merveilles (cataloged as Français 2810) in the Bibliothèque Nationale de France consists of 299 parchment folios, each measuring about 42 by 30 centimeters and featuring two columns of text. According to the library, the manuscript was commissioned by John the Fearless, Duke of Burgundy (1371–1419), who had it transcribed and illustrated between 1410 and 1412. In early 1413, he presented it as a gift to his uncle, the Duke of Berry (1340–1416). The manuscript is famous for its 265 magnificent color illustrations, leading one scholar to call it the grandest of all medieval European works that used both text and images to introduce the wonders of the Far East.

The Livre des merveilles contains French transcriptions of seven different works. The first is The Travels of Marco Polo (under the title Le livre de Marc Paulet et des Merveilles), which runs from the first folio to the back of the 96th. This section is adorned with 84 color illustrations, three of which depict Hangzhou. Although the images are untitled in the manuscript, the accompanying text allows us to name them: The Queen's Surrender of the City (folio 64r), The Celestial City (folio 67r), and Tax Collection in Quinsai (folio

69r). For the sake of narrative clarity, let us begin with The Celestial City.

1. The Celestial City

The red text below the illustration reads: "Here is told of the very noble city of Quinsai, which is the capital of the kingdom of Mangi." A few lines down, it adds: "The name of this city means in French the City of Heaven (la Cité du Ciel)." As noted, "Quinsai" is a transliteration of the Chinese Xingzai, while the name "Celestial City" is a creative interpretation of proverbs like "Heaven above, Suzhou and Hangzhou below."

The 157 lines of text that follow, running to the top of folio 69v, are all dedicated to describing Hangzhou. The account highlights several key features: (1) "It is the most magnificent and noble city in the world." (2) "The city is built in the water and is surrounded by it, so one must build 12,000 stone bridges to get from one place to another." (3) "In the city there is a beautiful great lake, around which are built grand palaces, luxurious mansions, and many temples. In the middle of the lake are two islands." (4) "There are many fine houses in the city with tall stone towers, where people can move their valuables for safety in case of fire." (5) "The city also contains the palace of the king of Mangi, which is incredibly lavish and grand," with

The Celestial City, from the Collection of the Bibliothèque Nationale de France

"a thousand rooms, all very beautiful and spacious, decorated entirely in gold and brilliant colors." The "beautiful great lake" is of course West Lake, and the "palace of the king of Mangi" refers to the Southern Song Imperial Palace. While Polo's descriptions may contain some hyperbole, they accurately capture the main characteristics of Hangzhou.

The illustration of The Celestial City was created to bring these descriptions to life, capturing the city's crisscrossing canals, its extensive network of bridges, and its magnificent architecture. Extensive research has identified the artist as an anonymous Flemish painter active in Paris in the early 15th century. Because he also contributed illustrations to a popular French book of hours, the Egerton Hours (now in the British Museum), modern scholars have named him the "Egerton Master." Having never been to China, the Egerton Master depicted the Celestial City entirely through the lens of European architecture. The buildings in his painting feature steep-pitched roofs and dormer windows. The stone towers that Polo described for storing valuables become European-style chimneys and castle turrets. A large, dome-roofed building in the upper right is reminiscent of a great European cathedral, particularly St. Mark's Basilica in Venice. The painting is thus less a depiction of Hangzhou than a beautiful fantasy, embodying a European artist's romantic vision of a far-off Chinese metropolis.

2. The Queen's Surrender of the City

The red text under this illustration reads: "How le grant Kaan conquered the land of Mangi." Le grant Kaan is Kublai Khan, founder of the Yuan Dynasty. The text that follows tells the story of the conquest of Hangzhou. The king of Mangi, it says, "was very powerful, with great wealth, many subjects, and vast lands," but his people were devoted to pleasure rather than arms, "and the king most of all." The king had once consulted an astrologer, who told him, "Your kingdom will be taken from you by a man with a hundred eyes." Believing a hundred-eyed man to be an impossibility, the king felt secure. But in 1268, the Great Khan sent a baron named Baian Tinesan to conquer Mangi, and "Baian means 'a hundred eyes.'" (Scholars long ago identified "Baian" as a transliteration of Bayan (1236–1295), the Yuan chancellor, and "Tinesan" as a rendering of chengxiang, the Chinese word for chancellor.) The story continues: Bayan led his great army to Quinsai, the capital. "The king of Mangi, terrified by the sight of Bayan's mighty host, fled with his subjects in a thousand ships to islands in the ocean." The queen, however,

The Queen's Surrender of the City, from the Collection of the Bibliothèque Nationale de France

"remained behind and bravely led the people to defend the city." When she asked an astrologer the name of the enemy commander and was told it was Bayan, or "Hundred Eyes," she recalled the prophecy and surrendered. "Later, the queen was brought before the Great Khan, who received her with great respect and honor, treating her as a great lady and providing for her generously."

According to Chinese historical sources, in 1275, under orders from Kublai Khan, General Bayan led a three-pronged invasion against Hangzhou, the Southern Song capital. In the first month of 1276, his army reached Gaoting Mountain, about 30 li (15 km) northeast of the city. At the time, the Song emperor, Zhao Xian (1271–1323), was only five years old. The government was run by his grandmother, the Grand Empress Dowager Xie Daoqing (1210–1283). Faced with the overwhelming Yuan army, officials in Hangzhou abandoned their posts and fled. With no other choice, the Song court surrendered to Bayan. The child emperor and his mother, Empress Quan, were taken captive and sent to the Yuan capital, Dadu. The Empress Dowager Xie, who was ill, remained in Hangzhou for several months before she too was taken to Dadu, where she died seven years later. Meanwhile, the emperor's two half-brothers, Zhao Shi (1269–1278) and Zhao Bing (1272–1279), fled south under the protection of loyal ministers. Zhao Shi later died of illness on an island off the Guangdong coast, while Zhao Bing perished during the naval Battle of Yamen, when a minister leaped into the sea with the boy in his arms.

Cross-referencing with Chinese history, it becomes clear that the "queen of Mangi" in Polo's story was Grand Empress Dowager Xie, wife of the former Emperor Lizong(1205–1264). The "king" who fled to the islands was likely the young prince Zhao Shi. Empress Dowager Xie was, in fact, the grandmother of the last three Song rulers (Zhao Shi, Zhao Xian, and Zhao Bing), who were all just children when Bayan conquered Hangzhou and were therefore unmarried. The fact that The Travels not only transliterates Bayan's name but also includes the "hundred eyes" pun suggests Polo picked up the story from local Chinese lore. Such legends were apparently common. A late-Yuan text, Nancun Chuogeng Lu, records a contemporary saying: "When Jiangnan is to be broken, a hundred wild geese (bǎi yàn) will pass over." The prophecy's meaning only became clear after the fall of the Song, when people realized it referred to Chancellor Bayan. Clearly, Polo's account of the fall of Hangzhou is a blend of historical fact and romantic folklore.

The illustration, The Queen's Surrender of the City, is even more fanciful. Also the work of the Egerton Master, it depicts Hangzhou as a European castle with Gothic spires and a Romanesque stone gate. The Mongol army is portrayed as a host of medieval knights with European armor and weapons. The Mongol commander is shown not as the 40-year-old Bayan, but as a dignified and benevolent old man wearing a crown—almost certainly representing Kublai Khan himself. The most fascinating figure, however, is the queen. The historical Xie Daoqing was 66 at the time of the surrender, described in the History of the Song as "old and sick," "dark-skinned, and blind in one eye." The artist, however, portrays her as a beautiful young woman in a crown and a red robe, mounted on a great dapple-gray horse. She holds a silver key to the city, which she offers to the Mongol commander. While the text of The Travels makes no mention of a key, the gesture was a European symbol of surrender, and so the artist added it to the scene. The entire illustration is a perfect example of the romantic European imagination of the East.

3. Tax Collection in Quinsai

The red text beneath this illustration reads, "How Quinsai pays great tribute to the Great Khan." The text explains that the Khan's domains are divided into nine parts, one of which is Mangi. This region, it notes, is exceptionally productive: "The amount of silk produced here is astonishing," and "more sugar is produced here than in all the rest of the world combined."

With its additional abundance of salt, charcoal, and other resources, the region paid an "almost incredible" amount of tax revenue to the Great Khan each year.

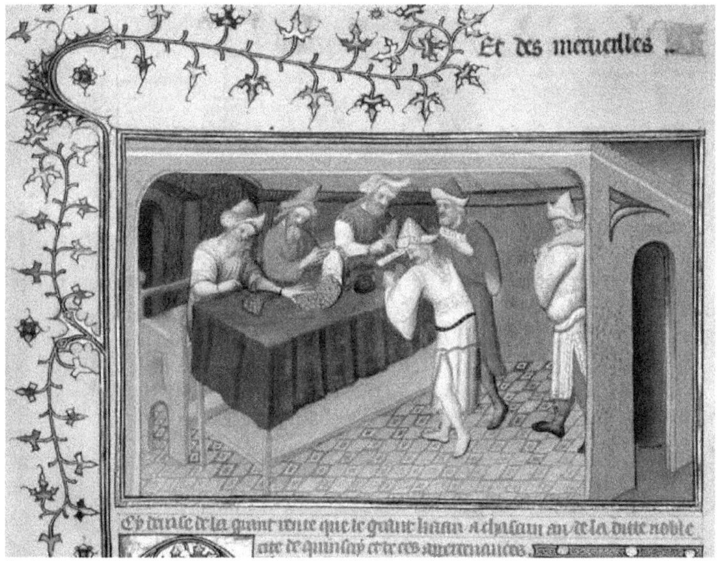

Tax Collection in Quinsai, from the Collection of the Bibliothèque Nationale de France

Tax Collection in Quinsai, also by the Egerton Master, portrays the city's residents paying their taxes. The setting is a square, single-story hall with Romanesque stone doorways and a geometrically patterned floor, bearing no resemblance to Chinese architecture. The three tax officials are all depicted as Europeans, with prominent noses, deep-set eyes, and thick beards, and they wear various styles of European hats. The taxes are being paid in gold coins, the currency of medieval Europe. The officials are seated together: one records the payment in a ledger, another pours coins from a bag, and a third counts them. The three taxpayers are also shown as Europeans in European dress. Despite the text's claim that Quinsai's tax payments were "almost incredible" in size, the artist, having never seen China, could not imagine the splendor and solemnity of an imperial government office (yamen). Compared to the real thing, the scene he painted appears humble and plain, lacking any sense of official majesty.

7.3 Odoric's Journey Through Zhejiang

Marco Polo traveled to China via the overland Silk Road, eventually making his way south to Hangzhou in Zhejiang. From there, he journeyed west up the Qiantang River, through Jinhua and Quzhou, into Fujian province, and finally set sail for home from Quanzhou along the Maritime Silk Road. Another European traveler, Odoric of Pordenone (c. 1286–1331), would later trace this route in the opposite direction, traveling from Fujian into Zhejiang and following the Qiantang River to Hangzhou.

A Portrait of Odorico da Pordenone

Odoric was born in Villanova, a small Italian village near the town of Pordenone in the Friuli region. A popular theory once held that his family was of Czech origin, descended from a soldier sent to garrison Pordenone by the King of Bohemia; this was based on a Latin document in which Odoric refers to himself as a Bohemian. More recent research, however, has revealed that the word "Bohemian" was a later interpolation into the text. Modern scholars now believe Odoric's family was native to the Friuli region.

As a young man, Odoric joined the Franciscans, a Catholic monastic order known for its asceticism. Around 1318, he left Italy and set out for the East. Unlike the merchant Marco Polo, who had traveled to China overland and returned by sea, the friar Odoric did the reverse: he journeyed to China via the Maritime Silk Road and returned to Europe overland. Odoric's route took him from Italy across Western Asia to the Persian Gulf, and from there to India. Around 1322, he sailed to Guangzhou in China. He then traveled north, passing through Quanzhou, Fuzhou, Hangzhou, and Yangzhou on his way to Beijing. Around 1328, he began his return journey overland, finally reaching Venice in 1329.

In May 1330, at a monastery in Padua, Odoric dictated the story of his travels in Asia to a fellow friar, William of Solagna, who recorded it in Latin. The resulting book is known in English as The Travels of Odoric. A few months later, Odoric set out for Avignon, the seat of the papacy at the time, to report on his journey. On the way, however, he fell ill in Pisa and was forced to return to the town of Udine, where he died on January 14, 1331.

In the days after Odoric's death, miraculous stories began to circulate in

Udine; it was said that the chronically ill could be cured simply by touching

The Sarcophagus of Odorico da Pordenone, surmounted by his sculpted effigy

his body. The legends spread quickly, growing more fantastic with each telling, and soon drew crowds of pilgrims from the surrounding countryside. The leaders of Udine built a shrine in Odoric's honor and sent a delegation to Pope John XXII (reigned from 1316 to 1334) to request that he be made a saint. The delegation brought with them a book of Odoric's miracles compiled in Latin, titled *De reverentia magni Chani* (On Reverence for the Great Khan). It was not until 1755, however, that Pope Benedict XIV officially beatified Odoric, declaring him "Blessed." Because of his travels in China, Odoric is considered the first person in the history of Chinese Catholicism to be beatified. Catholics in Taiwan and Hong Kong still commemorate him every year on January 14.

According to his Travels, Odoric's first port of call in China was Guangzhou. From there, he traveled through Quanzhou to Fuzhou. He then writes, "Leaving this place and traveling for eighteen days, I passed through many towns and saw many things, and I came to a great mountain." Eighteen days later, "having passed through many more towns, I came to a great river and stayed in a city [called Belsa] that had a bridge across it. The inn where I lodged was at the end of the bridge, and my host, wishing to amuse me, said, 'If you would like to see some fine fishing, come with me.' He led me onto the bridge, and I saw that he had several boats there, with water-birds tied to perches. He tied a cord around the birds' throats so they could not swallow the fish they caught. Then he put three large baskets in a boat... and let the birds loose. They immediately dove into the water and began to catch a great quantity of fish, and as soon as they caught one, they would put it in one of the baskets themselves, so that in a short time all three baskets were full."

The "water-birds" Odoric described were, of course, cormorants. Odoric was the first to introduce this unique fishing method to European readers; Marco Polo makes no mention of it. In China, fishing with cormorants dates back to at least the Tang Dynasty (618–907). The Song dynasty scholar Shen Kuo (1031–1095) wrote in his famous Dream Pool Essays, "The people who live by the water in the region of Shu all raise cormorants. They tie a cord around the bird's neck so it can catch fish but not swallow them; when it has a fish, they simply lift it up and take the fish out. This is still done today." The location where Odoric witnessed this, "Belsa," does not appear in all manuscripts of his travels. While some versions omit it, others mention "a city called Belsa." For over 150 years, scholars have debated its identity. In

1866, Sir Henry Yule (1820–1889) considered Wenzhou a possibility but concluded, "I find myself unable to identify the city." More recent proposals have included Lishui and Jinhua, but none of these names are a good phonetic match for Belsa. The Chinese translator of Odoric's travels, He Gaoji, notes that the great river was probably the Qiantang in Zhejiang, but "the name Belsa has no suitable phonetic equivalent... so we can only transliterate it and await further research." For a century and a half, Belsa has remained a puzzle for scholars both in China and abroad.

A review of ancient Chinese sources suggests a solution: Belsa is likely a transliteration of Baisha, the site of Baisha Ferry in what was then Jiande County, Zhejiang. The earliest surviving local history, the Chunxi Yanzhou Tujing, mentions Baisha Ferry, noting it was on a major transport artery connecting Zhejiang with the provinces of Jiangxi and Fujian. The ferry was a popular subject for Song and Yuan dynasty poets. For example, the Southern Song poet Yang Wanli (1127–1206) wrote in his poem "Arriving Late at Yanzhou after Buying a Boat at Baisha": "Heavy fog feels like morning rain, but the setting sun clears to a fine evening. Beyond the river, the countless mountains disappear; a single pagoda gleams on a distant peak. My boat is small and I feel cramped,

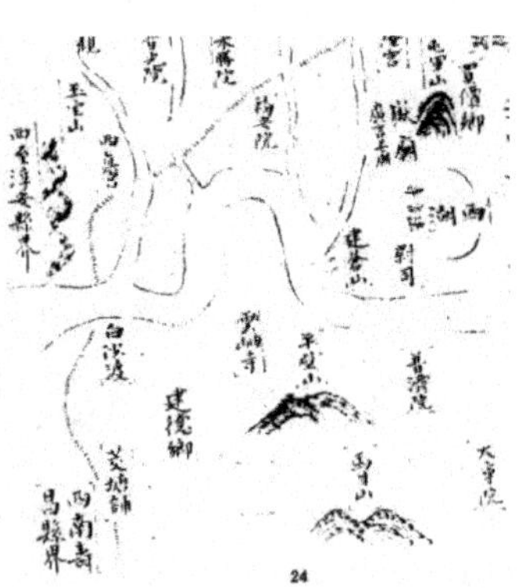

The White Sands of Jiande, as Depicted in the the Chunxi Yanzhou Tujing

and I am weary from the long journey. But the water below Ziling Terrace refreshes my spirit before I have even tasted it."

Odoric mentions staying at an inn in Baisha. Coincidentally, the Southern Song scholar Hong Mai (1123–1202) left a similar record: "When I was about ten years old, I passed through Baisha Ferry in Quzhou and saw two poems written on the crumbling wall of a tavern... The second had a certain profundity. It read: 'A single drop of oil on a white robe leaves a mottled stain that troubles the eye. You can wash it in a thousand rivers, but how can it compare to when it was never stained at all?' I loved these words at the time, and now, more than sixty years later, I remember them vividly." Although Baisha Ferry was technically in Yanzhou prefecture, it was close to Quzhou, and it is plausible that Hong Mai misremembered the location decades later. Similarly, Odoric's mention of a bridge was likely a lapse in memory; no bridge was built there until 1960. But it is perfectly natural that a busy ferry crossing in the Song and Yuan eras would have had inns and taverns. It was precisely because this area had been a small town since the Song and Yuan dynasties that the Baisha Township was established here during the Republic of China era. Later, it was upgraded to the Xin'anjiang District, directly under the Jiande Prefecture in 1957, renamed Xin'anjiang Town the following year, and finally became the seat of Jiande County in 1960 when the county government moved from Meicheng. It is now known as the Xin'anjiang Subdistrict.

Odoric's report of cormorant fishing at Baisha Ferry was one of the details that most captivated his European readers. Local histories confirm the practice. The Chunxi Yanzhou Tujing lists the cormorant first in its section on local birds. A Qing dynasty gazetteer from the area even quotes a poem on the subject: "The fishing skiff plies the evening mist, while cormorants dry on the nets in the setting sun." Because the birds were so useful, the local county gazetteer from the Republican period notes that fishermen along the Qiantang River "treated cormorants as domestic animals." Odoric's account of seeing cormorant fishing at Baisha is therefore entirely credible.

On his journey from Baisha Ferry to Hangzhou along the Qiantang River, Odoric observed another fishing method: "This time the fishermen were in a boat which had a tub of hot water in it. The men were stripped naked, with a bag over their shoulders. They then dove into the water for about half an hour, catching fish with their bare hands and putting them into their bags. When they came out of the water, they threw their bags into the boat and jumped into the tub of hot water. Others then took their turn, doing the same as before; and in this way they caught a great many fish." While catching fish by hand has always been common throughout China, the detail about the fishermen jumping into a tub of hot water on the boat is not corroborated by any records from the Zhejiang region. Why Odoric included this detail remains a mystery.

Immediately after his description of hand-fishing, Odoric begins his account of Hangzhou, which he calls "Cansay." "The name," he says, "means

'City of Heaven.' It is the greatest city in the whole world." He writes that "the city is situated on a tranquil lagoon and has canals, just like Venice. There are twelve thousand bridges in the city, and on every bridge there are guards."

Like Marco Polo's book, Odoric's Travels was widely copied upon its release, resulting in many different versions. According to a recent survey by the Czech scholar Lucie Olivová (Li Shijia), there are 133 known manuscripts of the work in Italian, French, German, Spanish, Welsh, and other languages. The differences between the versions grew as the book was copied and recopied over the years. Some scribes even added illustrations. A parchment manuscript in the Bibliothèque nationale de France, for example, contains two such images, which, based on the text, can be titled Fishing by Hand and Feeding the Creatures at the Temple.

The six lines of text above the illustration Fishing by Hand are Odoric's description of the event. The artist is anonymous, but because he also illustrated a 1415 book of hours now in the Bibliothèque Mazarine in Paris, scholars have dubbed him the "Mazarine Master." Like the Egerton Master, the Mazarine Master had never been to China and relied entirely on his imagination. Although Odoric stated that he saw this fishing method in the countryside near Hangzhou, the illustration shows a group of people fishing in a river just outside the city walls, which are depicted as a European castle. The river is teeming with large, silvery fish, suggesting the region's abundance. The "bags" that Odoric mentioned, likely traditional Chinese fish baskets made of woven bamboo, are missing; the artist simply depicts two naked fishermen in the water. The figure in the upper left, fishing with a rod and reel, is not mentioned in Odoric's text at all and was evidently an invention of the artist.

Fishing by Hand, from the Collection of the Bibliothèque Nationale de France

The red text below Fishing by Hand reads: "The great city of Casaie, also called Catusaie." Both names are variant spellings of "Quinsai," or Hangzhou. The text goes on to describe the city, calling it the "City of Heaven" (Cité du ciel) and "the greatest city in the world." It says that it "is situated in a gulf of the sea, and is surrounded by many lakes, ponds, and pools, just like Venice," and that it has twelve great gates.

The text related to the Feeding the Creatures at the Temple illustration appears on both sides of the folio. In it, Odoric recounts meeting a Christian in Hangzhou who was "a man of great authority." One day, this man took him to visit a temple. There, a monk carrying two baskets of food led them into a garden with a small hill. "The monk rang a bell, and about twenty four-legged creatures with human faces immediately came down from the hill very obediently and gathered quietly together. The monk mixed the food in a large silver basin and set it before the beasts to feed them. After the beasts had eaten, the monk rang the bell again, and the four-legged monsters returned to their places. I found this to be truly amazing."

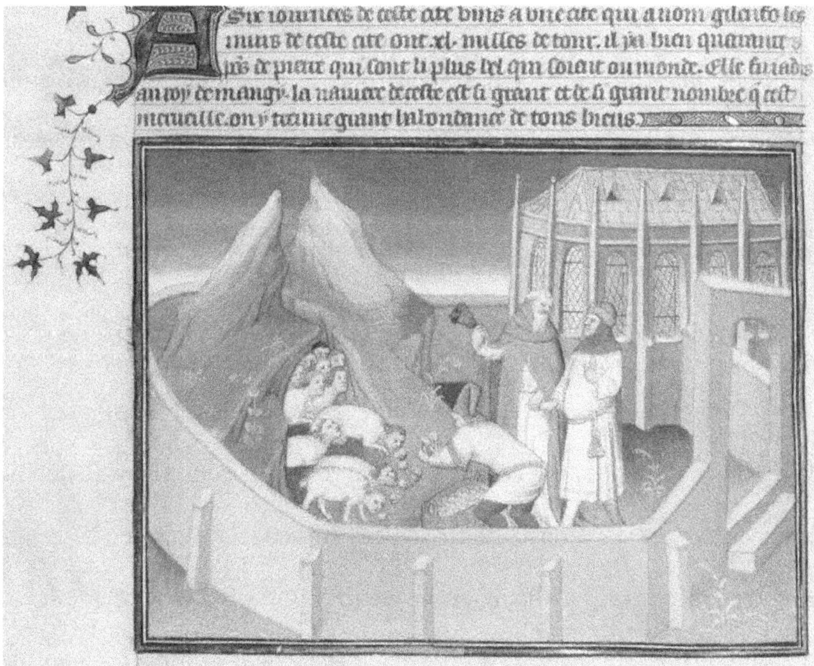

The Feeding the Creatures at the Temple, from the Collection of the Bibliothèque Nationale de France

The Mazarine Master also painted Feeding the Creatures at the Temple.

The temple where Odoric saw the strange creatures was likely Buddhist, but the artist has depicted it as a Gothic church with Romanesque arched windows. The human-faced, four-legged creatures themselves are drawn with the faces of men and the bodies of sheep, a common motif in medieval European art. While Odoric said the creatures came down from a small hill, the illustration shows them emerging from a cave. The artist has also chosen to depict their food as a type of fruit. On the right of the illustration, two men are shown in conversation. One, an old man with a white beard, wears a white robe with a rope belt and a grey cloak—the typical traveling attire of a Franciscan friar. This is undoubtedly Odoric himself. The man he is speaking with, the Christian from Hangzhou, is shown wearing a red hat and a money pouch at his waist to symbolize his wealth and power. He, too, is depicted as a European. The monk feeding the creatures, whom the artist would have considered a pagan, is drawn as a clown-like figure in a pointed hat—a far cry from the appearance of a real Buddhist monk.

After his stay in Hangzhou, Odoric traveled to Chilenfu (Nanjing). From there, his account says, one comes to a great river called the Talay. Following this river downstream, one reaches the city of Iamzai (Yangzhou). Leaving Yangzhou, he writes, "at the mouth of the river Talay is a city called Menzu. The ships in this city are probably better and more numerous than in any other city in the world. They are painted white as snow on the outside and have halls and chambers and all kinds of amenities, all very beautiful and clean. The number of ships here is so great that you would not believe it if you heard of it, and you might have trouble believing it even if you saw it with your own eyes."

The "great river" Talay is undoubtedly the Yangtze; the name comes from the Mongolian word for "sea," dalai (as in Dalai Lama). The city of Menzu (also spelled Mezu, Mensy, etc.) has been identified by scholars as Mingzhou (modern-day Ningbo), as there is no other port city on China's southeastern coast with a similar-sounding name. The problem is that Ningbo is not located at the mouth of the Yangtze, nor is it north of Yangzhou. There are several possible explanations for this discrepancy. Odoric may never have actually visited Ningbo, but only heard about it. It is also possible that his memory failed him as he dictated his story while ill. Perhaps it was a combination of both factors. After all, Odoric's account is not entirely factual; it contains many unreliable and even absurd stories. He claims, for instance, to have found a nation of pygmies along the Yangtze where women married at the age of five and gave birth to palm-sized children. It is entirely plausible, then, that he simply misremembered the location of Mingzhou.

Marco Polo left China by the Maritime Silk Road, and Odoric of Pordenone arrived by it. Both men visited Zhejiang, and their accounts fired the imagination of Europe with visions of the East. The illustrations in the Bibliothèque Nationale de France—The Queen's Surrender of the City, The Celestial City, Tax Collection in Quinsai, Fishing by Hand, and Feeding the Creatures at the Temple—are echoes of Zhejiang's connection to the world, a lasting legacy of the Maritime Silk Road in medieval Europe.

Chapter 8. Japanese Tribute Delegations in Zhejiang

Marco Polo and Odoric of Pordenone both visited Zhejiang during the Yuan Dynasty and enjoyed considerable freedom of movement—a privilege made possible by the Yuan government's generally open policy toward foreign contacts. After Zhu Yuanzhang overthrew the Yuan and founded the Ming Dynasty, however, this openness gave way to a far more restrictive approach. The Ming court established a tribute trade system that redefined China's relations with the outside world. Its core features were as follows:

First, foreign merchants were prohibited from engaging in private trade with Chinese citizens. Only a small number of states, officially recognized by the Ming government, were permitted to send tribute missions—nominally acts of political homage—which also served as the sole channel for conducting trade. In this way, commerce was tightly bound to diplomacy, and overseas trade became an extension of state-to-state political relations.

Second, the Ming court restricted foreign exchanges to just three designated ports: Ningbo, Quanzhou, and Guangzhou. Each port served specific partners—Japanese envoys were received only at Ningbo, Ryukyuan envoys at Quanzhou, and Southeast Asian envoys at Guangzhou. Strict regulations governed the frequency of tribute missions, the number of ships, and the size of delegations. Initially, Japan enjoyed relatively lenient terms; some missions brought as many as 1,200 participants, and during the Yongle reign (1403–1424), Japanese tribute ships arrived almost annually. In 1453, a Japanese delegation comprised nine ships. Thereafter, restrictions grew increasingly severe: Japan was allowed to send tribute only once every ten years, with no more than three ships and 300 people per mission.

Third, to verify the legitimacy of tribute envoys, the Ming government issued official credentials known as *kanhe* (tally certificates). A copy was given to each tribute state, while the court retained a matching counterpart. Upon arrival, envoys presented their *kanhe*, which Chinese officials compared with the court's own copy to confirm authenticity. One scholar vividly described the *kanhe* as "a certificate stamped with a seal across the fold," a metaphor for the Ming government's meticulous control over foreign contacts.

Foreign tribute missions to China presented the Ming court with local specialties such as spices, medicinal herbs, and precious gems. In return, the court, following the principle of "giving generously while receiving modestly," bestowed gifts—silk, porcelain, and other treasures—worth far more than the tributes received. Tribute ships also carried large quantities of so-called "accompanying goods," nominally the private property of foreign monarchs, their consorts, or members of the delegation. The Ming government often purchased these goods at exceptionally high prices. Because tribute trade was an unequal exchange unconstrained by market value, it yielded extraordinary profits for foreign states. As a result, they sought every opportunity to increase the frequency of their tribute missions or to enlarge the scale of their delegations.

Ningbo was designated by the Ming government as the sole port for official contact with Japan. To oversee these exchanges, the court established the Zhejiang Maritime Trade Superintendency (*shibosi*), headquartered in what is now the Nine-Bend Corridor area of Zhongshan Park, Haishu District. Under its administration were the Guest Hall (Jiabin Tang), a lodging facility for Japanese tribute envoys, and the Maritime Trade Warehouse (Shibo Ku) for storing goods. The reception of Japanese tribute missions followed a set protocol. When tribute ships entered the Zhoushan Archipelago, Ningbo officials dispatched vessels to greet them, offering wine and food before escorting them into the Yong River. Upon arrival, the envoys presented the *shibosi* with a formal letter from the Japanese government along with their Ming-issued *kanhe* (tally certificate). The *kanhe* recorded precise details such as the number of ships, personnel, official tribute items, and "accompanying goods." These documents were forwarded to the Ministry of Rites in Beijing for authentication. While awaiting the ministry's decision, the envoys stayed at the Guest Hall and were strictly prohibited from carrying weapons. If approved, the delegation was summoned to the capital, with all travel and hospitality expenses for the round trip between Ningbo and Beijing covered by the Ming government. After completing their audience and tribute presentation in Beijing, the envoys returned to Ningbo. Before their departure for Japan, local officials provisioned their ships with roughly a month's worth of food for the voyage. Each such mission thus represented a considerable expense for the Ningbo authorities.

Between 1401 and 1549, Japan sent 20 diplomatic missions to the Ming court, while the Ming dispatched eight missions to Japan. All 28 delegations passed through Ningbo, underscoring the city's central role in Sino-Japanese relations of the time. The Japanese missions included not only government officials but also scholars, Buddhist monks, and other notable figures. Among them, two monks in particular developed especially close ties with Zhejiang: Sesshū (1420–1506) and Sakugen Shūryō (1501–1579).

Sesshū (1420–1506) was born in what is now Sōja, Okayama Prefecture, and was sent to a Buddhist temple in his youth. While pursuing his Buddhist studies, he also distinguished himself as an exceptional painter. In 1467, Sesshū traveled to Ningbo as part of a Japanese diplomatic mission. During his stay, he visited many of the region's celebrated scenic sites, recording them in his art. His painting *View of Mount Yuwang* vividly portrays the celebrated Ayuwang Temple in Ningbo. In 1992, drawing on Sesshū's depiction, the city of Ningbo reconstructed the temple's East Pagoda. The original painting is now housed in the Tokyo University of the Arts Museum.

Sesshū's *Map of Ningbo Prefecture*

During his stay in China, Sesshū also produced the *Draft of Tangshan's Scenic Splendors*, vividly portraying the landscapes of Dinghai (present-day Zhenhai), Ningbo, and Shaoxing. The original work has since been lost, but a copy by an anonymous artist survives and is now housed in the Museum of Fine Arts, Boston. One section, the *Map of Ningbo Prefecture*, takes the entire eastern city wall and the eastern stretch of the northern wall as its central axis, presenting a sweeping panorama of Ningbo's urban landscape in the Ming period. The city's long, continuous walls encircle and protect it, with three imposing gates—Lingqiao Gate (East Gate), Yancang Gate (North Gate), and Dongdu Gate—standing prominently. Within the walls, houses crowd together in dense rows, while the pavilions of Tianning Temple and the Twin Buddha Tower rise above the rooftops. The map also labels the "Siming Post Station" and mistakenly marks Moon Lake as "Nan Hu," with "Hu" being an error for "Lake." Outside Lingqiao Gate, a pontoon bridge of linked boats spans the water, and beyond the northern and eastern walls, the Yao River and Fenghua River teem with vessels—an animated testament to the vitality of maritime trade. Another section, the *Map of Shaoxing Prefecture*, depicts

the lofty slopes of Mount Kuaiji, compact clusters of dwellings, and a network of canals, bridges, and small boats, capturing the quintessential charm of a Jiangnan water town.

In 1469, before Sesshū departed Ningbo for his return to Japan, the local scholar Xu Lian composed a farewell poem and inscribed a long preface in regular script. This piece, now housed in the Mōri Museum in Japan, is known as the *Preface to the Poem Sending Sesshū Back to His Homeland*. In it, Xu Lian praised Sesshū as "gifted in both poetry and painting" and presented him with the following verses:

Your home lies by the tranquil waters of Penglai,

Your graceful bearing transcends the mortal realm.

Long have I heard your verses rise beyond the world of men,

While your brush leaves colors drifting among the clouds.

From the thousand peaks of Vulture Mountain you set forth with staff in hand,

Across the whale-ploughed seas you sail home, cup in tow.

I know where our thoughts will meet when we are apart:

The moon high in the heavens, the clouds upon the hills.

In these lines, the farewell of a Ningbo scholar to a Japanese monk is conveyed with unfeigned warmth, natural ease, and heartfelt sincerity.

Sakugen Shūryō, the third abbot of Myōchi-in, a subtemple of Tenryū-ji in Saga, Kyoto, was a man of profound learning in Chinese culture. In 1539, he served as vice-envoy in a Japanese tribute mission to China, with Hoshin Shakudō as chief envoy. This was his first diplomatic journey to China. In his *Record of the First Voyage*, Sakugen kept a detailed diary of the mission. These entries are of great value for studying Zhejiang's role in the Maritime Silk Road and preserve a wealth of information about the region.

The delegation set sail from Japan in April 1539. Strong northerly winds pushed them slightly southward, and on the second day of the fifth lunar month they entered the waters off Wenzhou. Local fishermen told them, "With fair winds, it takes five days; without them, ten" to reach Ningbo. Continuing north through the waters of Taizhou, they anchored on the seventh near an island south of Changguo Garrison, a coastal stronghold in Xiangshan County under Ningbo's jurisdiction. The garrison commander sent men to guide them to Shipu Port, where they were warmly received with fine wine and delicacies. On the twelfth, the commander, Liu Dongshan, presented the Japanese envoys with a poem:

In the wide Damu Sea your treasure ship lies moored,

Sweet winds and gentle waves—there is nothing to fear.

Heaven surely blesses the virtuous in this very place,

Loosen your ropes and set forth without delay.

The "Damu Sea" refers to the offshore waters near Xiangshan.

On the sixteenth day of the fifth month, under escort from the Ming navy, the Japanese delegation reached Dinghai—present-day Zhenhai—at the mouth of the Yong River. Local officials supplied them with fresh water, poultry, pork, and other provisions, along with seasonal fruits such as loquats. Lu, a deputy inspector of the Ningbo maritime circuit, asked whether they had brought the *kanhe*—the official tally certificate—and cautioned the Japanese merchants traveling with the mission to abide by Chinese law, trade fairly, and guard against being cheated by Chinese merchants. Sakugen Shūryō observed that each day, some three to four hundred fishing boats entered the Yong River, bound for Ningbo to sell their catch.

On the twenty-second day of the fifth lunar month, Sakugen Shūryō and his party, escorted by Ming troops, traveled by boat from Dinghai to Ningbo. Upon landing, the magistrate of Yin County sent a delivery of provisions: one *dan* of white rice, a side of pork weighing twenty *jin*, two jars of wine, one hundred *jin* of bamboo shoots, and two hundred *jin* of firewood. The next day,

Ningbo officials sent an interpreter surnamed Zhou to deliver a notice reminding the Japanese envoys to comply with Chinese laws. Sakugen Shūryō and his companions passed these instructions on to the Japanese merchants accompanying them. On the twenty-fourth, as the ships were "thirsty," they urgently requested fresh water—preferably well water—to be sent promptly and in repeated deliveries. The Ningbo authorities complied. That same day, the Ningbo Maritime Trade Office (*shibosi*) sent an official document requesting a report on the exact number of people in the mission and the quantity of grain they required.

On the twenty-fifth day, Sakugen Shūryō and his entourage went ashore to pay their respects to various Ningbo officials before taking up lodgings at the Guest Hall (Jiābīn Táng). Above its main entrance hung a plaque inscribed "Cherishing the Distant with Virtue," while the east gate bore the inscription "Beholding the Splendor of the Superior Kingdom."

Inside the hall were two additional plaques. One read "Beware of Fire by Day" on the front and "Beware of Fire by Night" on the reverse; the other read "Guard Against Theft by Night" on the front and "Guard Against Theft by Day" on the reverse. From Sakugen Shūryō's account, we learn that the gate of the Ningbo Prefectural Office bore the three large characters for "Ningbo Prefecture." In the main hall hung a plaque reading Hall of Upright Mind, and on a pillar to the left dangled a key with a small tag marked "Main Gate Key." The Zhejiang Maritime Trade Superintendency displayed a plaque with its full name above the main gate, while a frequently used side entrance bore simply Maritime Trade Office. Outside the main hall, a notice was posted: All travelers, regardless of rank, are strictly forbidden to enter the public hall without permission, to loiter, sit, or cause a disturbance. At the time, the superintendent was Wei Huang, reporting to a eunuch surnamed Liu, whose full title was Imperial Commissioner Guarding Zhejiang and Other Regions, Concurrently in Charge of Maritime Trade, of the Directorate of Imperial Stables. The Yinxian County Office bore a plaque with the two characters for "Yinxian." Inside were two small side doors—one to the east inscribed Practice Benevolence, and one to the west inscribed Uphold Virtue. The plaque above the front of the main hall read Hall for Protecting the People, while the rear door was inscribed Hall of Self-Reflection. Inside, a horizontal plaque declared Watched Over by the Spirits. Most strikingly, the main hall of the Ningbo Prefectural Office displayed a moral couplet: Show an extra measure of kindness, and the people will receive an extra measure of benefit; Covet a single coin, and the official is worth less than that single coin. These plaques and couplets, preserved for more than 480 years, vividly reflect the ethos and long tradition of Chinese officialdom.

Sakugen Shūryō's *Record of the First Voyage* offers a vivid portrait of Ningbo's cityscape and street life in his day. The eastern city gate, Lingqiao Gate (Spiritual Bridge), bore its name above the entrance. Beside it hung a plaque inscribed Inspection, indicating that all entrants were subject to security checks. The western gate was named Wangjing (Gazing Toward the Capital), a reference to Beijing, and just beyond it stood an outer gate with the inscription Safeguard the Nation's Lifeblood. By the banks of the Yao River rose a building called Yinen Tower (Tower of Imprinted Grace). The southern gate was marked with the characters Changchun (Eternal Spring).

Ningbo was adorned with countless gate towers and ornamental archways. Sakugen Shūryō remarked that "in some places a gate stood every five paces, in others every ten, their number beyond reckoning." The plaques on these structures carried inscriptions—some in four characters, such as Siming Weiguan (Magnificent Sights of Siming), Siming Fudi (Blessed Land of Siming), and Penglai Zhenjing (True Realm of Penglai); others in two characters, such as Xuanhua (Proclaiming Transformation), Chengliu (Carrying Forward the Legacy), and Guilin (Cassia Grove). Within the City God Temple stood an image of the Lord of the Northern Dipper, before which hung a plaque inscribed with seven large characters reading The City God of Ningbo Prefecture.

In the Ming dynasty, Ningbo was renowned for its flourishing scholarly culture and was among the most advanced regions in China in terms of the imperial examination system. Its number of successful jinshi—the highest degree in the system—far outstripped that of other regions. Records suggest that in Yinxian County alone, more than 250 men attained the jinshi title during the Ming period. To bring glory to their ancestors, families of new jinshi often erected memorial archways and similar structures. Thus, Sakugen Shūryō saw numerous such arches in Ningbo. He remarked that their inscriptions "shone brilliantly before the eyes." Some bore two-character titles, such as Jieyuan ("Top Provincial Graduate"), Wenxian ("Literary Eminence"), and Xiangfeng ("Soaring Phoenix"). Others carried three-character names, such as Jinshi Fang ("Archway for Jinshi"), Dengying Lou ("Tower of Ascending to Yingzhou"—a mythical isle symbolizing transcendence and success), Sanfeng Jie ("Three Phoenix Street"), and Jukui Fang ("Archway of Gathered Brilliance," denoting brothers as jieyuan or a father and son both as jinshi). Four-character inscriptions included Yunlong Jiahui ("Auspicious Gathering of Clouds and Dragons"), Jiawu Binxing ("Scholarly Success in the Jiawu Year"), Kuibi Jiaohui ("Radiant Convergence of Literary Stars"), Sanshi Jinshi ("Three Generations of Jinshi"), and Caifeng Lianfei ("Twin Phoenixes in Flight," likely celebrating two brothers passing in the same year).

From Sakugen Shūryō's accounts, we see that Ningbo was a bustling hub of commerce, its streets lined with shops and signs "too numerous to count." Fan-makers advertised with plaques reading: "Self-made, fashionable fans of ingenious design in every color," "Gilt fan faces in various hues," "All kinds of fan faces for sale," "Replacement of fan faces in any color," and "Exquisite fans in all varieties." Some shop signs were more refined, bearing names such as Far-Spreading Breeze of Benevolence and Half a Bright Moon Accompanies the Traveler. Pharmacies displayed signs like

Shen's Medicine Chamber and Annals of the Apricot Grove—a poetic allusion to the healing arts. Bamboo-blind weavers simply hung a sign reading Sunshade, while hat sellers wrote Cool Hats. Brush shops offered Finely Crafted Superb Brushes and Zhongshan's Finest Tips (referring to the region famed for brush-making). Other signs announced goods and services such as Horsehair for Sale, Wine Lees for Sale, Cottonseed for Sale, Binding and Printing Sutras and Books, and Interpreting the Changes to Resolve Doubts (for fortune-telling). The tavern signs were the most intriguing. Some were straightforward—Fragrant Aged Wine, Finest Distilled Spirits, Five-Spice Flavored Wine, New Wine for Sale, Lotus White Wine. Others adopted a literary touch, such as Yu's Aversion (referring to the legendary ruler Yu's dislike of excessive drink) and Poetry-Fishing Hook. One even proclaimed: Travelers Dismount at the Scent, Passersby Halt for the Taste. This recalls the famous couplet of Hangzhou's century-old Zhiweiguan restaurant—Halt for the Taste, Dismount for the Fragrance—showing that, as Sakugen recorded, such poetic signboards were already gracing Ningbo's streets as early as the late Ming dynasty.

However, Sakugen Shūryō also witnessed the darker and more brutal side of Chinese society. In the sixth lunar month of 1539, during a spell of continuous rain and stifling humidity, he had just arrived in Ningbo and was walking through the streets when he saw several prisoners by the roadside, shackled in heavy cangues and already tortured to the brink of death. Unable to bear the sight, he feared they would not survive and wrote to the local officials, pleading for their release as an act of compassion and mercy. Perhaps, as a devout Buddhist, Sakugen was overly idealistic—unaware that for ordinary people living in the so-called "Celestial Empire," compassion and mercy were luxuries rarely afforded.

During his stay in Ningbo, Sakugen Shūryō kept a busy schedule, frequently calling on officials, monks, and scholars. Take, for instance, the 29th day of the sixth lunar month. His activities that day unfolded as follows:

> "Around mid-morning, I visited Moon Lake with San'ei and Sōkei—a site once visited by the Tang poet He Zhizhang. There stood a shrine in his honor, its gate inscribed with six characters: 'Shrine of the Tang Secret Inspector He.' Inside, the main hall was solemn, with a statue of He at the center. A stone bridge arched over the lake, bearing the name 'Minister's Bridge' in three large characters.
>
> Next, we visited the Confucius Temple, where a tablet at the center bore eight characters: 'Spirit Seat of the Most Sacred Teacher Confucius.'
>
> Later, we stopped by the residence of Fan Nangang. Above the gate were two characters: 'Soaring Phoenix.' I brought him a Japanese fan. Old Fan greeted me with a smile, as though we were friends reuniting after a decade. He served a fine meal and poured excellent wine. We enjoyed white cloud mushrooms and drank

from cups of the same name. I first tasted pine blossom cakes. In a dish, I noticed flowers resembling impatiens; when I asked their name, Fan replied, 'Full Pond Red.'

In the afternoon, I visited Yanqing Temple, home to the spiritual descendants of the Tiantai master Zhizhe. A welcoming monk greeted us and led us into a room. One elderly monk held my hand warmly, spoke about the temple's history, and offered us watermelon and northern tea. I gifted him a simple fan, and in return, he presented me with four paintings of birds."

Through his talent and literary refinement, Sakugen Shūryō earned the admiration of Ningbo's scholars. Many composed poems in his honor. One such verse reads:

Long have we revered your distant land's extraordinary gift;

Your noble spirit seems heaven-sent.

In your traveler's lodge, we spoke through wind and rain,

And your writings dazzled the entire hall.

A particularly treasured testament to his bond with the Ningbo literati is the *Preface to the Linked Verses of the Western City* (Jōsai Renku Jo), now preserved at Myōchi-in, a sub-temple of Tenryū-ji in Kyoto.

While residing at Myōchi-in, a sub-temple of Tenryū-ji in western Kyoto,

Sakugen Shūryō gathered fellow poets to compose a vast linked-verse sequence totaling 9,000 lines, later compiled into the *Linked Verses of the Western City* (Jōsai Renku). The name "Western City" referred to Myōchi-in's location in Kyoto's western quarter. In 1539, Sakugen brought this manuscript with him to Ningbo. That autumn, during the ninth lunar month, he had the collection professionally mounted and sought a distinguished literary figure to write a preface for it. While in Ningbo, he and his companions frequently interacted with the local scholar Ke Yuchuang.

At the time, one of Ningbo's most renowned scholars was the calligrapher Feng Fang (c. 1500–1570), whose works are still preserved in the Tianyi Pavilion Museum. Sakugen Shūryō learned about him through Ke Yuchuang, and before leaving Ningbo, he asked Ke to invite Feng to write a preface for his *Linked Verses of the Western City*. Initially reluctant, Feng eventually agreed after Ke's earnest and persistent persuasion. In his preface, Feng Fang warmly praised Sakugen's achievement in "honorably continuing the work of his predecessors" and offered a high appraisal of his poetry:

"Reading your poems, I find language that is plain yet profound, concise yet deeply thoughtful. You depict elusive scenes with vivid clarity, and your words carry boundless meaning beyond their surface. True insight resides in your heart, and your elegant phrases shine with brilliance—resonating through time. Surely, this is the work of one who aspires earnestly and lives up to the legacy of his masters."

That such refined prose by a Ningbo scholar would appear as the preface to a Japanese poet's work was a perfect literary match. One can only hope that this collaborative creation between Chinese and Japanese literati—the Linked Verses of the Western City—will be cherished for generations to come.

On the 19th day of the tenth lunar month in 1539, Sakugen Shūryō and his companions bid farewell to their friends in Ningbo and boarded tribute vessels at the Yancang Gate (also known as Heyi Gate) in the city's north, beginning their journey northward along the Grand Canal to Beijing. The ship carrying Kosodai bore a yellow flag reading "Principal Envoy," while Sakugen's ship flew a similar flag marked "Deputy Envoy." After traveling forty li, they reached Xiba. On the 20th, with overcast skies and unfavorable winds, they were forced to anchor and await the tide. Not until the third watch of the night did they "ride the wind beneath the moon," continuing north. By dawn, they had arrived at Cheju Relay Station.

On the 21st day of the tenth lunar month, the Japanese delegation was received by officials at Cheju Relay Station and disembarked for a brief visit. Sakugen Shūryō noted: "There is a small hill here called Cheju—it is said to be where King Goujian of Yue once rested his chariots and horses." That afternoon, around the hour of *shēn* (3–5 p.m.), the Japanese tribute ships departed Cheju and by the hour of *xū* (7–9 p.m.), they arrived at Yaojiang Relay

Station. The waterway between the two stations spanned sixty *li*. The following day, on the 22nd, the envoys went ashore to meet with the local officials at Yaojiang. Along the road, they noticed numerous ceremonial archways. One in particular bore the four large characters "Jinshi Jidi" (Successful Imperial Scholar), flanked by the characters "Yuan" (First) and "Kui" (Top Candidate). The inscription also included: "14th year of the Hongzhi reign, xinyou (1501), First Place in the Shuntian Provincial Examination." This arch was most likely erected in honor of Xie Pi, a native of Yuyao (courtesy name Yizhong, sobriquet Ruhu). In 1501, he placed first in the Shuntian provincial examination, earning a place among the revered "Five Champions." In 1505, he ranked fourth in the metropolitan examination, and during the final palace examination, he distinguished himself further by winning third place in the top tier—known as a Tanhua or "Flower of the Court," one of the elite "Three Laureates" along with the Zhuangyuan (Champion) and Bangyan (Second Place). The characters "Kui" and "Yuan" on the arch commemorate Xie Pi's exceptional achievements in both provincial and national civil service examinations.

On the 22nd day of the tenth lunar month, around the hour of *wèi* (1–2 p.m.), the Japanese delegation departed from Yaojiang Relay Station. After traveling 40 li by water, they arrived at Xiaba around *yǒu* hour (5–6 p.m.). However, the tide was too low for further navigation, so they had to wait. By *xū* hour (7–8 p.m.), when the tide had risen, "strongmen used a windlass to haul the ships across the dam." In other words, the vessels had to be manually winched through the sluice gate. After continuing another 18 *li* by water, the mission reached Zhongba around *chǒu* hour (1–2 a.m.). There, the boats were once again manually hauled through the sluice. Following an additional 10 *li* of travel, they arrived at Shangyu around *yín* hour (3–4 a.m.)—concluding an arduous night journey through three dam stages.

Around 10 a.m. on the morning of the 23rd day of the tenth lunar month, Sakugen Shūryō and his party departed from Shangyu, continuing their journey northward along the canal. After traveling 30 *li* by water, they arrived at Cao'e Relay Station around noon. The station's gatehouse prominently displayed the three characters: "Cao'e Relay Station." The next day, the 24th, they set off from Cao'e and alternated between traveling by boat and riding sedan chairs overland. By afternoon, they reached Dongguan Relay Station.

At around 3–4 a.m. (*yín* hour) on the 25th day of the tenth lunar month, the Japanese delegation set off by boat from Dongguan Relay Station. After traveling 40 *li*, they arrived at Taojiayan. Along the way, they passed a location marked by three large characters: "Guashanpu" (Guashan Station). From Taojiayan, they continued for another ten *li*, passing by Fanjiang Temple. By noon, they had reached Shaoxing. According to Sakugen Shūryō, the journey from Taojiapu to Shaoxing covered a total of 40 *li* by boat. Within Shaoxing's boundaries, they passed several notable sites, including Yingchun Pavilion and Penglai Relay Station.

On the 26th day of the tenth lunar month, the Japanese tribute ships continued their journey through Shaoxing, passing by numerous stone bridges along the way. That day, the delegation traveled in sequence past Lingtou Bridge, Meishi Station, Tongji Bridge, Keqiao Station, and Qianqing Relay Station, finally arriving at Feng Relay Station in Xiaoshan.

On the 27th day of the tenth lunar month, Sakugen Shūryō and his entourage disembarked and continued their journey overland by sedan chair. By the 28th, they had arrived at Xixing Relay Station, where they saw an imposing gate tower bearing the inscription "Capital of All Yue" (Quán Yuè Dūhuì). This gate stood about one *li* (roughly 500 meters) from the Qiantang River. They then boarded boats to cross the river and arrived at the outskirts of Hangzhou. According to Sakugen's account, near the Qiantang River outside Hangzhou stood another gate tower, inscribed with three large characters: "Yingri Tower" ("Sun-Reflecting Tower").

On the 29th day of the tenth lunar month, officials in Hangzhou arranged for the Japanese envoys to travel by boat to the North Gate. Upon arrival, they noted that "laborers were as numerous as clouds," a vivid image that reflected the bustling transport of goods along the canal at the time. On the first day of the eleventh lunar month, the Japanese delegation disembarked and entered Hangzhou to pay an official visit. On the second day, Hangzhou officials paid a return visit. On the third day, the delegation departed the city by boat and arrived in Deqing.

Continuing their journey along the Grand Canal, the delegation passed a number of post stations, including Tiaoxi Station in Huzhou Prefecture and Gusu Station in Suzhou Prefecture. On the second day of the third lunar month in 1540, they arrived in Beijing, entering the city through Chongwen Gate. They were accommodated at the Huitongguan, the official guesthouse designated by the Ming court for hosting foreign tribute missions. Although the Ming government bestowed generous gifts upon the Japanese envoys and purchased their accompanying trade goods at high prices, it remained inwardly unwelcoming. As a result, the overall reception was noticeably cold and formal. On the ninth day of the fifth lunar month in 1540, the Japanese delegation departed Beijing and began their return journey south along the canal.

On the third day of the ninth lunar month, they re-entered Hangzhou through the Wulin Gate. Two days later, on the fifth, they witnessed the spectacular tidal bore of the Qiantang River. Overwhelmed by the sight, Sakugen Shūryō exclaimed, "What a truly magnificent spectacle!"

On the early morning of the sixth day of the ninth lunar month, the Japanese delegation crossed the Qiantang River and proceeded along the Eastern Zhejiang Canal toward Ningbo. On the twelfth, they disembarked outside Lingqiao Gate in Ningbo. *Portrait of Master Sakugen Shūryō.* In the days that followed, Sakugen Shūryō and his companions made preparations for their return to Japan while also engaging in poetic exchanges with local literati. Two cultural artifacts resulting from this period are still preserved at Myōchi-in, a sub-temple of Tenryū-ji in Japan. One of these is the *Portrait of Master Sakugen Shūryō*. In the painting, he is depicted wearing a square cap and monastic robes, holding a book in his left hand while his right rests naturally on his knee. He sits with calm composure, his expression both benevolent and solemn. Above the portrait, Ke Yuchuang inscribed a eulogy:"The Master is a distinguished Japanese monk. As an envoy to China, he resided in Mingzhou, embodying both dignified presence and literary elegance." He further offered his wishes:"May he enjoy long life and enduring health."

The second artifact is a calligraphic and pictorial work titled *Returning Home in Glory*, created by Ke Yuchuang. The piece is composed of two parts. The upper section features large semi-cursive script reading Returning Home in Glory, signed "Written by Ke Yuchuang, Recluse of Siming in the South." The lower section is an ink painting depicting a harmonious landscape: distant peaks and nearby hills layered with natural rhythm; below, a small boat is moored by the shore, where several figures stand to welcome someone. Behind them, houses are partially hidden among trees, and in the lower right corner stands a flat bridge. According to Liu Hengwu, Ke Yuchuang painted this scene based on Sakugen Shūryō's descriptions of Tenryū-ji Temple. The composition is believed to portray the temple itself along with its surrounding mountains, waterways, and bridge structures.

On the twenty-third day of the fifth lunar month in 1541, Sakugen Shūryō and the other Japanese envoys departed Ningbo by boat, beginning their return journey to Japan. They reached Japanese waters by the end of the sixth month, enjoying smooth sailing along the way. Although Sakugen Shūryō served only as deputy envoy on this mission to China, his deep mastery of Chinese culture made him the leading figure in cultural exchanges with Ningbo's literati, earning their heartfelt admiration. His travel diary, *Record of the First Voyage*, along with the valuable cultural artifacts he brought back to Japan, remain important primary sources for the study of the Maritime Silk Road in Zhejiang.

During their tribute mission in Beijing, Ming officials explicitly instructed Sakugen Shūryō and his delegation that they could not return for another ten years, that the number of tribute ships must not exceed three, and that the delegation must be limited to no more than 100 members. However, just six years after returning to Japan, Sakugen Shūryō sailed back to the coast of Zhejiang in the sixth month of the 26th year of the Jiajing reign (1547), this time as chief envoy, leading more than 600 people aboard four tribute ships—violating all the agreed limits. As a result, the Ming authorities denied them entry into Ningbo Port, and the delegation was forced to anchor in the Zhoushan Islands. Sakugen documented this second mission to China in his diary *Record of the Second Voyage*.

Although the Ming court placed numerous restrictions on Sakugen Shūryō and the other Japanese envoys, local officials in Ningbo did their utmost to offer assistance. During the delegation's stay offshore, Ningbo authorities continually sent them essential daily supplies. According to Ming regulations, Japanese missions were only allowed to communicate with official Chinese representatives and were strictly prohibited from engaging in private trade. Yet for the coastal residents of Ningbo, the arrival of the Japanese tribute ships presented a rare and valuable commercial opportunity. Defying government prohibitions, they repeatedly approached the ships to conduct trade. In *Record of the Second Voyage*, Sakugen Shūryō recorded these transactions in brief but telling detail. Nearly every few days, merchant boats arrived to trade alongside the tribute ships. On the first day of the eleventh lunar month in 1547: "a small trading boat arrived." On the third: "one small boat came, carrying fresh wine, tangerines, and other items." On the fifth: "a small trading boat arrived." At times, multiple boats came in succession, or even simultaneously. For instance, on the twelfth: "Morning frost, white like snow. At the hour of mǎo, a merchant boat arrived… At noon, another boat arrived. The weather threatened rain." On the seventh day of the twelfth month: "At the hour of chén, six or seven boats came, loaded with rice, wine, and more." On the twenty-first: "Clear skies, but the wind had not calmed. At the hour of sì, a small boat arrived with scallions, vegetables, vinegar, and more. A north wind blew. That night, the cold was bitter." On the twenty-fourth: "By evening, a light rain fell. A small trading boat arrived." These sparse notes reflect the harsh realities of life for ordinary Chinese people. They braved the bitter cold and stormy seas, risking their lives among the waves to trade their humble goods for a bit of money or goods from the Japanese. Even more perilously, they did so knowing they could face government punishment at any time.

To expedite their audience with the Chinese emperor and fulfill their tributary mission, the Japanese envoys anchored off the coast of Ningbo actively sought various pretexts to persuade the Ming authorities to grant them permission to disembark. Fearing that their prolonged presence at sea might provoke unrest, the Grand Coordinator, Zhu Wan, also petitioned the imperial court on their behalf. Eventually, the court granted approval for Sakugen Shūryō to land in Ningbo as a duly recognized envoy.

On the tenth day of the third lunar month in 1548 (the 27th year of the Jiajing reign), after drifting at sea for ten months, Sakugen Shūryō and his fellow envoys were finally escorted into Ningbo by Ming naval vessels and accommodated at the Jiabinguan Guesthouse. During his first diplomatic mission to China, things had gone relatively smoothly, and his diary from that journey, *Record of the First Voyage*, is filled with light-hearted and joyful prose. By contrast, his second visit was marked by frustration: the Ming authorities kept him stranded outside the mouth of the Yong River for ten months. The resulting diary, *Record of the Second Voyage*, reveals his deep sense of gloom and helplessness. Many entries are sparse, even perfunctory—just a few words or dull, repetitive notes. It was only after he was allowed to re-enter Ningbo and reunited with old acquaintances that his writing regained its vitality and expressive richness. On the twentieth day of the ninth lunar month that year, Sakugen visited the scholar Feng Fang in Ningbo. That day, he recorded an unusually long and exuberant entry: Feng Fang came out to greet him with a bow; once inside, they bowed again. "We took our seats. After sitting down, we drank tea. After tea, we engaged in brush conversation for a while. Then the master invited me and the officers to dine in his quarters. After ten rounds of wine, musicians performed, and the banquet continued until evening before we departed."

A few days after Sakugen Shūryō visited Feng Fang, the latter composed a special essay in his honor titled *Record of the Humble Studio* (Qianzhai Ji). This treasured piece, along with the *Preface to the Linked Verse West of the City* (Chengxi Lianju Xu), is preserved today at Myōchi-in, a sub-temple of Tenryū-ji in Japan. At the beginning of the essay, Feng Fang wrote that Japan, under the influence of Chinese culture, had also become a land of propriety, where "people are often fond of learning, respectful of ritual, and marked by loyalty, righteousness, and sincerity." He offered a brief overview of the historical ties between China and Japan, before turning to Sakugen's arduous journey: "Drifting at sea for over a year, he endured the dampness of frost and dew, the shocks of crashing waves, the lurking dangers of jackals and tigers, and the surging rise and fall of whales and sea beasts—he experienced them all." Feng then used Sakugen's change of literary name as a thematic pivot for heartfelt praise, drawing upon deeply rooted Confucian values. He noted that Sakugen's original sobriquet had been Yizhai ("Studio of Harmony"), which he later changed to Qianzhai ("Studio of Humility")—a name inspired by the *Book of Changes* (Yijing), where "a mountain within the earth" symbolizes modesty and inner strength. Quoting the Commentary on the *Book of Changes*, Feng wrote:

> *"Heaven diminishes the proud and favors the humble. Earth shifts from fullness to flow toward the humble. People disdain arrogance and esteem modesty. Spirits bring calamity to the proud and blessings to the humble. Humility brings honor and radiance. Though lowly, it cannot be surpassed—this is the true path of the gentleman."*

Finally, by tracing Sakugen's scholarly lineage, Feng Fang concluded with firm affirmation:"The roots of the master's learning undoubtedly lie in our Middle Kingdom, and he has been truly shaped by the Way of the ancient sages."Having endured long months of hardship at sea, Sakugen must have been deeply moved upon reading such words

On the sixth day of the tenth lunar month, Sakugen Shūryō led part of the Japanese envoy in departing from Ningbo. They left the city in sedan chairs through Dongdu Gate and boarded boats at Yancang Gate, retracing the same route along the Grand Canal that they had followed during their previous journey to Beijing.

In the fifth lunar month of the 28th year of the Jiajing reign (1549), the Japanese delegation arrived in the capital and was hosted and rewarded by the Ming court. Later that same year, Sakugen and his party returned to Ningbo. In the summer of the 29th year of Jiajing (1550), the Japanese mission finally departed China and set sail back to Japan.

Before Sakugen Shūryō and his companions departed Ningbo, many local literati composed poems to bid them farewell. One remarkable work commemorating this moment—a collaboratively created painting titled *A Farewell to Special Envoy Master Qianzhai on His Return to Japan*—is preserved today at Myōchi-in, a sub-temple of Tenryū-ji in Saga, Kyoto. In the painting, four Ningbo scholars—Fang Meiya, Tu Yuelu, Dong Qiutian, and Bao Jishan—stand outside Dongdu Gate with hands clasped in farewell, accompanied by two attendants. Behind them rise groves of trees, along with the city walls and gate towers of Ningbo. On a slowly departing boat, Sakugen, dressed in a yellow robe, returns the gesture, bowing toward the shore. Behind him, a figure shades him with an umbrella. Around them, boatmen are shown in vivid detail—some hoisting sails, others rowing—rendered with remarkable vitality. Inscribed above the painting is a farewell poem praising Sakugen Qianzhai:

Master Qianzhai, a hero among men,

His brush flows like Jin and Tao of old.

Twice he bore royal mandate to the Celestial Court,

Ten thousand leagues of whale-ridden waves, endured without complaint.

A sealed letter delivered to the Sage Son of Heaven,

Whose dragon gaze and lightning glance hailed him as the style of the age.

Great imperial favor spared no golden gift,

An edict declared this worthy envoy deserved highest praise.

Now his sails are raised—he cannot be held back.

We offer fine dishes in farewell at the banks of the Yin River.

A decade may pass before we meet again, and time will age us all—

So tonight, let us drink deep and lose ourselves in wine.

This poem reflects not only the heartfelt respect of the Ningbo literati for Sakugen, but also the deep friendship forged between them.

"Though we may hope to meet again in ten years, time does not wait—So tonight, let us drink ourselves into cheerful oblivion." When Ye Yinzhai and the others raised their cups with the Japanese guests at the confluence of the Three Rivers, they likely still held hope for a reunion a decade hence. But the course of history is rarely predictable, and cherished hopes are often dashed by its cold and indifferent hand. After this parting, Sakugen Shūryō never returned to China. In fact, his delegation marked the final Japanese tribute mission to China during the Ming dynasty. From that point onward, Ningbo would never again host such an embassy from Japan.

Farewell Portrait for the Special Envoy Master Qianzhai on His Return to Japan

Meanwhile, as the tide of globalization gathered momentum, a new wave of foreign visitors arrived. From the late sixteenth century onward, increasing numbers of Europeans began setting foot on the soil of Zhejiang.

Chapter 9. Matteo Ricci and Francisco Cabral's Affection for Zhejiang

9.1 A Monk Travels from the Western Regions to the Heavenly India

In the 16th century, alongside wealth-seeking European explorers and merchants, Catholic missionaries also undertook long and arduous journeys to China. The first European missionary to set foot in Zhejiang was the Italian Jesuit, Michele Ruggieri (1543–1607).

Michele Ruggieri was born in Naples, Italy. Gifted with intelligence and a passion for learning, he joined the Society of Jesus in 1572. In March 1578, he set sail from Lisbon, Portugal, together with fellow Italian Jesuit Matteo Ricci (1552–1610), and arrived in Goa, India, in September that year. In July 1579, Alexandre Valignano (1539–1606), the Jesuit superior overseeing missions in the East, transferred Ruggieri to Macao to study Chinese in hopes of opening the tightly sealed gates of the Chinese empire. To support this endeavor, Valignano also sent Matteo Ricci to Macao. On April 26, 1582, Ricci departed Goa aboard a Portuguese vessel and arrived in Macao on August 7.

Since the Ming government strictly forbade foreigners from entering the Chinese interior, Michele Ruggieri and Matteo Ricci were constantly searching for opportunities to gain access. In September 1583, with the assistance of Wang Pan, the prefect of Zhaoqing, they were finally granted permission to reside in the city of Zhaoqing in Guangdong. Wang Pan hailed from

Shaoxing in Zhejiang province. According to Zhaoqing's local gazetteer, Wang was known for being "compassionate and gentle," "committed to public welfare," and "honest and upright in office." So highly respected was he that during his lifetime, the people of Zhaoqing built a shrine in his honor. This shrine was located in what is now the Chongxi Pagoda Scenic Area on Tajiao Road in Duanzhou District, Zhaoqing, and was designated a municipal-level protected cultural site in 2003. In 2011, during restoration work on the rear hall of the shrine, a stele titled *Record of the Living Shrine of Inspector Wang of Shanyin*, dated to the sixteenth year of the Wanli reign (1588), was discovered. In Wang Pan's hometown of Shaoxing, two surviving stone rubbings associated with him are also preserved. One is *Record of the City God Temple of Shanyin County*, and the other is *Record of the Black Dragon Spirit*. In the latter, Wang wrote: "I relocated to the left side of Huozhu Mountain. Behind my residence stood a government granary, within which was an old shrine dedicated to the Black Dragon King." From this, we know that Wang Pan's home was situated near Huozhu Mountain, within the city of Shaoxing.

Wang Pan held a favorable view of the two Western missionaries, Michele Ruggieri and Matteo Ricci, and even permitted them to choose a plot of land for the construction of a church. It was thanks to Wang Pan's welcoming attitude that Ricci and his companions were able to establish a foothold in China's interior and build a church later known as Xianhua Monastery. In 1584, Wang Pan was promoted to Vice Commissioner of Surveillance in

Guangdong, but his post remained in Zhaoqing, allowing him to continue supporting Ricci and his colleagues. His successor as prefect of Zhaoqing was Zheng Yilin, a native of Shangyu in Zhejiang province. Under the protection of these two Zhejiang-born officials—Wang Pan and Zheng Yilin—Ruggieri and Ricci not only lived comfortably in Zhaoqing, but also saw their missionary work begin to flourish. Still, they were not content to remain in Zhaoqing. Their greater ambition was to reach Beijing, the capital of the Ming Empire, and they continued to search for opportunities to make that journey.

According to Ming dynasty regulations, local officials like Zheng Yilin were required to travel to Beijing for an imperial audience once every three years. The year 1586 happened to be Zheng Yilin's turn to make the journey. Upon learning of this in early 1585, Michele Ruggieri expressed his desire to accompany Zheng to the capital. However, since the Ming authorities strictly forbade bringing foreigners to Beijing without special permission, Wang Pan and the others devised a workaround. Wang told Ruggieri, "If you're willing, we can take you to Zhejiang instead." For Ruggieri, that was more than enough.

The missionaries attached great significance to the journey to Zhejiang and hoped that the Portuguese Jesuit Antonio de Almeida (1557–1591) could accompany Michele Ruggieri. However, Almeida was still in Macau at the time and had not yet been granted permission to enter China. To get around this restriction, Ruggieri resorted to a clever ruse: he told Zheng Yilin that he needed to bring a disciple "to recite scriptures with him." In this way, Almeida's name was added to Ruggieri's travel permit as his apprentice.

To prepare for the journey to Zhejiang, Ruggieri traveled to Guangzhou to purchase essential supplies. By coincidence, Almeida was also in the city among the Portuguese merchants conducting business and unexpectedly ran into Ruggieri. While at the Guangzhou market, they happened upon a fortunate opportunity: one of Wang Pan's brothers had transported a shipment of high-quality silk from their hometown in Zhejiang to Guangzhou, but had been unable to sell it. Upon hearing of this, Ruggieri and his companions arranged for the Portuguese to buy the entire batch at a relatively high price. In gratitude, Wang Pan's brother warmly invited Ruggieri and his party to travel with him aboard his ship back to Shaoxing. Thus, by a stroke of luck, all the conditions for the journey to Zhejiang came together. According to the *List of Metropolitan Graduates from the Second Year of the Wanli Reign* preserved at the Tianyi Pavilion Museum in Ningbo, this brother of Wang Pan was named Wang Lian. He is also one of the earliest recorded Zhejiang merchants known to have engaged in lawful international trade with Europeans in Guangzhou.

At the end of 1585, Michele Ruggieri and Antonio de Almeida set out for Zhejiang together with Zheng Yilin and Wang Lian, the brother of Wang Pan. In January 1586, they arrived in Shaoxing, where they were warmly received by Wang Pan's father, Wang Yu, and stayed at the Wang family residence.

For a long time, it was believed that Ruggieri had only visited Shaoxing during his time in Zhejiang, and not Hangzhou. However, newly discovered materials from recent years confirm that he did, in fact, travel to Hangzhou. Evidence comes from three Chinese poems Ruggieri himself composed during his stay, which are transcribed below:

Touring Hangzhou Prefecture

Unafraid of traveling ten thousand li,

I wandered through Zhejiang to reach Hangzhou.

Why carry ten thousand volumes of sacred texts?

To spread the name of the Lord of Heaven alone.

Two Poems Composed at Tianzhu Temple in Hangzhou, in Reply to Various Gentlemen

I

A monk comes from the Western Paradise to Tianzhu,

Undaunted by three years of long and weary travel.

After reading the books of sages and worthies,

He shares the holy teachings with the common folk.

II

A single boat sails past the sea's edge,

Three years on water to arrive in Cathay.

My heart, like autumn water, always reflects the moon;

My body, like the bodhi tree, bears no blossoms.

Your noble province allows me to set foot here—

This humble monk now calls it home.

Should you ask about the truths of the Western Heaven,

They speak not of the Buddha Shakyamuni.

遊到杭州府
不憚驅馳萬里程　雲遊浙省到杭城
携經萬卷因何事　只為傳揚天主名

寓杭州天竺詩答諸公二首
僧從西竺來天竺　不憚驅馳三載勞
時把聖賢書讀罷　又將聖教度凡曹

Two Poems on Touring Hangzhou by Michele Ruggieri

These three poems by Michele Ruggieri are likely the earliest known Chinese-language poems about Hangzhou written by a European.

From the Middle Ages to the present day, many Europeans—Marco Polo among them—have left behind vivid accounts of Hangzhou, but all in Western languages. Westerners capable of writing about the city in Chinese have always been exceedingly rare, and those able to do so using classical Chinese verse are rarer still. That Ruggieri composed such poetry in Chinese makes these three works especially valuable.

From a content perspective, Ruggieri's three poems are of considerable significance, as they reveal his vague and ambiguous understanding of the distinctions between Buddhism and Catholicism, as well as his rather superficial grasp of Chinese culture at the time.

Although Ruggieri was aware that Catholicism—the faith he sought to spread—differed from Buddhism, he struggled to articulate the deeper theological divergences between the two. For instance, he referred to the divine figure he worshipped as "Tianzhu" (Lord of Heaven), rather than "Fo" (Buddha), and in his second poem, Composed at Tianzhu in Hangzhou, he wrote: "If you gentlemen ask about Western Heaven, it is not the Tathagata Buddha Shakyamuni."

Yet, paradoxically, Ruggieri's poems are filled with Buddhist terminology. He referred to himself as a "seng" (monk) or "pin seng" (poor monk), described his travels as "yunyou" (cloud-wandering), called Catholic scriptures "jing" (sutras), and even used the Buddhist term "du" (to ferry or deliver souls) to express the Catholic notion of salvation.

From an artistic perspective, Ruggieri's classical-style Chinese poems are of remarkable quality and stand as a testament to the progress he made in learning the language. For a European with no prior knowledge of Chinese to compose such verses within just a few short years is nothing less than extraordinary. These poems also reflect, from another angle, the dedication and perseverance with which he pursued his Chinese studies.

Yet Ruggieri remained dissatisfied with his command of the language, believing that his limited proficiency hindered his missionary efforts in China. After leaving Hangzhou, he composed a poem titled *Lamenting My Inaccurate Chinese*, in which he wrote:

For years I've lived here, yet still the Way is hard to convey—

Simply because the words of China and the West are not the same.

Only when I fully grasp the Chinese tongue,

Will I preach the Way with calm and ease.

In August 1586, Ruggieri and Almeida returned to Zhaoqing. Although their stay in Zhejiang was brief, they were the first Catholic missionaries to enter the province following the Age of Discovery. On November 20, 1588, acting on the orders of Alessandro Valignano, Ruggieri boarded a Chinese junk in Macao and set sail for Europe to report on the state of the Catholic mission in China to the Pope. After a long and arduous journey, he arrived in Lisbon, Portugal, on September 13, 1589. At the time, the Roman Curia was preoccupied with other matters, and the major European powers showed little interest in China. As a result, Ruggieri's return to Europe was met with indifference. Back in Europe, Ruggieri hoped to compile an atlas of China. However, he died in May 1607 in the city of Salerno, Italy, before the project could be completed. In 1987, a draft of this Chinese atlas was discovered in the National Archives in Rome. Among its contents were two maps of Zhejiang Province, now referred to as Zhejiang Map A and Zhejiang Map B.

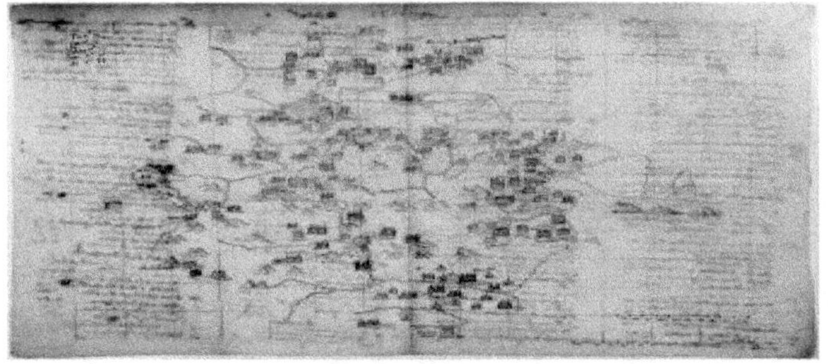

Zhejiang Map A from Michele Ruggieri's *Atlas of China*

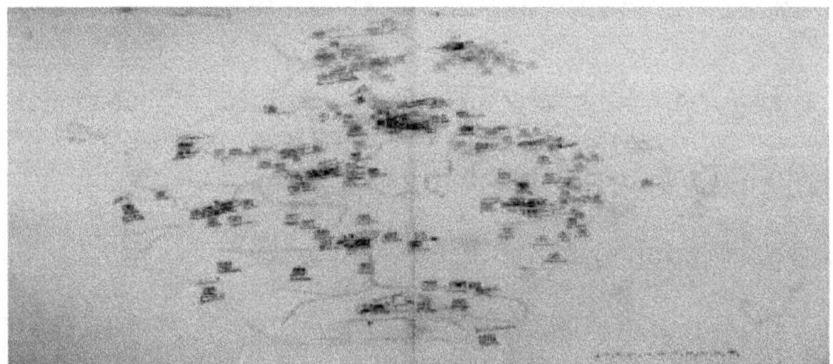

Zhejiang Map B from Michele Ruggieri's *Atlas of China*

On both of Michele Ruggieri's maps of Zhejiang Province, the region is labeled as Cechian. The maps depict major mountain ranges, waterways, and cities throughout the province, with each city illustrated as a European-style fortress. Around Hangzhou, a dense cluster of urban settlements is shown. On Zhejiang Map A, "Han ceu" (Hangzhou) is faintly identifiable. To the west of the city, the shimmering waters of West Lake are depicted, with the Latin label Sicu Lacus (West Lake) inscribed within the lake. The Qiantang River appears as Cien tam, and just above it, Xiaoshan is labeled Siau Scian. The names of several prefectures, including Chia Hhin (Jiaxing), Cu ceu (Huzhou), Gnien ceu (Yanzhou), Ninpo (Ningbo), Toi ceu (Taizhou), Uuon ceu (Wenzhou), Chin cua (Jinhua), Ciu ceu (Chuzhou), and Hhin ceu (Quzhou), are visible but not very distinct. On Zhejiang Map B, the names of many counties are depicted more clearly. These include Linngan (Lin'an), Tapin (Taiping), Tum Hhian (Tongxiang), Zum te' (Chongde), Pincu (Pinghu), Hai Hhien (Haining), Ci Chi (Cixi), Fun Cua (Fenghua), Sian Scian (Xiangshan), Nin Hai (Ninghai), Scian Iu (Shangyu), Sien Chiu (Xianju), Quam Gnien (Huangyan), Lan Chi (Lanxi), Tumiam (Dongyang), Tum Lui (Tonglu), Ciongan (Suian), Suonpin (Xuanping), Sumiam (Songyang), Juon Ho (Yunhe), Ciuingan (Ruian), and Taisuon (Taishun). However, both maps mistakenly depict Xiangshan County—located on a peninsula—as an island. This error can be traced back to inaccuracies commonly found in popular Ming dynasty maps of the time.

9.2 Martino Martini's Map of Zhejiang

Michele Ruggieri's two maps of Zhejiang are the earliest known maps of the province created by a European. However, as they remained buried in archives and largely unknown to the public for centuries, they had little impact. About fifty years later, another Italian missionary residing in Zhejiang—Martino Martini (1614–1661)—also produced a map of the province, which went on to exert a wide influence in Europe.

Martino Martini was born in Trento, in present-day Italy, and enter the Society of Jesus in 1632. In 1639, he departed from Lisbon bound for Asia, but his ship encountered a storm near the Gulf of Guinea off the coast of Africa and was forced to return. In March 1640, he set sail again, this time accompanied by over twenty Jesuit missionaries, including the Italian Giulio Aleni and the Portuguese Simão da Cunha (1589–1660), both of whom would later work closely with him. They arrived in Goa, India, in September of that year. Unable to find a vessel to China, they were compelled to remained in Goa until the following year. On August 4, 1642, they finally arrived in Macao.

In 1643, Martino Martini disguised himself as a Chinese soldier and traveled into the Chinese interior aboard local vessels, accompanied by Giulio Aleni and Simão da Cunha. They journeyed by water from Guangzhou to Nanxiong, crossed the Meiling Pass, reached Nanchang in Jiangxi Province, and continued along the Yangtze River to the regions of Nanjing and Shanghai. In Shanghai, Martini began his formal study of the Chinese language and adopted a Chinese name, Wei Kuangguo (卫匡国, meaning "To Protect and Save the Country"), with coutersey name Jitai. In October 1643, he arrived in Hangzhou.

During Michele Ruggieri's time in Zhejiang, Ming society still presented the appearance of peace and prosperity. But by the time Martino Martini arrived, the dynasty was already teetering on the brink of collapse. Peasant uprisings led by Li Zicheng and Zhang Xianzhong were sweeping across the country with unstoppable momentum, while bandits and looters took advantage of the chaos to pillage. Outside the Great Wall, Qing forces were gathering strength, poised to strike. Amid such upheaval, the challenges faced by a European like Martini—who had yet to master the Chinese language—can only be imagined.

In 1644, a series of pivotal events took place in Beijing that reshaped the course of Chinese history. In April, Li Zicheng's rebel forces captured the capital, prompting the Chongzhen Emperor to hang himself. By June, Qing troops had entered and taken control of the city. When this shocking news reached Nanjing—the Ming dynasty's secondary capital—Martino Martini was living there. In July, he returned to Hangzhou from Nanjing.

On July 4, 1645, the Qing army captured Hangzhou, forcing Martino Martini to flee into the mountainous border region between Zhejiang and Fujian. There, he may have served in the remnants of the Southern Ming's Longwu regime (1645–1646), possibly overseeing cannon production. He maintained close ties with the Ming general Liu Zhongzao. It was during his harrowing flight through the Zhejiang-Fujian mountains that Martini first encountered Qing soldiers in Wenzhou. According to accounts, he was sheltering with a group of people in a large mansion when the Qing army arrived, striking fear into everyone present. In an effort to distinguish himself, Martini inscribed the phrase "Residence of a Scholar of Western Heavenly Learning" on the gate, arranged his European books, telescope, and other foreign items on a table, and set up an altar displaying an image of Jesus. The Qing soldiers, intrigued by these unfamiliar objects, were filled with curiosity rather than hostility. Their commander received Martini politely, questioned him, and ultimately asked him to change out of Han Chinese attire into Manchu dress and return to Hangzhou as soon as possible. It is said that when Martini returned to Europe in 1653, he brought with him the red paper bearing the inscription "Residence of a Scholar of Western Heavenly Learning," and proudly displayed it to others. However, his 1654 first edition of *De Bello Tartarico Historia* (*The History of the Tartar War*) made no mention of this encounter. Martini only added the story in later editions, reportedly at the suggestion of others.

In May 1647, in Lanxi, Zhejiang, Martino Martini encountered a remarkable scholar named Zhu Shi (courtesy name Zijian), to whom he dictated a text titled *The Chapter on Choosing Friends* (*Qiu You Pian*). In the preface he wrote for the work, Zhu praised Martini as "noble in bearing and refined in form, with a divine and compassionate presence—appearing like a celestial being, truly a sage among men." In 1648, while in Hangzhou, Martini intended to translate a work by a Spanish scholar into Chinese, though the project was never completed. In 1650, Martini was appointed Jesuit Superior of the Hangzhou region. Between March and April of that year, he left Hangzhou for Beijing, where he visited the famed Great Wall. With a strong European education and mastery of mathematics, Martini had hoped to assist the German Jesuit Johann Adam Schall von Bell (1592–1666), who was serving at the Imperial Astronomical Bureau. However, Schall—concerned that Martini's prior association with the Longwu regime might attract scrutiny from the Qing court, and amid growing internal disputes within the Jesuit community—did not support his stay. As a result, Martini was unable to remain in Beijing and returned to Hangzhou later that same year.

Toward the end of the Ming dynasty, several Catholic religious orders arrived in China, including the Jesuits, Dominicans, and Franciscans. Among them, the Jesuits were the most influential, with prominent members such as Michele Ruggieri, Matteo Ricci, and Martino Martini. Beginning with Ricci, the Jesuits adopted a strategy of cultural accommodation, using classical Chinese terms like Tian ("Heaven") or Shangdi ("Supreme Deity") to refer to the Christian God. They also permitted Chinese converts to participate in traditional practices such as honoring Confucius and performing ancestral rites. In contrast, the Dominicans and Franciscans strongly opposed these accommodative methods. The Dominicans even sent envoys to Europe to lodge complaints with the Roman Curia, thereby initiating what would become the centuries-long "Chinese Rites Controversy." In September 1645, the Roman

Curia issued a formal decree prohibiting Chinese Catholics from taking part in Confucian and ancestral rites.

The decree was a significant setback for the Jesuits. In response, the Jesuit missionaries in China resolved to send Martino Martini to Europe to personally present their case to the Roman Curia. In January 1651, Martini quietly arrived in Anhai, Fujian. Two months later, in March, he boarded a Chinese junk bound for Manila in the Philippines. He remained there for nearly a year before setting sail again in January 1652. While passing through Batavia (present-day Jakarta), which was under Dutch control at the time, Martini was detained by the Dutch authorities for eight months. It was not until February 1653 that he was able to resume his journey to Europe. In August of that year, he landed at the port of Bergen in Norway. From there, he traveled through Belgium, the Netherlands, and other European countries, finally arriving in Rome in October 1654. Martini provided the Roman Curia with a detailed explanation, arguing that ancestor worship and Confucian rites were long-standing cultural practices in China rather than expressions of religious belief. On March 23, 1656, the Roman Curia issued a ruling favorable to the Jesuits, permitting Chinese converts to participate in the veneration of Confucius and their ancestors.

During his time in Europe, Martino Martini published his Latin work *De Bello Tartarico Historia* (*The History of the Tartar War*) in Antwerp in 1654. The book vividly chronicled the turbulent situation in China at the time, especially the Qing conquest. As a firsthand witness to these dramatic events, Martini provided Europeans with one of their most authoritative and accessible accounts of China's transition from Ming to Qing. The book was soon translated into French, German, English, Portuguese, Danish, and other languages. Between 1654 and 1706, it went through more than twenty editions. Many subsequent European writings on China drew heavily from this work. In *De Bello Tartarico*, Martini gave a striking account of the Qing army's occupation of Hangzhou:

> *Hangzhou is the capital of Zhejiang Province. The city was filled with remnants of Chinese forces, including regular soldiers as well as many generals and officials who had retreated there. They resolved to proclaim a new emperor: the Prince of Lu, a member of the Ming imperial family. However, the prince refused to take the imperial title, believing that retaining his princely status was preferable to the disgrace and violent death that might come from falling from the throne. Later, in an effort to boost military morale, he promised that if they succeeded in recapturing the imperial capital, he would accept the crown.*
>
> *Less than three days after he ascended the throne—a reign shorter than that of the tragic 'emperor' he sought to replace—the Tartar army (i.e., the Qing troops) arrived. The disorganized soldiers, seizing the moment of crisis, demanded payment from the*

prince and his commanders, refusing to fight without receiving their wages first. At this critical juncture, the Prince of Lu, unwilling to witness the destruction of his people, his officials, and the entire city, carried out an act of compassion and self-sacrifice unparalleled in Europe. He ascended the city wall, knelt, and cried out to the Tartar generals, pleading for mercy on behalf of his people: 'Do not spare me—I am willing to die for my people.'

Having spoken these words, he left the city and approached the Qing army, where he was promptly detained. His noble devotion to his people, had it been met with the magnanimity of an Alexander or a Caesar, would surely have been rewarded as a heroic act deserving of honor.

After capturing the prince, the Qing immediately ordered the city gates to be closed and guarded, preventing both their own troops and the prince's supporters from entering. They then launched a brutal assault on the prince's forces. Many of the defenders, however, perished not by sword or arrow, but by drowning: vast numbers hurled themselves into the great Qiantang River, which flows past the city and is about a league wide.

Some attempted to escape aboard boats, but the vessels quickly sank from overcrowding. Others, in a frenzy of fear and panic, trampled each other at the riverbanks, pushing many into the water. Thousands perished. The Tartars, lacking boats to cross the river, waited until the enemy had been routed and then entered the city in triumph—without further violence or atrocities. In this way, the noble city of Hangzhou was spared.

As for the city's grandeur, beauty, and wealth—I shall describe them elsewhere. What I report here is based not on hearsay, but on my own eyes. I lived in Hangzhou for three years before departing for Europe from there.

This account offers a rare glimpse into the Qing army's entry into Hangzhou through the eyes of a European eyewitness. When compared with Chinese historical sources, it reveals a vivid and authentic dimension of the event—alongside certain touches of European romanticism.

After entering mainland China in 1643, Martino Martini began collecting Chinese texts on geography and cartography. His extensive travels across many provinces gave him valuable opportunities to conduct firsthand surveys of China's geographical landscape. When he set sail for Europe in 1651, he used the long voyage to organize his collected materials and compile them into an atlas of China. At the time, Amsterdam in the Netherlands was the center of European cartography. Many influential modern maps were produced and printed there, including the renowned *Theatrum Orbis Terrarum, sive Atlas Novus* ("*New Atlas of the World*"), a monumental series launched in 1635 by the prominent map publisher Joan Blaeu. In the first half of 1654,

Martini traveled to Amsterdam specifically to negotiate the publication of his Chinese atlas with Blaeu. In 1655, Blaeu published Martini's *Novus Atlas Sinensis* ("*New Atlas of China*") in Latin as the sixth volume of the *Theatrum Orbis Terrarum*.

Martino Martini's *Novus Atlas Sinensis* was an exquisitely produced, large-format atlas (32.5 cm × 50 cm). The first edition included one general map of China, fifteen provincial maps, and a map of Japan, along with explanatory texts and a table listing the latitudes and longitudes of major Chinese cities. As the first atlas of China to be published in Europe, it marked a significant milestone in the history of Western cartography. The atlas featured a dedicated map of Zhejiang Province, titled CHEKIANG PROVINCIA. All eleven Ming-era prefectures of Zhejiang were represented: HANGCHEU (Hangzhou), Vencheu (Wenzhou), Kiahing (Jiaxing), Kinhoa (Jinhua), Kiucheu (Quzhou), Niencheu (Yanzhou), Hucheu (Huzhou), Xaohing (Shaoxing), Chucheu (Chuzhou), Taicheu (Taizhou), and Ningpo (Ningbo). Surrounding Hangzhou, several other locations were also marked, including Xiaoxan (Xiaoshan), Fuchun F. (Fuchun River), Fuyang, Juhang (Yuhang), and Haining. Major geographical features such as the Tienmo Montes (Tianmu Mountains), Tientai Montes (Tiantai Mountains), and Cientang F. (Qiantang River) were clearly depicted. Particularly noteworthy is Martini's detailed rendering of the Canalis (Eastern Zhejiang Canal), highlighting its strategic importance. Jesuit symbols appear on the map at Hangzhou, Ningbo, and Lanki (Lanxi), indicating that these were key centers of Jesuit missionary activity in the region.

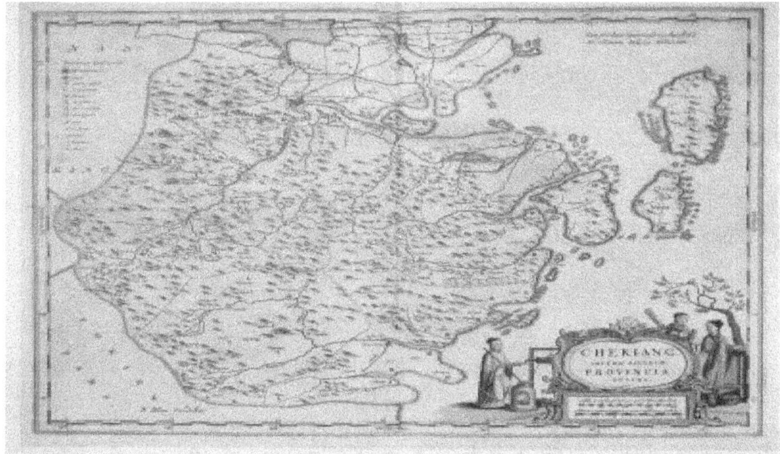

The Zhejiang Province Map in Martino Martini's *Novus Atlas Sinensis*

In the textual section of the *Novus Atlas Sinensis*, Martino Martini provides a detailed account of Zhejiang Province, including its geography, administrative divisions, local products, and military garrisons. He writes:"Zhejiang faces the sea to the east. Departing from the port of Ningbo, one can reach the Japanese archipelago in just a day—or even less—if the winds and currents are favorable." Martini describes Zhejiang as a province of "both mountains and plains, with a mild climate, fertile soil, numerous rivers and lakes, and abundant rainfall—conditions well-suited for the cultivation of a variety of crops." He praises the region's exquisite silk, noting that it is "of exceptional quality and reasonably priced," widely sold throughout China and also exported "to neighboring Japan and the Philippine Islands, and even further abroad to India and continental Europe." Martini attributed the superiority of Chinese silk over European varieties to the excellence of

Chinese mulberry leaves, which were, in his view, better than those grown in Europe. He notes that Chinese silk had already reached Europe in antiquity, during the Greco-Roman period, when the Chinese were referred to as the "Seres." However, Europeans remained unclear for centuries about how silk was produced. The Roman author Pliny the Elder (AD 23–79) wrote that the Seres "were famed for the wool that grew on their trees. They would spray water on the branches to collect the white down from the leaves, and their wives would spin and weave it into cloth." Martini corrected this longstanding misconception, explaining to his European readers that silk was not gathered from trees in this manner, but rather painstakingly produced through the cultivation of mulberry trees and the rearing of silkworms—a process deeply rooted in Chinese agricultural labor and expertise.

In *Novus Atlas Sinensis*, Martino Martini also described the renowned scenic sites and distinctive local products of various regions across Zhejiang. When writing about West Lake in Hangzhou (lago Si), he remarked:"Many lofty bridges have been built across the lake, allowing boats to pass underneath while also enabling people to stroll freely above." He went on to describe the lake's pleasure boats as "lavishly adorned and resplendent in gold—worthy of the name palazzi d'oro ('golden palaces')." To drift across West Lake aboard such a vessel, he wrote, was "a supreme delight." Outside the city, the Qiantang River (Cientang) was famed for its dramatic tidal bore, a natural spectacle known throughout the world."Each year, on the eighteenth day of the eighth lunar month, the surging tide of the Qiantang River reaches its peak. Accompanied by a thunderous roar, the mighty wave charges upriver with the force of mountains crashing into the sea—powerful enough to overturn any vessel."

In his description of the water chestnuts (Peci) produced in Jiaxing, Martino Martini wrote:"If one places a copper coin and a water chestnut in the mouth and chews them together, the coin can be bitten through effortlessly, using no more force than that needed to chew the chestnut." He continued:"I have personally attempted this many times and have confirmed this extraordinary power of nature." As water chestnuts were unknown in Europe, Martini's account became increasingly exaggerated as it was retold by others. In reality, his statement stemmed from an ancient Chinese belief that water chestnuts could dissolve copper. For example, Effective Prescriptions from Generations of Physicians by Wei Yilin (1277–1347) from the Yuan dynasty recorded that if someone accidentally swallowed a copper coin or similar object, one could "grind raw water chestnuts into a paste and ingest it, and the copper would naturally dissolve." Likewise, Wang Kentang (1549–1613) wrote in Standards for Diagnosis and Treatment that "eating water chestnuts or arrowheads would cause the coin to dissolve on its own."

Martino Martini spoke highly of Shaoxing, writing:"Shaoxing enjoys nationwide renown as a cradle of distinguished figures and accomplished scholars. Nestled in a region of rivers and wetlands, the city naturally invites comparisons with Venice—yet its waters are clearer, and its scenery more graceful." He further noted, "The entire city is built from a kind of white, square-cut stone," and "every street crosses a canal, with the banks on either side also faced with the same white stone blocks." Shaoxing lies along the Eastern Zhejiang Canal, and the canal's lock system left a lasting impression on Martini. He wrote:"Thanks to this system of locks, boats are raised to higher levels, enabling them to continue their journey through the canal. Small vessels can travel all the way to Ningbo, while larger ones may pass directly out to sea."

In *Novus Atlas Sinensis*, Martino Martini also gave accounts of several other cities in Zhejiang. He noted that Huzhou was "famous for its abundant silk production" and "well-known for its high-quality writing brushes." Yanzhou was recognized for its local specialties, including paper, copper ore, and lacquer. In Jinhua, residents extracted a fine oil called Kieuyeu from Chinese tallow tree seeds. "The white candles made from this oil," Martini wrote, "are of excellent quality—they don't stain the hands and give off no unpleasant odor when extinguished." To the south of Quzhou stood Mount Lanke (Lano), "the eighth most sacred mountain in Taoism." The key overland route from Zhejiang to Fujian passed through Jiangshan County in Quzhou, "a rugged path that winds through steep mountains, the most treacherous of which is Xianxia Pass (Sienhoa)." In Chuzhou, Martini highlighted Mount Kuocang (Hoçang), "the eighteenth sacred Taoist mountain," said to stretch for 300 li (stadi). Chinese geographers believed it reached a height of 1,000 zhang (mille), and that "its summit has a constant climate, free from wind or rain."

Ningbo, he observed, was rich in marine resources, offering a wide range of fresh and dried seafood—including many types of crab, shrimp, and shellfish—that were highly sought after across the country. Fish like mullet could be caught year-round, but the prized yellow croaker (Hoang), "named for its golden hue," could only be fished in early summer. Near Taizhou, Martini described Mount Chicheng (Cheching) as "the sixth sacred Taoist mountain," distinguished by its nearly all-red appearance. Mount Tiantai (Tientai), he wrote, was "regarded as the foremost of China's Taoist mountains and believed to be the most auspicious." The nearby Tiantai County derived its name from the mountain. "The temples on Mount Tiantai are extraordinarily magnificent—too many to count." Finally, Wenzhou, "the most remote coastal city in Zhejiang," was described as resembling Hangzhou with its "dense network of waterways." Its urban landscape featured "numerous and exquisitely built structures," earning it the nickname "Little Hangzhou." The harbor bustled with "a great number of deep-sea junks," and the city was "teeming with residents and merchants."

On April 4, 1657, Martino Martini set sail from Lisbon, Portugal, accompanied by more than a dozen fellow Jesuits on his second journey to China. The voyage was perilous—they were seized by pirates, struck by violent storms, and several of their companions died en route. Martini finally returned to Hangzhou on June 11, 1659. By then, Qing forces had largely solidified their control over Zhejiang Province, and society had entered a period of relative stability. For Martini, there was an additional stroke of good fortune: Tong Guoqi, the provincial governor and highest-ranking official in Zhejiang, was notably sympathetic toward missionaries.

Tong Guoqi, a relative of the Qing Emperor Shunzhi, was appointed Governor of Zhejiang in recognition of his distinguished military service. He first came into contact with missionaries when he entered Beijing with the Qing army. Although he did not convert to Christianity due to his status as an imperial kinsman, his wife was baptized and became a devout Catholic. Because his wife regularly attended Mass at Martini's church, Tong often visited Martini. Finding the original chapel too small, he provided funds for the construction of a new one. Martini used this support to purchase a plot of land in Hangzhou—just south of Tianshui Bridge inside the northern city gate—and likely contributed to the church's architectural design himself. Construction began in 1659, and Tong personally visited the site to inspect its progress. By that time, however, Martini was suffering from a severe gastrointestinal illness, contracted during his second voyage from Europe to China in 1658. As construction intensified, his condition worsened. Chinese doctors prescribed a slow-acting restorative treatment, but Martini, perhaps impatient with the pace of recovery, took a strong dose of rhubarb as a laxative. The excessive amount worsened his condition dramatically. By the time the doctors arrived, it was too late. On June 6, 1661, Martino Martini died in Hangzhou.

When Martino Martini passed away, the Catholic church in Hangzhou had not yet been completed. The French missionary Humbert Augery, who had arrived in the city in 1658, continued the construction and brought it to completion in 1663. The newly completed church was built in the Baroque style, with a splendid exterior modeled after the Jesuit headquarters in Rome. Its interior featured lofty vaulted ceilings and a symmetrical, harmonious layout that evoked a powerful sense of solemnity and grandeur.

Hangzhou North Zhongshan Road Catholic Church

Interestingly, the church also incorporated distinctively Chinese elements, such as circular windows—features not typically found in European churches. At the time, it was widely acclaimed as one of the most magnificent churches in China and remained a prominent landmark in Hangzhou for many years.

Martino Martini was widely admired for his erudition and affable nature.

During his final illness, officials and longtime friends in Hangzhou frequently visited him. After his death in 1661, he was buried at the Dafangjing Cemetery, on the northern slope of Taoyuan Ridge in Hangzhou. To residents of Qing-era Hangzhou, Martini's body became the subject of miraculous legends. By the early 19th century, it was said that his corpse had remained perfectly preserved, with hair and nails that continued to grow—requiring regular trimming throughout the year. On Catholic feast days, believers would wash his face, tidy his appearance, and place his body on a chair for prayer. Such marvels drew even local Buddhists, who came to burn incense and seek blessings at his tomb. For many Chinese, religious affiliation mattered less than the pursuit of tangible blessings in daily life. Owing to the sacred aura surrounding his remains, the cemetery was left undisturbed for over two centuries—even as Catholicism in Hangzhou experienced repeated waves of prohibition and revival.

By 1877, however, Martini's body had severely decomposed. Missionaries placed his remains in a coffin and reburied them beneath a small chapel built on the cemetery grounds. By the 1930s, the precise location of his remains within the chapel had already been lost to time.

In addition to Martino Martini, several other missionaries were also buried in the Dafangjing Cemetery. In 1736, during a period when the Qing government was enforcing strict prohibitions against Catholicism, the Catholic community in Hangzhou undertook a renovation of the cemetery. However, between 1860 and 1864, the cemetery sustained damage when the Taiping Army occupied the city. In 1874, Hangzhou Catholics once again repaired the site.

During the Cultural Revolution of the 1960s, the cemetery was subjected to severe destruction. Part of the grounds was absorbed into a neighboring brewery. By the 1980s, all the original structures on the site had vanished, leaving behind only collapsed burial vaults.

The Dafangjing Missionary Cemetery Before 1949

Entrance to the Martino Martini Memorial Garden for Missionaries

After the end of the Cultural Revolution, China entered a new era of reform and opening-up, and Hangzhou once again reconnected with the world. Against this backdrop, renewed attention—both domestic and international—was drawn to Martino Martini and his burial site. In September 1980, during a state visit to China, Italian President Sandro Pertini traveled to Hangzhou and expressed a desire to pay tribute at Martini's grave. However, since the cemetery had already been destroyed, local authorities were unable to fulfill his request. In 1984, the Hangzhou municipal government initiated the restoration of the cemetery, completing the project in 1986. The scattered remains of the missionaries were collected and placed into approximately a dozen ossuaries. As the bones had become intermixed and could no longer be individually identified, the ossuaries were left unnamed. In 1989, Martini's cemetery was officially designated a Key Cultural Heritage Site under provincial protection in Zhejiang. Further renovation work was carried out in 2008 by the Culture and Sports Bureau of Xihu District in Hangzhou.

Since the beginning of the 21st century, Hangzhou's rapid urban expansion has transformed Dafangjing from a once-remote suburban area into a vital part of the city. Now located at No. 549 Xixi Road in Xihu District, the site has been renamed the Martino Martini Missionary Memorial Park.

Façade of the Stone Archway

In 2015, Hangzhou launched the Xihu Ant Town initiative, centered on Xixi Road, with the aim of establishing a national hub for technological innovation. The area has since become home to numerous high-tech enterprises at the forefront of industrial development. Built upon cutting-edge global scientific advancements, these enterprises rely heavily on robust international exchange and collaboration as the foundation of their success. Situated at the heart of Xihu Ant Town, the Martino Martini Missionary Memorial Park has become a significant cultural and historical landmark, symbolizing Hangzhou's inclusive and outward-looking spirit. The park's dignified, time-worn architecture stands in striking contrast to the modern, thriving high-tech firms that surround it—together reflecting a powerful truth across time: only by remaining committed to reform and opening up, and by confidently embracing the world, can a radiant future be realized.

Part III. The Commerce of the Ancient Zhejiang Maritime Silk Road

Zhejiang's Maritime Silk Road was a conduit for the movement of both people and goods. As merchants, monks, diplomats, and other travelers plied these sea routes, they carried a vast array of items to distant lands, many of which were produced in Zhejiang. In turn, a diverse range of foreign products flowed into Zhejiang through this same maritime network, creating a dynamic, two-way channel of exchange.

Chapter 10. Zhejiang Ceramics on the World Stage

Zhejiang is a pivotal cradle and production hub of Chinese porcelain. As early as the Western Zhou period, the region of eastern Zhejiang, centered on the Ningshao Plain, was already firing proto-porcelain. By the Eastern Han dynasty, mature porcelain had emerged. The ceramics produced in this region are known collectively as Yue ware, and numerous Yue kiln sites have been unearthed in areas like Shanglin Lake in Cixi. During the Tang and Five Dynasties periods, Yue ware was esteemed as imperial tribute and, simultaneously, became a major commodity for overseas trade via the Maritime Silk Road. The Korean Peninsula was one of its earliest and most important foreign markets.

10.1 The Spread of Zhejiang Ceramics to the Korean Peninsula and the Japanese Archipelago

The introduction of Yue ware to the Korean Peninsula can be traced to the late 3rd or early 4th century CE. At the time, China was fragmented. Zhejiang was ruled by a succession of six dynasties—the Eastern Wu(AD 222–280), Eastern Jin(AD 317–420), Liu Song(AD 420–479), Southern Qi(AD 479–502), Liang(AD 502–557), and Chen(AD 557–589)—all of which were based in the capital of Jiankang (modern Nanjing) and are thus known collectively as the Six Dynasties. This era in Korea was also one of division, the Three Kingdoms period, with Goguryeo(37 BC–AD 668),

Baekje(18 BC–AD 660), and Silla(57 BC–AD 935) vying for dominance. Situated in the southwest of the peninsula, the kingdom of Baekje faced the Six Dynasties regimes across the sea and maintained contact via the Maritime Silk Road. To counterbalance the strategic alliance between its rival Goguryeo and the Northern Wei dynasty in northern China, Baekje cultivated exceptionally close diplomatic ties with the southern Chinese courts. These geopolitical circumstances made the Baekje kingdom the earliest and foremost importer of Yue ware.

Archaeological finds confirm that the earliest Yue ware in Baekje—and indeed on the entire Korean Peninsula—dates to the Six Dynasties period. Key early sites include the elite fortifications of Mongchon Toseong and Pungnap Toseong, located in modern Seoul. Mongchon Toseong, a military fortress from the Three Kingdoms period enclosed by an earthen wall and moat, has yielded shards of Yue celadon jars, inkstones, and bowls, as well as fragments of black-glazed pottery. Nearby lies Pungnap Toseong, which many scholars believe was a royal capital of Baekje. In addition to Yue ware fragments, a relatively intact glazed pottery jar was unearthed there. Although the quantity of ceramics from these two sites is modest, the artifacts provide crucial physical evidence for studying the initial phase of Yue ware importation and help establish the chronology of these ancient Baekje centers.

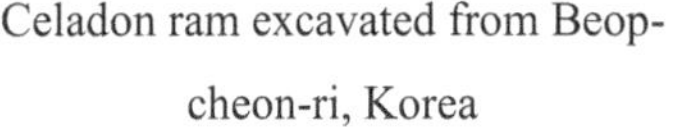

Celadon ram excavated from Beopcheon-ri, Korea

Yue kiln Celadon "Tiger" Spout discovered in Korea

Yue ware has also been unearthed at other Baekje sites, including Seokdong-ri in Seoul, Hwasang-ri in Cheongyang County, Sucheong-ri in Gongju, Jingmok-dong in Buan, and Beopcheon-ri in Wonju County. The Beopcheon-ri site yielded a particularly charming and well-preserved celadon sheep figurine, a style also found in China's Jiangsu and Zhejiang provinces. Based on comparisons with artifacts in Chinese collections, this figurine is clearly a product of the Eastern Jin period (AD 317–420). Another remarkable find, this time in Kaesong, North Korea, was an exquisite Yue celadon huzi, a vessel in the shape of a tiger commonly identified as a chamber pot. Although it was a surface find rather than an excavated piece, its resemblance to similar vessels unearthed in Shaoxing and Huangyan suggests it dates to the early Six Dynasties period.

How did this Yue ware reach Baekje from southern China? Two main theories exist. The first posits a maritime route, with the ceramics arriving either as diplomatic gifts from Six Dynasties rulers or as commodities traded by private merchants. The second suggests an overland route, where the ceramics were gifted by northern Chinese regimes to Goguryeo or Baekje and then transported south. Many scholars have dismissed the maritime theory, arguing that Baekje lacked the capacity for large-scale seafaring. This view, however, overlooks the advanced nautical capabilities of the Chinese; merchants from the Six Dynasties were perfectly capable of exporting these goods to Baekje via the sea. More importantly, the archaeological record contradicts the overland theory. If the ceramics had traveled by land, far more examples should have been found in neighboring regions, especially in Goguryeo to the north. In reality, fewer than ten pieces of Yue ware have ever been discovered in Goguryeo territory. This scarcity strongly indicates a maritime path. As direct sea routes from the Zhejiang coast to Korea had not yet been established, these wares were likely shipped from major ports near the mouth of the Yangtze River, which served as collection and distribution hubs.

Beginning in the late 8th century, exports of Yue celadon to the Korean Peninsula increased, reaching a commercial scale by the 9th century. In the southeastern Gyeongju region—the capital of the Silla and later Goryeo dynasties—75 pieces have been unearthed from at least 20 different sites. Bowls are the most common find (54 pieces), supplemented by basins, dishes, jars, ewers, and censers. Most date to the late Tang and Five Dynasties periods, with a few from the Northern Song. These were generally exquisite, high-quality items used by Gyeongju's aristocracy and high-ranking monks. Comparative studies confirm that the shapes and decorative motifs of the

Gyeongju finds have direct parallels at Yue kiln sites in Zhejiang, such as Shanglin Lake. The National Museum of Korea also holds superior examples, including a celadon ewer discovered near Seoul that realistically imitates a leather flask, down to the meticulously rendered stitching.

During the Five Dynasties and Ten Kingdoms period, the Wuyue Kingdom of Zhejiang (AD 907–978) established close maritime links with the Goryeo dynasty of Korea (AD 918–1392). As large quantities of Yue ware flowed into Goryeo, the relationship evolved from simple trade to a full-scale transfer of industrial technology. Goryeo artisans not only copied the styles but also imported production techniques directly from Zhejiang, a development evident in the roughly 1,700 kiln sites discovered in Korea. Many of these share striking similarities with the Yue kilns of eastern Zhejiang. For instance, Goryeo potters adopted the wood-fired longyao ("dragon kiln"), a long, sloping structure built into hillsides, which was characteristic of southern China. This stood in contrast to the coal-fired, circular mantou ("steamed bun") kilns of northern China and the earlier pit kilns used in Korea. By the 10th century, the dragon kiln had become standard. Goryeo dragon kilns mirrored their Zhejiang counterparts in design, with a firebox at the lower end, a flue at the upper end, and stoking ports along the sides.

To ensure stability on the inclined floor, Goryeo potters also adopted the Zhejiang practice of laying down a bed of sand and using angled supports to level the wares. Furthermore, they used saggars—refractory boxes of similar shape and size—to protect pieces from contamination and damage during firing. Early Goryeo ceramics also mimicked distinctive Yue ware features, such as the yubi base, a foot-ring shaped like an ancient jade disc, and decorative parrot motifs. It is clear, therefore, that Goryeo's porcelain technology was profoundly shaped by the techniques of Zhejiang's Yue kilns.

By the 12th century, Goryeo ceramic technology had matured into its own distinctive style. Xu Jing, a Northern Song envoy who sailed from Ningbo to Goryeo in 1123, praised its characteristic blue-green glaze—which he called feise and is now known by its Korean name, bisaek ("kingfisher color")—writing that "in recent years, the craftsmanship has become exquisite, and the glaze color especially fine". This jade-green ware became famous as Goryeo celadon. It was used by Goryeo royalty and also sent as tribute to the Song imperial court. Simultaneously, both Goryeo and Chinese merchants traded it as a luxury commodity in China, creating a reverse flow of high-value goods. During the Song and Yuan dynasties, Ningbo served as the primary port for trade with Goryeo, and Goryeo celadon was imported in significant numbers. This trade is documented in texts like the Yuan-era gazetteer Zhi Zheng Siming Xuzhi and corroborated by archaeological evidence. For example, five celadon fragments were found in the city's

Goryeo celadon excavated in Ningbo in 1995

Yuan-dynasty wall stratum in 1993. More significantly, a damaged Goryeo celadon lid (10 cm in diameter) was discovered in 1995 at the site of the Song-Yuan Maritime Trade Office. Now in the Ningbo Museum, the lid is decorated with chrysanthemums and two male figures, variously interpreted as depicting sumo wrestling or taekwondo. This exceptionally rare artifact demonstrates that the Maritime Silk Road had become a two-way channel, facilitating not only the export of Zhejiang's ceramics but also the import of Goryeo wares. It was this dynamic, reciprocal cultural exchange that infused Zhejiang's history with such vitality.

In 1975, South Korean fishermen discovered Chinese ceramics on the seabed near Dodeok Island in Sinan County, prompting an official investigation that located a shipwreck at approximately 35°N, 126°E. The surviving hull, identified as a Chinese-built vessel, measured 28 meters long with eight compartments; it is estimated to have originally been 34 meters long and 11 meters wide, with a 200-ton capacity. The cargo was overwhelmingly Chinese but also contained Japanese items, including sake, swords, Go stones, bronze mirrors, and wooden tags inscribed with "For official use by Tōfuku-ji Temple," a famous monastery in Kyoto. A crucial piece of evidence, a wooden tag found in 1983, was inscribed with "Third Year of the Zhizhi Reign." As the Zhizhi reign corresponds to the Yuan emperor Yingzong, this dates the cargo to 1323 CE. The scholarly consensus is that this vessel, known as the Sinan Shipwreck, departed from China bound for Hakata, Japan, in or shortly after 1323, but sank en route.

The Sinan wreck yielded a vast cargo, including over eight million copper coins (weighing 28 tons) minted across various Chinese dynasties from the Tang to the Yuan. The most recent coins were the Zhi Da Tong Bao of the Yuan. The ceramic find was even more staggering: over 20,000 pieces from renowned kilns such as Jingdezhen, Cizhou, Jizhou, Jian, and Jun. Wares from Zhejiang's Longquan kilns were by far the most numerous, accounting for over 12,000 items. While most were from the Yuan dynasty, a small portion dated to the Southern Song. This Longquan celadon can be divided into two broad categories: utilitarian items such as bowls, dishes, jars, ewers, medicine grinders, and water droppers for inkstones; and decorative objects like vases, censers, flowerpots, flower holders, and Bodhisattva statues.

The Longquan celadon from the Sinan wreck includes many masterpieces of superb quality and glaze. One striking example is a celadon statue of the bodhisattva Guanyin. Though its crown is missing, the figure's serene facial expression remains intact. Its deep-set eyes gaze forward, seemingly contemplating the joys and sorrows of the mortal world. The bodhisattva sits upright with the right leg raised and the right hand resting on the knee (the forearm is now missing); the left hand rests

Longquan celadon Guanyin statue from the Sinan shipwreck, Korea

on the left knee, and a lotus flower blossoms beside the exposed toes of the left foot. In Indian Buddhist scripture, Guanyin's sacred abode, Potalaka (transliterated into Chinese as Putuoluojia Shan or Putuoshan), is an island in the Indian Ocean. With the Sinicization of Buddhism during the Tang dynasty, this mythical dwelling became identified with an island off the

Zhejiang coast—modern-day Mount Putuo. This statue from the wreck thus embodies the Yuan-dynasty conception of Guanyin held by the people of Zhejiang. Similar Guanyin figures from the Longquan kilns have been found in Zhejiang itself, with a fine example housed in the Longquan Celadon Museum. Such statues offer invaluable physical evidence for tracing the evolution of Guanyin worship in the region.

While scholars universally agree that the Sinan ship's destination was Hakata, Japan, its port of origin remains a subject of debate, with Ningbo in Zhejiang and Fuzhou in Fujian being the two main candidates. However, two key artifacts from the wreck point strongly to Ningbo. The first is a piece of Longquan ware inscribed Shi Si Shuai Fu Gong Yong, meaning "For Official Use by the Command Headquarters." A fragment with the identical inscription was discovered in Ningbo in 2001. This "Command Headquarters" (Shuai Fu) was the common name for the Yuan dynasty's military and administrative authority for the Eastern Zhejiang Circuit (Zhedong Dao Xuanweishi Si Du Yuanshuai Fu), which was based in Ningbo. The ceramic pieces were therefore likely special commissions for official use by this government body. The second artifact is a bronze scale-weight bearing the inscription Qingyuan Lu, or "Qingyuan Circuit," which was the official Yuan-dynasty name for Ningbo. Together, these two invaluable artifacts provide powerful evidence for the Ningbo-origin theory. A voyage from Ningbo to Japan that passed by the Korean Peninsula would confirm the existence of a sophisticated trade network connecting China, Goryeo, and Japan, with Ningbo serving as a pivotal hub.

Celadon marked "for the use of the Marshal's office" from the Sinan shipwreck, Korea

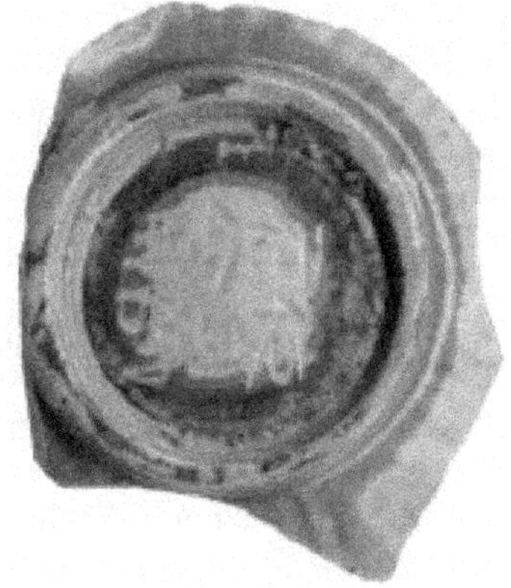

Ceramic shards marked "for the use of the Marshal's office," excavated from Tianyi Square in Ningbo

Given the wreck's intimate connection to Zhejiang, the Zhejiang Provincial Museum and the Gwangju National Museum of Korea collaborated on a special exhibition in Hangzhou from December 2012 to March 2013 titled "Sailing Under the Yuan: Masterpieces from the Sinan Shipwreck," the event commemorated the 20th anniversary of diplomatic relations between China and South Korea. It offered visitors a glimpse into the splendor of

"Made in Zhejiang" products from 700 years ago and highlighted the far-reaching influence of Zhejiang's Maritime Silk Road throughout East Asian waters.

As the preceding account shows, Yue ware from Zhejiang was being imported into the Korean Peninsula as early as the Six Dynasties period, and these exports grew steadily over time. In stark contrast, imports to Japan during the same era were exceptionally rare—the only known example is a single Eastern Jin celadon jar found in Matsuyama City, Ehime Prefecture. The reason for this scarcity remains something of an enigma to scholars. Later, during the Tang dynasty, the Japanese government dispatched numerous official missions to China, the kentōshi envoys, beginning in AD 630 to absorb Chinese culture. These missions returned with diplomatic gifts from the Tang court as well as goods they purchased themselves. While their cargo included Chinese ceramics, it consisted mainly of Tangsancai (three-color) wares; Yue celadon was seldom, if ever, among them.

Beginning in the 9th century (late Tang dynasty), private maritime trade between China and Japan flourished. Zhejiang's coastal ports—Ningbo, Taizhou, and Wenzhou—became vital hubs for this commerce, with local merchants such as Zhou Guanghan, Yan Shengze, Li Da, and Zhan Jingquan playing key roles. Against this backdrop, Yue ware began to be imported into Japan as a major commodity. Archaeological excavations have since uncovered Yue ware pieces dating from the 9th to the mid-11th centuries at over

200 sites across Japan. These sites are concentrated in Kyushu, the island closest to Zhejiang and connected by the maritime routes. The port of Hakata (in modern Fukuoka) was particularly important, as it housed both the Dazaifu, the government office for foreign affairs and trade, and the Kōrokan, an official guesthouse for foreign envoys and merchants. Consequently, the richest finds of Yue ware have come from the Dazaifu and Kōrokan sites. Numerous pieces have also been found in western Japan, particularly around the ancient capital, Heian-kyō (modern Kyoto).

The Yue ware unearthed in Japan is dominated by bowls, but also includes dishes, ewers, water droppers, boxes, and censers. In general, pieces from the Kōrokan site are of higher quality and often feature carved decorations, whereas those from the Dazaifu and other sites in western Japan tend to be coarser and undecorated. Through comparative analysis, experts have even traced some pieces to specific kilns. For example, certain celadon bowls with bi-disc style bases, lamps, and water droppers from the Kōrokan are believed to have originated from the Shanglin Lake kilns in Yuyao, while a dish with incised floral patterns found in Heian-kyō was likely produced at a kiln in Yin County. Two other characteristics of these finds

Yue Kiln ceramics excavated from the Korokan in Fukuoka, Japan

are noteworthy. First, the ceramics were discovered almost exclusively at the sites of former government offices, temples, and elite mansions, indicating they were luxury goods for the upper echelons of society—officials, monks, and aristocrats—rather than for common use. Second, the pieces are generally of ordinary quality; true masterpieces are rare. Why did merchants not transport the finest Zhejiang wares to Japan? Scholars speculate this may relate to a combination of Japanese consumer tastes and purchasing power. This question turns Yue ware into a key line of inquiry for understanding the consumption culture of the era, a fascinating topic worthy of deeper research.

10.2 Zhejiang Ceramics in the Arab World

In addition to its eastward export to Korea and Japan via the East China Sea routes, Yue ware also traveled westward to distant markets via the South China Sea branch of the Maritime Silk Road. Discoveries from the burgeoning field of underwater archaeology, particularly several key shipwrecks, have provided a wealth of evidence about this westward trade. The most significant of these finds is the Batu Hitam ("Black Stone") shipwreck.

The Batu Hitam wreck was discovered in 1998 off Indonesia's Belitung Island and named for a black reef it likely struck before sinking. Its diverse cargo included gold, silver, glassware, and spices, but it was dominated by over 67,000 pieces of Chinese ceramics. The vast majority were from the Changsha Kiln (over 60,000 pieces), with a smaller collection of nearly 200 Yue wares. Other ceramics included Gongxian white ware, blue-and-white porcelain, and Lingnan celadon. A key dating artifact is a Changsha bowl inscribed with a date corresponding to the second year of the Baoli reign, or 826 CE, firmly placing the shipwreck in the first half of the 9th century. The Yue ware pieces from the wreck, though few, are significant. For example, they include celadons with incised floral patterns, challenging the previous scholarly view that such decoration was a rare exception in the late Tang period and compelling a revision of our understanding of Yue ware's stylistic evolution.

Yue Kiln censers from the "Belitung" shipwreck

Scholars have long debated the origin of the "Belitung" shipwreck, also known as "Heishihao." Research suggests the ship, nearly 20 meters long, was built with timber sourced from India. Its hull shape and construction point to an Indian or Arabian origin, with the Persian Gulf as its intended destination. The question remains: from which port did it set sail? Many hypotheses have been put forward. One theory suggests the ship departed from Guangzhou, given the presence of Lingnan celadon on board. However, this is unlikely. Late Tang dynasty porcelain found in Guangzhou rarely includes Changsha and Yue wares, and there is a notable absence of Gongxian kilns' white and blue-and-white porcelain. This contrasts sharply with the "Belitung's" cargo, which closely matches the ceramic assortment found in Yangzhou. Furthermore, a bronze mirror recovered from the wreck bears an inscription: "Forged from a hundred refinements on the 29th day of the 11th lunar month in the Wuxu year of the first Qianyuan era at the heart of the Yangzhou Yangtze River." As the first year of Qianyuan corresponds to AD 758,some scholars believe the ship was loaded in Yangzhou before sailing to Guangzhou to take on additional Lingnan wares. Another theory proposes that Chinese goods were first transported to a Southeast Asian port, such as Palembang (Srivijaya), and then consolidated onto the "Belitung." This is also considered improbable, as the ship would have carried a wider variety of non-Chinese goods, yet the vast majority of its cargo is of Chinese origin. While the ship's exact port of departure remains undetermined, one thing is certain: the more than 200 Yue kiln celadon pieces found on board could not have been loaded at the port of Ningbo. These wares were likely first shipped to Yangzhou or another port city before being loaded onto the "Belitung."

Although Yue ware was only a minor part of the Batu Hitam cargo, it took center stage in another discovery: the Cirebon shipwreck, found off the coast of Indonesia in 2004.

Cirebon is a port city on the north coast of Java. Local fishermen began reporting an ancient wreck in the area in 2001, and between 2004 and 2005, a commercial salvage company conducted a scientific excavation under license from the Indonesian government.

The Cirebon wreck's cargo was immense and varied, containing ivory, gemstones, glass, Buddhist and Islamic objects, and even a Chinese bronze mirror with Daoist trigrams. Yet Chinese ceramics formed the bulk of the find. Of the more than 490,000 artifacts recovered, 75% were Chinese ceramics, and of those, the vast majority—estimated at over 300,000 pieces—were Yue celadons. The sheer scale of this find has been described as "earth-shattering." The Yue ware includes rare treasures like deer-shaped boxes, makara appliqués, phoenix-head ewer lids, and large octagonal ewers. Crucially, one bowl is inscribed Wuchen Xu Ji Zao, meaning "Made by the Xu workshop in the Wuchen year." The cyclical year wuchen corresponds to 968 , when Zhejiang was part of the Wuyue Kingdom. Further dating evidence comes from a large cache of lead coins inscribed Qianheng Tongbao, minted by the Southern Han regime(AD 917–971) between AD 917 and AD 925 . Together, these artifacts securely date the shipwreck to the second half of the 10th century.

Yue Kiln ceramics from the Cirebon shipwreck

Excavation revealed that the cargo was systematically packed, preserving its original arrangement. This raises the question: was this ship loaded in Ningbo and bound for Southeast Asia? The answer is almost certainly no. The vessel carried not only Yue ware but also goods from Southeast Asia, the Middle East, and even East Africa, as well as inbound cargo like raw glass intended for the Chinese market. A port like Ningbo would not have handled such a diverse collection of foreign goods, nor would it be loading China-bound cargo for an outbound trip. The ship's construction also refutes a Chinese origin. It was a locally built Southeast Asian shuttle boat, or perahu, about 30 meters long, designed to ferry goods between islands and larger ocean-going vessels. Furthermore, the 300,000 pieces of Yue ware were not produced at the same time; they span a period of nearly a century, from the late Tang to the early Northern Song. The most plausible explanation is that the Cirebon wreck was one such shuttle boat, operating out of a major regional entrepôt like Srivijaya. It was carrying Chinese goods (like the ceramics) to be loaded onto larger ships bound for Southeast Asia and the Indian Ocean, and foreign goods (like ivory and glass) to be transferred to ships sailing for China. Tragically, the vessel sank before reaching its destination. While the ceramics were not loaded directly from Ningbo onto this shuttle boat, the vast majority must have originally been exported from there. The sheer quantity of these wares powerfully attests to the steadily increasing capacity of the port of Ningbo from the late Tang dynasty onwards.

Although the ceramics on the Batu Hitam and Cirebon wrecks were not loaded directly from Ningbo, the two ships together reveal a critical shift in China's export economy. In the early 9th century, as shown by the Batu Hitam, Changsha ware dominated the market while Yue ware was a minor export. By the latter half of the 10th century, the era of the Cirebon wreck, Changsha ware had all but disappeared from foreign trade. In its place, Yue ware had surged to become not only the premier export ceramic but one of China's most important bulk commodities traded overseas.

Besides Indonesia, numerous Yue Kiln ceramics have been found in other Southeast Asian countries along the Maritime Silk Road's South China Sea route, including Thailand, Malaysia, and the Philippines. After passing through the northwestern tip of Sumatra, the route entered the Bay of Bengal, proceeded through Sri Lanka, and arrived at the ancient kingdom of Quilon (present-day Kollam) on India's southern coast before continuing into the Arab world.

The Arab Empire, which rose in the 7th century and reached its zenith in the 8th, once stretched from the Indus River to the Atlantic. By the time of China's Song dynasty, however, this empire had fragmented into numerous states. The most prominent included the Abbasid Caliphate (750–1055), centered in Baghdad; the Fatimid Caliphate (909–1171), centered in North Africa; and the Umayyad Caliphate (756–1236) on the Iberian Peninsula. Ancient Chinese referred to this vast region collectively as Dashi, a term derived from the Persian name for Arabs.This "Arab world" encompassed Central and West Asia as well as parts of North and East Africa. As the Southern Song official Zhou Qufei (1135–1189) wrote in his geographical treatise *Lingwai Daida* (*Representative Answers from the Region beyond the Mountains*): "Dashi is the collective name for many nations. There are over a thousand, of which only a few are known to us by name".

Chinese ceramics began arriving in the Arab world during the Tang dynasty. Over 160 archaeological sites from the 8th to 10th centuries, from Samarra in Iraq to Nishapur in Iran, have yielded Chinese pottery. Zhejiang's Yue celadon formed a significant portion of these early imports, alongside white wares and Tang sancai. This trade, conducted primarily by sea, accelerated dramatically during the Song dynasty. Consequently, discoveries of Yue ware are concentrated in the ports and coastal regions of the Persian Gulf, the Red Sea, and the southern Arabian Peninsula. In Iraq, on the northern side of the Persian Gulf, numerous archaeological sites have yielded Yue kiln porcelain. Ctesiphon, located about 35 kilometers south of Baghdad and once the capital of the Persian Sassanian Empire, has produced celadon fragments from the Yue kilns of Shanglin Lake dating back to around the 10th century. The Baghdad Museum also houses Yue kiln porcelain from the 9th to 11th centuries. At the Sharmah site in Yemen, near the Gulf of Aden, more than 350 Chinese porcelain fragments were collected from the 1990s to 2005, and an additional 1,592 pieces were excavated. These artifacts date from the late Tang Dynasty to the Yuan Dynasty, and include a significant amount of Yue kiln porcelain, such as bowls, plates, and boxes. As only partial excavations have been conducted at this site so far, a full-scale excavation would undoubtedly reveal even more Yue kiln wares. Even farther away, at the Fustat site in Egypt, the quantity and variety of unearthed Yue kiln porcelain are even greater.

Fustat, founded on the Nile after the Arab conquest of AD 641, was Egypt's first Islamic capital. Even after the administrative center moved to nearby Cairo in AD 969, Fustat's economic power continued to grow. It evolved into one of the Arab world's great centers of craft production and international trade, reaching its apex in the 12th century. The city's prosperity came to a sudden end in 1168. In 1163, the Kingdom of Jerusalem, a Crusader state founded by Western European Catholics, launched repeated invasions into Egypt and advanced to the outskirts of Fustat by 1168. Facing the invasion, the ruling vizier ordered the evacuation of the population and set Fustat ablaze to prevent it from falling into enemy hands. The fire raged for over 50 days, leaving the once-thriving metropolis in ruins. Over time, the site became a desolate wasteland, parts of which were used as a garbage dump. Today, the area is a district of Cairo, and in 2017, the National Museum of Egyptian Civilization opened on the site of this historic city.

Commencing in the 20th century, archaeological excavations at Fustat have been continuously conducted by scholars from Egypt, Europe, the United States, and Japan. In recent years, a number of Chinese scholars have also begun to participate in the archaeological research at this site. One of the most significant results of this long-term research has been the discovery of vast quantities of Chinese ceramics. While a complete inventory is still lacking, the numbers are substantial. One late-20th-century Japanese study estimated that among the 350,000 unearthed ceramic fragments, more than 11,000 originated from East Asia (including China, Vietnam, Thailand, Japan, etc.), accounting for approximately 3% of the total. while recent fieldwork by Chinese scholar Qin Dashu suggests the number of Chinese pieces alone may exceed 20,000. Today, ceramics unearthed at Fustat are housed in museum collections across Europe, the United States, and Japan.

Yue Kiln ceramic shards excavated from the Fustat site in Egypt

The earliest Chinese ceramics at Fustat date to the late 9th century (late Tang) and come from various kilns, including Yaozhou, Changsha, Xing, and Ding. Yue celadon from Zhejiang was the most common type, though overall imports during this early phase were modest in both quantity and variety. Under Fatimid rule (969–1171), however, the volume of imported Chinese ceramics surged. Wares from all of China's major Northern Song kilns—including Yue, Ding, Cizhou, and Yaozhou—were shipped to Fustat. As the Yue kilns declined, they were supplanted by the rising Longquan kilns, also in

Zhejiang, whose products began to appear in increasing numbers. The Northern Song Longquan ware found at Fustat falls into two main types: those with carved lotus-petal motifs and those with incised floral designs.

During the Southern Song period, two major shifts occurred in the ceramics trade to Fustat. First, the ongoing conflict between the Song and the northern Jin dynasty severed export routes for northern Chinese kilns. As a result, ceramics from this period found at Fustat consist almost exclusively of southern wares: Longquan celadon and Jingdezhen qingbai (bluish-white) porcelain. Second, Chinese potters began producing wares specifically for the Arab market. Scholars have noted that among the Longquan finds at Fustat, standard vessel shapes are less common than large lotus-petal bowls. Roughly 75% of these bowls measure 160–240 mm in diameter, with 220 mm being the most common size—significantly larger than comparable bowls found in collections in China and the West. This demonstrates that merchants, learning from long-term sales experience, began commissioning larger vessels specifically tailored to the preferences of their Middle Eastern clientele.

Local artisans in the Arab world began imitating Chinese ceramics soon after they first arrived in the Tang dynasty. Song dynasty wares, especially Longquan celadon, were particularly sought after. Lacking the secrets to Chinese clays, glaze formulas, and firing temperatures, local potters were forced to innovate. Using local materials, they developed their own brilliantly colored glazes and unique application techniques. The resulting glazed earthenware, while inspired by Chinese porcelain, was not true porcelain itself but a distinct hybrid. This unique quality—neither fully pottery nor fully porcelain—gave it a special charm that made it a treasure of Islamic art. These traditions of colored glazes would, in turn, be transmitted back to China, influencing its own ceramic development in a remarkable cultural feedback loop.

Arabian glazed pottery discovered in Ningbo

Zhejiang's ceramics traveled east along the Maritime Silk Road to the Korean Peninsula and the Japanese Archipelago, and west to Southeast Asia, South Asia, the Middle East, and North Africa. Across this immense geographical expanse, people of every color, language, and faith used these wares, largely unaware of their specific origin. In effect, the world was using Zhejiang's products long before it knew the name "Zhejiang." Zhejiang porcelain was thus ancient Zhejiang's first calling card to the world, and the Maritime Silk Road was the channel that delivered it.

Chapter 11. The Origins of the Sacred Sandalwood Image of Seiryō-ji

11.1 The Sacred Image Journeys to Japan

In the late 10th century, as the Song dynasty was consolidating its rule over China, a Japanese monk from Tōdai-ji Temple named Chōnen (938–1016) was earnestly preparing for a pilgrimage to study Buddhism in the land of its transmission. On the first day of the eighth month of AD 983, Chōnen and his disciples, among them Jōzan, departed from Kyushu and reached the Chinese port of Taizhou on the eighteenth. According to Jōzan, they sailed aboard a vessel owned by the Wu-Yue merchants Chen Renshuang and Xu Renman. Chōnen's own account simply notes that he boarded a merchant ship of "traders from Taizhou" who were returning to China. These accounts confirm that the men were Taizhou merchants and mark Chōnen as the first Japanese monk to visit the Song dynasty.

Upon his arrival in Taizhou, Chōnen took up residence at Kaiyuan Temple. After receiving official travel permits, he set out for the Tiantai mountains on the ninth day of the ninth month. The pilgrims first visited Guoqing Temple, where they viewed a portrait of the great master Zhiyi. Chōnen was moved to describe the landscape as a place of "spectacular mountains and elegant trees, of deep streams and clear springs." From there, they ascended Mount Tiantai, crossed its famous Stone Bridge to pay homage at sites linked to the legendary Arhats, and visited the former hermitages of the three great

Tang monks Hanshan, Shide, and Fenggan. On the eighth day of the tenth month, they departed, arriving three days later at the Great Buddha Temple on Mount Nanming in Xinchang. There, they paid respects to Daoxuan (AD 596–667), founder of the Nanshan Vinaya School, and marveled at the colossal stone statue of Maitreya. Their journey then took them north through Hangzhou, finally bringing them to Kaiyuan Temple in Yangzhou on the eighteenth.

On the nineteenth day of the twelfth month of AD 983, Chōnen and his party arrived in the Song capital of Bianjing (modern Kaifeng). Two days later, he was granted an audience with Emperor Taizong in the Chongzheng Hall, where he presented tribute gifts of bronze vessels and books. Although Chōnen could not speak Chinese, his fluency in written characters allowed him to converse with the emperor through "brush talks." He provided a detailed account of Japan's geography, natural resources, and political system, which became the Song court's primary source of knowledge on the country; in fact, his testimony forms roughly eighty percent of the History of Song: Treatise on Japan. He also informed the emperor that many Chinese texts, including the Four Books and Five Classics, Buddhist sutras, and the Collected Works of Bai Juyi, had been transmitted to Japan. When Emperor Taizong learned that the Japanese imperial line had reigned in an unbroken succession, he sighed and remarked to his chancellor: "To think that this nation, which we considered a remote island of barbarians, should enjoy such a long and stable destiny, with its rulers and ministers passing down their positions for generations. China, by contrast, has been mired in chaos and division since the end of the Tang. If you wish for your own descendants to enjoy high office and its rewards, you must govern with the utmost diligence and never grow complacent."

Beginning in the third month of AD 984, Chōnen and his companions embarked on an arduous pilgrimage to China's most sacred Buddhist sites, including Mount Wutai, the White Horse Temple in Luoyang, and the Longmen Grottoes. They returned to Bianjing that summer, where they were received with great warmth by the Song government. In the third month of AD 985, Chōnen took his leave of Emperor Taizong. The emperor bestowed upon him the honorary title "Master Faji" (Master of Ferrying the Dharma) and lavished him with gifts, including a collection of Buddhist scriptures. Local officials provided an escort for his return journey, and on the twenty-seventh day of the sixth month, Chōnen arrived back at Kaiyuan Temple in Taizhou.

In the seventh month of AD 986, Chōnen departed from Taizhou with a wealth of treasures. After a successful voyage across the sea, he landed in Kyushu. The History of Song specifies that he returned to Japan aboard a ship belonging to Zheng Rende, a merchant from Ninghai County in Taizhou (part of modern Ningbo). The most precious and eye-catching of all the items Chōnen brought back from China was a 1.6-meter-tall wooden statue of Śākyamuni, the renowned "Udayana Sandalwood Auspicious Image."

This image is named for King Udayana, ruler of the ancient Indian kingdom of Kauśāmbī. Legend holds that he was initially hostile to Buddhism but became a devout follower after personally witnessing the miracles of Śākyamuni Buddha. Once, when the Buddha ascended to the heavens to preach the Dharma to his deceased mother, King Udayana grew so sick with longing that he felt he was near death. Desperate to save him, his ministers conceived a plan to carve a statue of the Buddha from precious sandalwood. To ensure a perfect likeness, the disciple Maudgalyāyana used his supernatural abilities to transport over thirty craftsmen to the heavens on three occasions, allowing them to study the Buddha as he preached. The completed statue was deeply venerated by the king and his subjects, becoming known as the "Udayana Sandalwood Auspicious Image," or the Sandalwood Image for short. It was believed to be the world's first statue of Śākyamuni, carved during his lifetime, capturing his true appearance, and possessing miraculous powers to heal the sick and avert disaster.

Upon returning to the mortal world, Śākyamuni is said to have seen the statue and, touching it, proclaimed: "One thousand years after my Parinirvāṇa, you shall journey to China to spread the Dharma." In fulfillment of this prophecy, the Sandalwood Image did eventually reach China. Several accounts of its journey exist. One popular version tells of an Indian named Kumārayāna who carried the statue on his back from India to Central Asia. The journey was long and arduous, yet legend says that while Kumārayāna carried the image by day, at night the image—an embodiment of the Buddha himself—carried him. When Kumārayāna passed through the Kingdom of Kucha (in modern Xinjiang), the local king, hoping to keep the statue, offered the monk his own sister in marriage. In Kucha, Kumārayāna fathered a son, the future master-translator Kumārajīva, to whom the statue was passed upon his death.

In AD 384, the Former Qin general Lü Guang (AD 337-399) conquered Kucha and seized both Kumārajīva and the Sandalwood Image as spoils of war, transporting them to Liangzhou (modern Wuwei, Gansu). In AD 386, Lü Guang established the Later Liang dynasty with Liangzhou as its capital. When the Later Qin conquered this state in AD 401, Kumārajīva and the statue were taken again, this time to the Later Qin capital of Chang'an (modern Xi'an). Thus, through the turmoil of war, the Sandalwood Image reached China's Central Plains. In AD 417, the Eastern Jin general Liu Yu (AD 363-422) defeated the Later Qin and had the statue moved to his capital, Jiankang (modern Nanjing), installing it in Longguang Temple. In AD 420, Liu Yu established his own dynasty, the Song (AD 420–479), known to historians as the Liu Song to distinguish it from later dynasties. From its new home in Jiankang, the statue would witness the rise and fall of four successive southern dynasties: the Song (AD 420–479), Qi (AD 502-557), Liang (AD 479-502), and Chen (AD 557-589).

In AD 589, Emperor Wen of the Sui dynasty sent his son, Yang Guang, to conquer the Chen dynasty. In AD 604, Yang Guang ascended the throne as

Emperor Yang. On a later southern tour, he had the Sandalwood Image moved from Jiankang's Longguang Temple to Kaiyuan Temple in Yangzhou, where he commissioned a special shrine for it. Long before his pilgrimage, Chōnen had heard that this legendary statue was enshrined in Yangzhou. He and Jōzan therefore made a special visit to Kaiyuan Temple on the eighteenth day of the eleventh month, AD 983. To their dismay, they discovered only the empty shrine—the image was gone. A monk explained its absence: "For centuries, the Sandalwood Image resided here, honored by emperors of successive dynasties. But then Li Yu (AD 937-978), the last ruler of the Southern Tang, moved it to his capital, Jiangning (modern Nanjing). In AD 975, Song armies conquered Jiangning, capturing Li Yu and seizing the statue. It was brought to the capital, Bianjing, and installed first in Yong'an Hall at Kaibao Temple, before Emperor Taizong moved it into the Zifu Hall of the imperial palace for his personal daily veneration." The monk added reassuringly, "When you reach Bianjing, you may have the chance to see it in the palace."

Disappointed by their failure in Yangzhou but hopeful of seeing the statue in the imperial palace, Chōnen and Jōzan continued their journey north to Bianjing. Jōzan's own records state that during their audience with Emperor Taizong on the twenty-first day of the twelfth month in AD 983, they requested permission to see and venerate the Sandalwood Image in Zifu Hall. The emperor granted their request. In the first month of the following year, AD 984, escorted by Song officials, Chōnen and Jōzan were led into Zifu Hall. There, at last, they laid eyes upon the legendary Sandalwood Image, fulfilling a lifelong dream.

When Chōnen's party returned to Bianjing in the summer of AD 984 after their pilgrimage to Mount Wutai and the Longmen Grottoes, the Sandalwood Image had already been moved from Zifu Hall to the newly built Qisheng Chan Monastery. Jōzan recorded that Chōnen, deeply desiring a copy of the statue, commissioned a "Master Carver of Buddhist Images" named Zhang Rong. Chōnen brought the master carver to Qisheng Chan Monastery to study the original and create an exact replica. This new statue was then painstakingly transported hundreds of miles from Bianjing back to the port of Taizhou. There, in AD 986, it was loaded onto the merchant Zheng Rende's ship for the final voyage to Japan.

The Sandalwood Image was held to be the world's first statue of the Buddha, a true embodiment of Śākyamuni imbued with miraculous powers. That Chōnen had commissioned a direct copy and brought it across the sea was an unprecedented event that caused a sensation throughout Japan. The imperial court spared no expense, mobilizing a vast workforce to overcome great difficulties and transport the statue and scriptures from Kyushu to the capital, Kyoto. In the second month of AD 987, a grand procession welcomed the treasures into the city. Entering through the Rajōmon gate, the parade proceeded north along the great Suzaku Avenue. It was led by a band, followed by porters carrying chests of scriptures—including 500 cases of the Tripiṭaka. Onlookers lining the route rushed forward to help carry the chests, hoping to absorb some of their sacred aura and receive the Buddha's blessing. Next came a cart bearing the Sandalwood Image, followed by another band. Chōnen himself, robed as a monk and surrounded by Jōzan and other disciples, walked at the heart of the procession. Greeted by jubilant crowds, the sacred image was ceremonially installed in Rendaiji Temple, which exists to this day.

Once installed at Rendaiji Temple, the replica image drew a ceaseless stream of worshippers, from the emperor and empress to court nobles and commoners alike. In AD 991, the statue was moved to Seikaji Temple in the northwest of Kyoto. Chōnen, however, harbored a grander ambition: to use the great prestige of the Sandalwood Image to establish his own temple, and with it, his own independent school of Japanese Buddhism. His inspiration was China's Mount Wutai, one of the Four Sacred Mountains of Chinese Buddhism and home to the celebrated Qingliang Temple. Since the Tang dynasty, Mount Wutai had been a hallowed destination for Japanese pilgrims. Upon his return, Chōnen petitioned the imperial court to rename Mount Atago, west of Kyoto, to Mount Godai (the Japanese reading of Wutai) and to grant him permission to build a new "Qingliang Temple"—Seiryō-ji in Japanese—on its slopes to permanently house his sacred image.

Although the court swiftly approved Chōnen's request, the project faced fierce opposition from rival Buddhist schools. His dream was deferred and remained unfulfilled at the time of his death in 1016. In the years that followed, his disciple Jōzan and others strove tirelessly to realize their master's vision. After extensive efforts, they finally secured court approval in 1019 to rename Seikaji Temple as Seiryō-ji. By renaming the existing temple, Jōzan and his followers substantially fulfilled Chōnen's ambition. The replica image, intended for only a temporary stay at Seikaji, now had a permanent home. It has been known ever since as the "Wooden Standing Image of Śākyamuni of Seiryō-ji," or more simply, the Seiryō-ji Śākyamuni.

The Śākyamuni statue that the monk Chōnen brought back to Japan from Taizhou, Zhejiang (now preserved at Seiryō-ji in Kyoto).

The Seiryō-ji Śākyamuni stands before a magnificent, boat-shaped mandorla, or kōhai. Its openwork surface is a dynamic interweaving of scrolling vines, bursting with vitality. Eleven smaller Buddhas—one at the apex and five on each side—adorn the mandorla, symbolizing the central figure's various manifestations. Against this backdrop, the Śākyamuni image stands with serene dignity. His hair is styled in ancient snail-shell curls, and atop his head, the cranial protuberance, or uṣṇīṣa, is inlaid with a red-tinted crystal. His long, compassionate eyes, inset with black lacquer pupils, give the face a striking spiritual intensity. Between his brows, a small, circular silver plaque represents the ūrṇā, one of the thirty-two major marks of a Buddha. His elongated earlobes, also set with crystal spheres, stretch down to his neck. His monastic robe, or saṃghāti, covers both shoulders, its fabric cascading in a series of concentric, U-shaped folds that flow smoothly down his body. Beneath the main robe, two undergarments with light, naturalistic folds cling to his legs. His right hand is raised in the abhayamudrā, the gesture of fearlessness that grants courage. His left hand is lowered in the varadamudrā, the gesture of wish-granting that signifies the fulfillment of all vows.

As Seiryō-ji's greatest treasure, the Śākyamuni image vastly elevated the temple's status and influence; to this day, it is honored in a special ceremony each October. Over the centuries, the statue's mystique deepened and new legends arose. Jōzan, who not only accompanied the statue from China but also witnessed its creation, had clearly stated that it was a replica carved in Bianjing by the master Zhang Rong. This account meant the Seiryō-ji statue was merely a copy, with the authentic original still in China—an admission that threatened the image's sacred status, as a copy's spiritual power could never match an original's. To resolve this conflict and satisfy the spiritual needs of the faithful, a miraculous new story emerged in the 12th century. The legend claims that while the replica was being carved, the original Sandalwood Image appeared to Chōnen in a dream and expressed its desire to go to Japan. On the very night the replica was completed, the original statue miraculously stepped down from its altar and switched places with the copy. Thus, the statue Chōnen brought to Japan was the true Sandalwood Image, while the one left in China was a mere imitation. This is why the Seiryō-ji image itself came to be called the "Sandalwood Auspicious Image" (Sendan Zuizō). A plaque with this title hangs today above the entrance to the Shakadō (Main Hall) where the statue is housed. Interestingly, the calligraphy was brushed by Yinyuan Longqi (Ingen Ryūki, 1592–1673), a monk from Fujian with close ties to Zhejiang. He once traveled to places like Putuo Mountain in Zhoushan, Xingshan Temple in Jiaxing, and Yunxiu Hermitage in Haiyan County. In the year 1654, at the juncture of the Ming and Qing dynasties, he traveled to Japan at an invitation and founded the Ōbaku school of Zen.

The transverse beam above the doorway of the Śākyamuni Hall at Seiryō-ji

According to this powerful narrative, the Sandalwood Image, symbolizing the Buddha himself, began its journey in India, the cradle of Buddhism.

It traversed the vast interior of Central Asia, circulated throughout China, witnessing the rise and fall of dynasties, and finally reached Japan. As a Japanese saying encapsulates it, the image "Originated in India, propagated the Dharma in China, and spread it throughout Japan." The Seiryō-ji statue thus came to be known as the "Śākyamuni Transmitted from Three Countries" (Sangoku Denrai Shaka), signifying its passage through India, China, and Japan. Visitors to Seiryō-ji today can see a large stone to the left of the main gate (as one enters) inscribed with the title "Śākyamuni Tathāgata Transmitted from Three Countries."

This version of events resonated deeply with the Japanese psyche, bolstering national religious confidence and gaining widespread acceptance. The story was famously immortalized in art. Seiryō-ji itself houses a six-volume set of narrative handscrolls titled Illustrated Legends of the Shakadō (Shakadō Engi Emaki), attributed to the painter Kanō Motonobu (1476-1559) and dated to 1515. The scrolls use text and images to recount the statue's origin. One scene depicts the carving of the replica: three artisans work meticulously before the original Sandalwood Image, their copy already nearly identical. To the right sit three observers—likely Chōnen and two disciples—watching with rapt attention. To the left sit two men in official robes and caps, presumably the Song officials escorting the monks. A subsequent scene shows two empty altars side-by-side. The two statues, however, have come to life; having stepped down from their respective bases, they are shown in the very act of switching places. The painting thus offers a vivid, visual confirmation of the legend that the Seiryō-ji statue is the one true Sandalwood Image instead of an duplicate.

The process of replicating the sacred statue (zuizō) as depicted in the Illustrated Scroll of *the Origins of Shakadō Hall*

The scene depicted in the Scroll of *the Origins of the Śākyamuni Hall* in which the newly traced sandalwood replica of the auspicious icon was secretly exchanged for the original

Because the Sandalwood Image was believed to depict the Buddha's true likeness, and the Seiryō-ji image was now regarded as that very statue, it attracted countless pilgrims. Furthermore, many prominent temples and wealthy patrons sought to commission their own copies. These replicas, all modeled on the Seiryō-ji Śākyamuni, are known collectively as "Seiryō-ji style" images. Nearly one hundred survive today, scattered across Japan. An early example, carved around the year 1100, is housed at Mimurodo-ji Temple in Uji. Other notable replicas can be found at Daien-ji in Tokyo, Jōraku-in in Kyoto, Saidai-ji in Nara, Enryaku-ji in Shiga, Enmei-ji in Osaka, Shinpuku-ji in Yokohama, and the Nara National Museum.

11.2 The Secrets Within the Image

For nearly a thousand years, it was believed that the Seiryō-ji Śākyamuni had been carved in the Qisheng Chan Monastery in the Song capital of Bianjing. This belief was shattered in 1954, when a rectangular cavity was discovered in the statue's back, filled with a trove of hidden artifacts. Scholars collectively refer to these as the "enshrined items" (nōnyūhin). Among them was a document written by Chōnen himself on the eighteenth day of the eighth month, AD 985—the day the statue was completed. This text, the Record of Chōnen's Pilgrimage to Song China and the Creation of the Auspicious Image, states explicitly that after returning to Kaiyuan Temple in Taizhou on the twenty-seventh day of the sixth month, AD 985, Chōnen resolved to commission a statue so the people of Japan could behold the true face of Śākyamuni. To fund the project, he sold his robes and personal belongings to purchase precious wood and hire artisans. The work began on the twenty-first day of the seventh month and was completed on the eighteenth day of the eighth—a date Chōnen must have chosen deliberately, as it marked the two-year anniversary of his first landing in Taizhou.

More importantly, an inscription was found on the interior of the panel covering the cavity: "Carved by Zhang Yanjiao and his younger brother Zhang Yanxi of Taizhou, Great Song State." This was definitive proof: the Seiryō-ji statue was carved not in Bianjing's Qisheng Chan Monastery but in Taizhou's Kaiyuan Temple. The artists were not the capital's famous Zhang Rong, but two brothers from Taizhou, Zhang Yanjiao and Zhang Yanxi. In another enshrined document, the Record of Items Placed Within the Auspicious Image, Zhang Yanjiao identifies himself as a "Master of Statue-Making." Furthermore, an inscription on the statue's pedestal reads, "Monk Baoning of Kaiyuan Temple, Taizhou, Tang State," confirming that the entire work, including its base, was made in Taizhou.

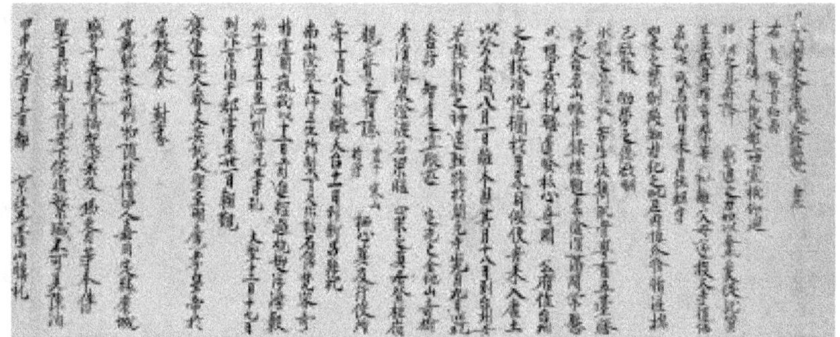

Partial Transcription of *the Record of Jōnen's Pilgrimage to the Song Dynasty for Buddhist Teachings, Pilgrimage, and the Erection of Sacred Statues*

Scientific analysis of the wood by Japanese scholars also disproved the claim on the Shakadō plaque. The statue was not made of precious Indian sandalwood, but of wood native to China. Twentieth-century studies concluded it was a type of Chinese bird cherry (Prunus wilsonii), referred to in Chinese as juanmao chouli. More recent analysis, however, suggests the wood is more likely a type of nanmu, a precious timber unique to China. One variety is even named Phoebe chekiangensis, or Zhejiang Nanmu, as it grows primarily in western Zhejiang and neighboring regions. It is hoped that scholars from Zhejiang may one day participate in future analysis, as the results could deepen our understanding of the region's ancient trade and transportation history.

Given that the statue was made in Taizhou, how did the Zhang brothers replicate the original in Bianjing so faithfully? Scholars have proposed three main theories. The first is that the master carver Zhang Rong created a small model in Bianjing, which Chōnen then brought to Taizhou for the brothers to copy. This seems improbable, as Chōnen's party spent at most a single day at Qisheng Chan Monastery—hardly enough time to produce a detailed model. A second theory suggests that Zhang Rong or another artist created a detailed drawing that served as a guide. The third theory posits that artisans in the Taizhou region already had a tradition of replicating the famous Sandalwood Image, and that the Zhang brothers may have possessed their own patterns or even carved similar statues before. Regardless, the fact that the Seiryō-ji image was produced in Taizhou makes it a crucial touchstone for studying the history of wood carving in Zhejiang.

The trove of items enshrined within the statue is remarkably rich, broadly categorized as follows: Documents: Six texts, including the aforementioned Record of Chōnen's Pilgrimage and Record of Items Placed Within, as well as a record of Chōnen's birth, a blood-oath pledge between Chōnen and his fellow monk Gizon, a register of Chōnen's patrons, and a list of donors. Buddhist Scriptures: Three sutras: the Suvarṇaprabhāsa Sūtra (Golden Light Sutra), the Lotus Sūtra, and the Diamond Sūtra. Woodblock Prints: Images of the Bodhisattvas Mañjuśrī, Samantabhadra, and Maitreya, as well as a depiction of the Vulture Peak Assembly. Votive Offerings: A wide array of small items including crystal, agate, vajra, and bodhi beads; a bronze mirror engraved with the Water-Moon Avalokiteśvara; glassware; foil fragments; calcite; silk replicas of the five viscera and six bowels (gozō roppu); and over 130 Chinese copper coins from more than forty devotees in Taizhou. Additionally, X-rays revealed a Buddha's tooth relic inside the statue's head. An addendum to the Record of Items, dated the eighteenth of the eighth month, notes a miracle: "The Buddha's tooth was placed inside the statue's face on the morning of the seventh. At noon, a drop of blood appeared on the statue's back. All who witnessed it were astonished, and so we record this miraculous sign."

The Record of Items Placed Within the Auspicious Image provides a detailed inventory of the enshrined objects and their donors, which corresponds almost perfectly with the items discovered. Some were personal mementos Chōnen brought from Japan. One was a tattered slip of paper bearing the date "24th day of the 1st month of the 8th year of Jōhei" (AD 938). The slip also bears several Japanese kana characters, believed to be the oldest extant example of the script. Scholars identify this as Chōnen's birth record, likely written by his mother, as the date matches his birthdate. His mother is thought to have sewn this slip together with his preserved umbilical cord and given it to him. Chōnen carried these precious keepsakes to China in AD 983 and placed them inside the statue before his return. When the statue was opened in 1954, only the paper remained; the umbilical cord had long since disintegrated.

Another document, *the Blood-Oath Pledge of Gizon and Chōnen*, was composed at Tōdai-ji in AD 972. The pledge is notable for Chōnen's statement that his "lay surname was Hata", leading many scholars to conclude his ancestors hailed from mainland China or the Korean peninsula. In the document, Chōnen and his fellow monk Gizon swear before "all Buddhas and Bodhisattvas, before Brahma and Indra, and all the gods of heaven and earth" to be of "one heart in life and death," to care for each other's welfare, to study the Dharma together, and to "join their strength" to one day build a temple on Mount Atago. They sealed the oath by cutting their fingers and stamping the document with bloody handprints. Chōnen's life became a struggle to fulfill this vow, and his pilgrimage to China was a crucial step. While he never built his temple on Mount Atago, he succeeded in establishing Seiryō-ji on the foundation of the former Seikaji.

According to the Record of Items, Chōnen himself donated a śarīra relic, a bodhi-bead rosary, a mirror, a copy of the Golden Light Sutra, Pāṭalī leaves, and various precious gems. Most of these were found, though the śarīra was difficult to identify and may have fragmented. The majority of items, however, were donated by local Chinese devotees. Monks from Taizhou's Kaiyuan Temple donated crystal and agate beads. Among the contents was also a woodblock print of Maitreya Bodhisattva (approx. 54x28 cm), showing Maitreya seated on a lotus throne beneath a canopy flanked by flying apsarasas. The print is dated to the tenth month of AD 984. The upper right corner attributes the painting to Gao Wenjin, a famous court painter, leading some to believe Chōnen acquired it in the capital. This is incorrect. The upper left corner clearly reads, "Carved by the Monk Zhili of Yuezhou." Zhili (960–1028) was a native of Yin County (modern Ningbo) and is revered as the 17th patriarch of the Tiantai school of Buddhism. Here, "Yuezhou" refers not to Shaoxing specifically but to the broader eastern Zhejiang region. It is possible Zhili, a great monk, was also a skilled carver, but more likely he commissioned a professional to do the work. In either case, the print was unquestionably produced in Zhejiang. Perhaps the most astonishing of the enshrined items is a set of miniature internal organs fashioned from silk, including a heart, liver, lungs, stomach, kidneys, and intestines. The creators used different colored silks for each organ—red for the heart, purple for the kidneys, and so on. Placed with the organs was a handwritten prayer. Though partially damaged, the text, cross-referenced with the official inventory, tells a poignant story. A nun named Qingxiao from Miaoshan Temple in Taizhou was suffering from a debilitating "wind illness" (likely a stroke). Together with her mother and disciple, she donated the funds to create the silk organs and have them sealed inside the newly completed statue. She prayed for a speedy recovery and a happy life, and for future rebirths blessed with "wisdom, fortune, and longevity." She also prayed that her deceased teachers and relatives might share in the merit generated by her pious offering.

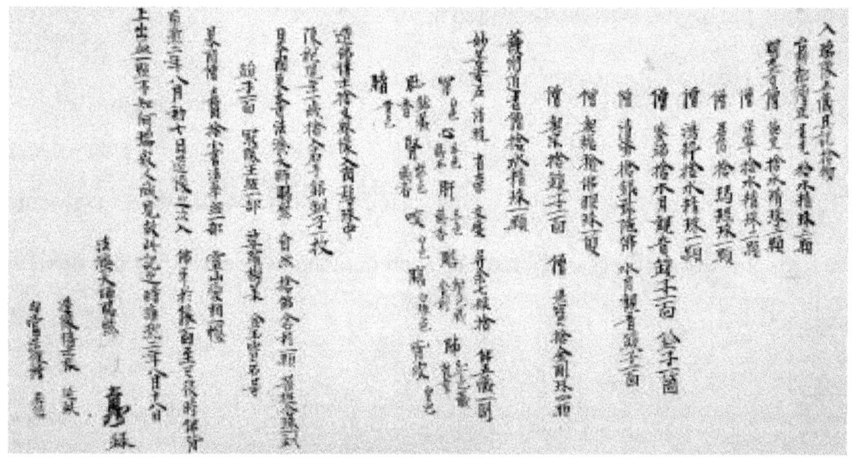

Record of the Enshrined Relics and Viscera Installation in the Sacred Buddha Statue

This set of organs was completed on the fifth day of the eighth month, AD 985, and placed inside the statue to serve as the Buddha's own viscera. This detail suggests that the people of Taizhou believed that even a Buddha required internal organs to be complete. The statue's makers, the Zhang brothers, noted in their donor record that they placed the organs inside on the eighteenth of the eighth month to repay the "Four Kindnesses": those of one's parents, of all sentient beings, of the sovereign, and of the Three Jewels (the Buddha, Dharma, and Sangha). In his own record, completed that same day, Chōnen wrote: "Now, as the Auspicious Image is complete, and the organs are placed within, I briefly record my purpose to explain its origins." This reveals that installing the organs was the final step in the statue's creation. After they were in place, Chōnen's newly written record was added to the cavity, and the back panel was sealed. The discovery offers invaluable insight into the process of creating sacred images in early Northern Song Zhejiang.

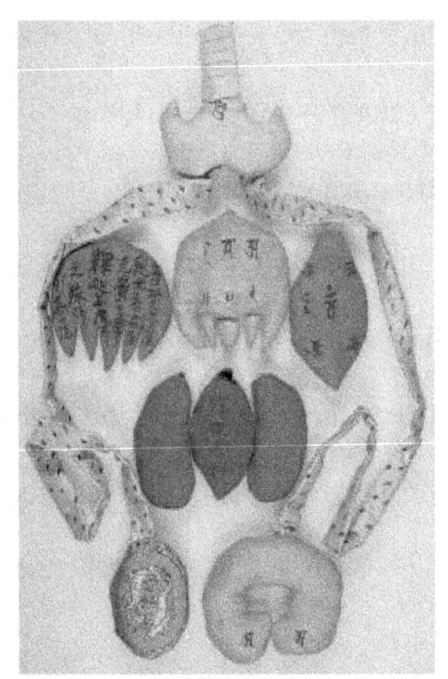

Silk-made human organ models (gozō) enshrined within the Buddha statue at Seiryō-ji Temple

In summary, though now a National Treasure of Japan, the Seiryō-ji Śākyamuni is a product of Zhejiang. It was carved in Taizhou by Taizhou artisans. Its enshrined items, including the Maitreya print and silk organs, were also made in Zhejiang, and most of the offerings were donated by the faithful of Taizhou. The statue is thus a rich time capsule of Zhejiang's culture in the 10th century, reflecting its advanced arts of sculpture, woodblock printing, silk weaving, metalwork, and even its understanding of medicine and folk religion. At the same time, this statue made in Zhejiang would have a profound and lasting impact on the art of Japan. It was so widely copied that it spawned an entire genre of Buddhist sculpture, the "Seiryō-ji style." While these copies have their own variations, they all share the same core features: the snail-shell curls, the robe covering both shoulders, the concentric U-shaped drapery, and the layered skirts visible at the ankles. These traits are a testament to the deep influence of Zhejiang's sculptural arts on the history of Japanese art.

The statue that Chōnen brought from Taizhou was revered in Japan for nearly a thousand years as the true Sandalwood Image. It remains a National Treasure, venerated to this day. But the original statue it was based on—the very one Chōnen saw in Bianjing's Qisheng Chan Monastery—suffered a very different fate.

In the winter of 1126, during the infamous Jingkang Incident, Jurchen armies sacked the Northern Song capital of Bianjing. Amid the chaos, a group of monks rescued the Sandalwood Image and transported it north to the area of modern-day Beijing. The temple housing this statue was first bestowed the name "Dayansheng Temple" by the Jin rulers, and in 1167, it was renamed "Dashengan Temple." It would remain there for centuries, a silent witness to the turbulent succession of dynasties: the Mongol conquest of the Jin, the Ming overthrow of the Mongols, and the Manchu conquest of the Ming. Throughout this time, the statue continued to receive imperial patronage, though its location changed several times. In 1665, the Kangxi Emperor moved it to the newly built Hongren Temple. In 1900, the temple was used as a base by the Boxers and was burned to the ground by the invading Eight-Nation Alliance. The original Sandalwood Image vanished in the blaze. While its fate is uncertain, some evidence suggests it was taken to Russia and may now reside in the Egituysky Datsan in Buryatia. The Kangxi Emperor once wrote of it: "This luminous, sacred image, born in the West and transmitted to the Central Kingdom, has remained bright, pure, and eternal through all the ages." Tragically, this great embodiment of the Buddha is no longer in China—a profound and lamentable loss.

The original Sandalwood Image arrived in China via the overland Silk Road, profoundly influencing Chinese Buddhism. Centuries later, a replica made by artisans in Zhejiang was carried to Japan along the Maritime Silk Road, where it had an equally profound impact on Japanese Buddhism. The story of the Seiryō-ji Śākyamuni thus encapsulates the intertwined histories of these two great channels of cultural exchange. It also stands as a powerful testament to the pivotal role Zhejiang played as a hub on the historic Maritime Silk Road.

Chapter 12. The Remarkable Overseas Journey of Southern Song Buddhist Paintings from Zhejiang

12.1 The Five Hundred Arhats of Daitoku-ji

In 1894, as the First Sino-Japanese War erupted on the western shores of the Pacific, the moribund Qing dynasty teetered on the brink of collapse amid the roar of cannon fire. In Ningbo, to forestall a Japanese invasion, naval mines were laid at the mouth of the Yong River. Consequently, steamships from Shanghai and other ports had to anchor offshore beyond the Zhenhai Estuary, forcing all cargo and passengers to rely on small wooden boats to reach land—a scene of utter chaos. Yet across the Pacific, in the United States, that very same year witnessed an event of profound cultural significance. Under the masterful curation of the American scholar Ernest Francisco Fenollosa (1853–1908), forty-four scrolls from the Five Hundred Arhats series were unveiled at the Museum of Fine Arts, Boston. Fenollosa, a leading expert on Japanese art history, a former professor at Tokyo University, and the inaugural curator of the MFA's Japanese Art Department, wrote in his introduction to the exhibition: "Such a monument of early Chinese religious art is of a type which can rarely, if ever, be seen in the West, either in its subject or in its execution. Indeed, there is no other series of Buddhist paintings of its class in any other part of the world." The following year, the exhibition traveled to the Pennsylvania Academy of the Fine Arts in Philadelphia and the Century Association in New York.

At the time, Bernard Berenson (1865–1959), the preeminent American authority on Western art history, viewed the Five Hundred Arhats with the collector Denman Waldo Ross (1853–1935), guided by Fenollosa himself. The encounter was an epiphany. In a letter to his fiancée dated October 26th, 1894, Berenson effused: "They have revealed a new world to me. For design, for subtility and perfection of puro-linear expression, they are on a level with the best that Europe has to show... as full of compassion and love as the most moving passages in the Gospels... I was prostrate with admiration. Fenollosa trembled with excitement, I was ready to squirm with delight and Ross was jumping about. We wept and we pinched each other to be sure we were not dreaming. I have never had a greater art-experience."

The paintings that so enthralled Fenollosa, Berenson, and their circle were the work of two Southern Song artists from Ningbo, Zhou Jichang and Lin Tinggui. The complete set comprised one hundred scrolls, each depicting five arhats. Originally enshrined in the Hui'an Cloister, a Buddhist monastery beside Dongqian Lake, the scrolls eventually made their way to Japan, though the history of their journey is shrouded in mystery. One long-standing theory, favored by Fenollosa, points to the eminent monk Lanxi Daolong, who sailed from Ningbo to Japan in 1246 after a long residency at Tiantong Temple. A more recent hypothesis, advanced by the Japanese scholar Kondō Kazunari, suggests another monk, Wuxue Zuyuan, is the more likely bearer.

A native of Xiangfeng Township in Yin County, Wuxue Zuyuan once served as abbot of Baiyun Yanxiang Temple, also near Dongqian Lake and not far from the Hui'an Cloister. After traveling to Hangzhou and Wenzhou, Zuyuan was residing at Tiantong Temple when the Southern Song dynasty fell. In 1279, he departed a war-torn Ningbo for Japan, first living at Kenchō-ji in Kamakura before becoming the founding abbot of Engaku-ji. Kondō theorizes that as Zuyuan prepared to leave, the precious scrolls were entrusted to him for safekeeping from the ravages of war. As this view is not yet substantiated by historical records, the precise story of how the Five Hundred Arhats were transmitted from Ningbo to Japan remains an open question.

According to Japanese records, what is known of the scrolls' provenance is that after arriving in Japan, they were first housed at either Kenchō-ji or Jufuku-ji. During the Warring States period, they came into the possession of the powerful Hōjō clan of Odawara and were stored at Zuisen-ji. After Toyotomi Hideyoshi defeated the Hojo clan in 1590, he brought the scrolls to Kyoto, initially placing them in Hōkō-ji before they were ultimately donated to Daitoku-ji. Six of the original scrolls were lost over the centuries; the Japanese painter Kimura Tokuō created replacements in 1638. By 1894, Daitoku-ji had fallen into disrepair and, unable to raise funds domestically, arranged through Fenollosa and with the approval of the Japanese government to send forty-four original scrolls to the Museum of Fine Arts, Boston for exhibition. Afterward, the museum and the collector Denman Waldo Ross each purchased five scrolls for $1,000 apiece. Ross later gifted his acquisitions to the MFA, bringing its total holdings to ten. In gratitude for his efforts, Japanese art dealers also presented Fenollosa with the scroll Arhats Washing, which he later sold to the American industrialist and collector Charles Lang Freer (1854–1919). In 1907, Freer acquired another scroll from the series in Tokyo, The Stone Bridge on Mount Tiantai. Both paintings were eventually bequeathed to the Freer Gallery of Art in Washington, D.C., where these two masterpieces by the Southern Song Ningbo artists became cornerstones of the collection. Today, Daitoku-ji holds 82 of the original scrolls. As all 94 extant original works were once part of the Daitoku-ji collection, scholars refer to them collectively as the "Daitoku-ji Five Hundred Arhats." To distinguish the various holdings, a cataloguing system is used: the 84 scrolls at Daitoku-ji (82 originals and 2 of the later replacements) are designated with a 'D,' the 10 at the MFA with a 'B,' and the Freer's The Stone Bridge on Mount Tiantai and Arhats Washing are designated F1 and F2, respectively.

Fenollosa was a pioneer in the study of the Daitoku-ji Arhats, laying the foundation for future scholarship. Berenson, the Renaissance expert, developed a profound interest in Chinese art after his encounter with the scrolls, undertaking comparative studies with Western painting that explored the shared spiritual pursuits of Eastern and Western cultures. In 1931, the Swedish scholar Osvald Sirén (1879–1966), already famous for his work on Renaissance art, viewed the paintings at the MFA with Denman Ross. He was so profoundly struck by the experience that he redirected his research to Chinese art history, a field in which his achievements were so monumental that he came to be hailed as an "encyclopedic expert on Chinese art history" and "the most comprehensive Western scholar of Chinese painting after World War II." In 1956, Wen Fong of Princeton University completed his doctoral dissertation, The Five Hundred Arhats at Daitoku-ji, elevating the study of these paintings to a new level of scholarly rigor.

Extensive research has confirmed that the Daitoku-ji Arhats were financed by numerous devout patrons, with details recorded in gold-ink inscriptions on some of the scrolls. Time has taken its toll, and today only forty-eight inscriptions remain legible. Written in a relatively standard format, they meticulously list the patron's name, residence, purpose of the donation, and date. The place of dedication is invariably the Hui'an Cloister, the artists are always Zhou Jichang or Lin Tinggui, and a monk named Yishao is always mentioned as the project organizer. For instance, the inscription on the Freer Gallery's The Stone Bridge on Mount Tiantai reads: "The wife of Gu Chunnian, Lady Sun the Twenty-eighth, and her entire family, residing in Beicangxia Hamlet, Cangmen Village, Xiangfeng Township, donated funds to have this painted for permanent enshrinement in the Hui'an Cloister, for the merit of protecting the family. Inscribed by the fund-raising monk Yishao in the wuxu year, the fifth year of the Chunxi reign. Painted by Zhou Jichang." The inscription on the MFA's Giving Food to Hungry Ghosts reads: "Painted by Lin Tinggui. The female disciple Zhang, with the Dharma name Faxi, from Baihuqiao Hamlet, Chicheng Village, Wanling Township, offered funds to have this painted for permanent enshrinement in the Hui'an Cloister, for the merit of the complete fulfillment of her wishes. Inscribed by the fundraising monk Yishao on the [...] day of the eighth month of the fifth year of the Chunxi reign ."

Arhats Washing Clothes from the "Five Hundred Arhats" series, Freer Gallery of Art, Washington D.C.

Cangmen Village in Xiangfeng Township was located west of Dongqian Lake. The place name Baihuqiao (White Falcon Bridge) is still in use today; it was here that Japanese invading forces surrendered to the Chinese army at the end of the War of Resistance against Japanese Aggression (1937–1945). The Hui'an Cloister was a monastery at the foot of Mount Yangtang, northwest of Dongqian Lake. Founded in AD 938 during the Later Jin dynasty, it was also known as the Arhat Cloister in the Southern Song, as legend held that sixteen arhats had once appeared on the summit of Mount Yangtang during the Tang dynasty. The term gānsēng refers to the fundraising monk responsible for soliciting donations. The fifth year of the Chunxi reign (wuxu) corresponds to 1178. We can thus deduce that in this year, with a donation from Gu Chunnian and his wife Lady Sun of Xiangfeng Township, the artist Zhou Jichang painted The Stone Bridge on Mount Tiantai. The artist of Giving Food to Hungry Ghosts was Lin Tinggui, and the patron was a lay Buddhist woman surnamed Zhang from the Baihuqiao area; "Faxi" (Dharma Joy) was likely her Dharma name. All these paintings were dedicated to the Hui'an Cloister, and the fundraising for the entire project was managed by one of its monks, Yishao.

By studying the forty-eight legible inscriptions, Japanese scholars determined that for a decade beginning in 1178, the monk Yishao tirelessly solicited donations for the Five Hundred Arhats project. The patrons were primarily devout men and women from the communities surrounding Dongqian Lake, with Xiangfeng Township contributing the most—funds for fifteen scrolls. Donations also came from the townships of Fengle, Yangtang, and Wanling. The patrons came from all walks of life: some were single women, such as Lady Cai the 102nd, Lady Xie the 20th, and Lady Li the 30th; many were couples, like Chen Shike and his wife Bi Baishou, Ye Wenyi and his wife Gu Bainiang, Gu Runeng and his wife Lady Zhang Wanyi, Gu Ruxian and his wife Lady Lu, and Wo Jingman and his wife Lady Zhang the 8th; others were mothers and sons, like Lady Ye the 27th and her son Bao Anli; still others were groups of men, like the brothers Shi Congxiang, Shi Congzhi, and Shi Congxiu, and their nephew Shi Jingmao. The most common motivations for these donations were for "the complete fulfillment of wishes through merit" and "the protection and peace of the family through merit," with some also inscribed for "adornment with blessings and longevity" or "the safeguarding of one's position." Many donations were explicitly for the salvation of deceased relatives: the widow Lady Qi the 106th prayed for her late husband, Attendant Huang Qisan, to ascend to the Pure Land; the three brothers Zhu Yunsong, Zhu Yunping, and Zhu Yunxi commissioned a work for the soul of their mother, Lady Hu Xiba (Dharma name Jiexiu); and the brothers Gu Renrui and Gu Rencong made a donation in memory of their deceased father, Assistant Instructor Gu Xishiba, and mother, Lady Wang the 43rd. Other commissions were made to pray for a son or for recovery from illness, as in the case of Lady Chen the 99th and her son Miao Jingqi, who sought a swift recovery from a "wind illness," an affliction likely akin to a stroke or paralysis.

Initially, the patrons of the Daitoku-ji Arhats were all residents of the area around Ningbo's Dongqian Lake. However, beginning in 1184, the donor base expanded beyond Zhejiang province to include residents of Huating County in Xiuzhou (modern Songjiang, Shanghai), Pingjiang Prefecture (modern Suzhou), and Jinghai County in Tongzhou (modern Nantong). For example, the patron of the MFA's Giving Alms to the Poor, Gao Zhiwen, was a native of Jinghai County but resided in Pingjiang Prefecture; he commissioned the work in 1184 in memory of his grandparents and father. The MFA's Arhats Crossing the Water was funded by the family of Gu Li from Huating County and was painted in the first month of 1188. In both cases, the artist was Zhou Jichang and the fundraiser was Yishao. Some scholars have posited that Yishao ventured into the regions of modern-day Jiangsu and Shanghai because local financial support had been exhausted after years of donations. The present author, however, believes the appearance of these non-local patrons was more likely due to happenstance—perhaps a personal connection Yishao had in those areas—rather than a depletion of local resources. If Yishao had truly needed to cast a wider net for funds, one would expect to see patrons from other affluent parts of Zhejiang, such as the capital Hangzhou, which are conspicuously absent from the inscriptions.

The scholar Kondō Kazunari discovered that several patrons noted their official titles. For instance, the Freer Gallery's Arhats Washing was donated by "Gentleman for Service" (jiangshilang) Chen Jingying and his wife. Other examples include the aforementioned "Attendant" (yuanwai) Huang Qisan and "Assistant Instructor" (zhujiao) Gu Xishiba. As Kondō points out, jiangshilang was the lowest-ranking official title in the Southern Song, carrying no actual duties, and was likely obtained through hereditary privilege. Similarly, Huang Qisan probably inherited the honorific "Attendant" from an ancestor who had been a Vice Director (yuanwailang). Gu Xishiba likely received the nominal title of "Assistant Instructor" through a special "grace examination" (tezouming) after multiple failures in the standard civil service examinations. In summary, the patron list for the Daitoku-ji Arhats includes only low-ranking officials with no real power; no mid- or high-ranking officials who passed the regular examinations are found, though their ancestors may have held such positions. These patrons were, in effect, the local elite of the Dongqian Lake region. It is particularly noteworthy that of the 48 inscribed paintings, 10 were donated by the Gu clan of Xiangfeng Township. The donor of Goats Offering (D33), in the Daitoku-ji collection, is identified as "Gu Rensheng, Gentleman for rendering service, military patrol of post stations for Guangde commandery of the new Ningguo prefecture." According to other historical records, this same Gu Rensheng was officially commended for his meritorious work in dredging Dongqian Lake. Some scholars thus argue that the Gu clan controlled the lake's water management and that the painting project was intended to support this dredging work. Other scholars believe that by commissioning the paintings, people sought both to honor the souls of deceased relatives and to pray to the arhats for favorable weather and bountiful harvests in the region.

The painting of the Daitoku-ji Five Hundred Arhats began in 1178. In that same year, Shi Hao (1106–1194), a native of Yin County and a powerful minister of the Southern Song court, founded Yuebo Temple about one li (roughly 500 meters) from the Hui'an Cloister. Some Japanese scholars have proposed that Shi Hao used both temples as centers to publicly hold Water-Land Dharma Assemblies (Shuilù Fǎhuì), using rituals for the souls of the war dead to express his political opposition to launching a major military campaign against the Jin dynasty. In this view, the Five Hundred Arhats were hung at these assemblies, making Shi Hao the secret patron of the project. The MFA's Guanyin in an Earthly Manifestation has become a focal point of this theory. In this painting, the figure seated on a chair is the monk Baozhi (AD 418–514), an incarnate arhat. According to legend, Emperor Wu of Liang (AD 464–549) once asked the most outstanding painter of his time, Zhang Sengyou, to paint Baozhi's portrait. Baozhi asked Zhang, "Do you wish to paint my physical form or my Dharma form?" Zhang replied, "I wish to paint your Dharma form." Baozhi then tore the flesh from his face to reveal the "wondrously beautiful" true face of Guanyin, leaving the artist unable to begin. The scholar Ide Seinosuke interprets the tall, dark-bearded elder holding an incense burner before Baozhi as Shi Hao; the black-robed monk with hands clasped in prayer behind Shi Hao as the fund-raiser Yishao; and of the two men conversing in front of Yishao, the elder holding a brush is Lin Tinggui, while the one holding a board is Zhou Jichang.

Manifestation of Guanyin from the "Five Hundred Arhats" series, Museum of Fine Arts, Boston

However, a growing number of scholars now believe that the Daitoku-ji Arhats are unrelated to Shi Hao, and they have proposed different interpretations of the figures. In the case of Guanyin in an Earthly Manifestation, for example, some scholars believe the dark-bearded elder before Baozhi is not Shi Hao but Master Fu (Fu Xi), a famous lay Buddhist from Yiwu during the Southern Dynasties period who was regarded by later generations as an incarnation of the bodhisattva Maitreya. In this interpretation, the figure holding the brush is the artist Zhang Sengyou, and the one with the board is Emperor Wu of Liang. Still others believe the figure with the brush is Emperor Wu, while the one with the board is Zhang Sengyou, its blankness signifying his inability to paint in the face of Baozhi's true Guanyin form. In short, scholars have not yet reached a consensus on the identities of the figures in this pivotal painting.

12.2 Arhat Veneration and the Legends of Mount Tiantai

According to recent scholarship, the Five Hundred Arhats paintings from Daitoku-ji were not created to be hung at Water-Land Dharma Assemblies but are instead connected to the veneration of arhats centered on Mount Tiantai. The word luohan is the Chinese transliteration of the Sanskrit Arhat and refers to a disciple of the Buddha Shakyamuni. During the Tang and Song dynasties, arhats were venerated in various groupings, including sixteen, eighteen, and five hundred. Puji Temple in Cixi even housed 516 arhat statues during the Northern Song. Although Buddhism originated in India, and the lives of the arhats initially had no connection to

Zhejiang province, the religion underwent a gradual process of localization after its introduction to China. It was through this process that the belief arose that Mount Tiantai in Zhejiang was the earthly dwelling place of the arhats—a tradition that originates with an eminent monk of the Eastern Jin dynasty named Tanyou.

During the Southern Liang dynasty (AD 502–557), the Buddhist scholar Huijiao (AD 497–554) of Shangyu, Zhejiang, wrote a foundational work of Buddhist history, the Biographies of Eminent Monks (Gaoseng Zhuan). This work records that Tanyou was a native of Dunhuang who studied the Dharma from a young age. Tanyou spent most of his life in Zhejiang, however, leaving behind many relics and legends. In Ninghai County, a place called Fengcha Mountain (Maple Raft Mountain) is said to be where Tanyou arrived by sea on a maple-wood raft (cha), which he cast aside upon landing, giving the ridge its name. The origin of the "Wind Cave" on Haiyou Ridge is similar: one sweltering summer, Tanyou was passing by and, feeling the heat, used his iron staff to carve a cave in the rock to catch a cool breeze. In the first year of the Yixi era of the Eastern Jin (AD 405), Tanyou arrived in what is now Gangtou Village. There, he struck the ground with his staff to open a spring and then founded a monastery, which came to be known as Shouning Temple and still stands today. Some legends also portray Tanyou as a gifted physician whose specialty was to cure illness by washing a living person's intestines to expel impurities. Next to Shouning Temple, there is a "Gut-Washing Well," and another such well and a "Gut-

Drying Rock" on Mount Tiantai are also said to be places where Tanyou practiced his healing arts.

Tanyou later traveled to Mount Tiantai and practiced asceticism in a cave. Though ferocious tigers and giant serpents constantly tried to frighten him, he remained steadfast, peacefully continuing his cultivation. Tanyou eventually ascended the mountain and came to the edge of the Stone Bridge. Also known as the Stone Girder (Shiliang), it is a natural monolith that stretches like a bridge across a steep gorge, with a waterfall cascading down the cliffs below. The Song-dynasty scholar Luo Shi (1029–1101) of Ninghai captured this in his verse: "A flying waterfall severs the cliff path; a natural stone resembles a girder." As early as the Northern and Southern Dynasties (AD 420–589), it was rumored that a hermitage of divine monks lay on the other side. But

Tiantai Stone Bridge (Shiliang)

because the narrow bridge was extremely treacherous and covered in slippery moss, no one had ever managed to cross it. When Tanyou reached the edge of the bridge, a voice from the sky declared, "I know you are a devout and sincere believer, but you cannot be allowed to cross this bridge now. Go back, and return in ten years." Hearing this, Tanyou was filled with sorrow and disappointment. He spent the night on the mountain, and in a dreamlike state, he heard the faint sound of Sanskrit chanting from a Buddhist service. The next morning, Tanyou set out for the Stone Bridge again but was met on the path by an old man with a white beard and eyebrows. "Why do you risk your life to go to the Stone Bridge?" the man asked. "I am the spirit of this mountain, and I am telling you not to go." Tanyou had no choice but to turn back, though his heart was heavy with regret. He then spent several days purifying his body and mind with sincere fasting and prayers before returning to the bridge once more. Suddenly, a small path materialized on the stone, allowing him to walk across. On the other side, he not only met the legendary divine monks but also joined them in their hermitage, where they burned incense and shared a meal. Afterward, the monks told him, "You cannot stay here yet. In ten years, you will naturally return." So Tanyou crossed back over the bridge. When he turned to look, he saw that the bridge had returned to its original state and the path had vanished.

While Tanyou was active in the Taizhou region, on the south side of Mount Tiantai, a monk from the Western Regions named Bosengguang was active in the area of Shan County, to the north. His surname, Bo, which can also be rendered as Bai, was a royal surname in the Western Regions, and many monks from that area adopted it. This Bosengguang was also a miraculous figure. Legend holds that upon his arrival, he lived in a remote cave. Local mountain spirits took the form of ferocious tigers and giant serpents to intimidate him, but he was fearless. He not only established a foothold but eventually founded a monastery. Furthermore, like Tanyou, Bosengguang is said to have died in a cave, after which his body turned green and did not decay. Because Tanyou and Bosengguang shared so many similarities, their stories were gradually conflated over time.

The conflation grew even more serious when Bosengguang and Tanyou were subsequently confused with Bo Daoyou, an eminent monk of the Eastern Jin. Bo Daoyou was a native of Shanyin (modern Shaoxing) in Zhejiang, and his original surname was Feng. A poet who loved to wander in the mountains, his verse describing Mount Ruoye (present-day Mount Hua) in Shaoxing—"Linked peaks stretch a thousand li; tall forests border the wide ford"—was widely celebrated by later generations. Because the names Tanyou and Daoyou are phonetically similar, people began to conflate the three figures—Tanyou, Bosengguang, and Bo Daoyou—starting in the late Southern Dynasties. Guanding, a disciple of the Great Master Zhiyi, founder of the Tiantai school, recorded that Zhiyi was inspired to travel to Mount Tiantai after hearing that a certain "Bai Daoyou"had crossed the Stone Bridge and met the divine monks. This "Bai Daoyou" was the result of the three-way conflation. Guanding also wrote that after Zhiyi arrived at

Tiantai, he did not know a suitable place to build a monastery. One night, while staying by the Stone Bridge, three divine beings appeared and showed him the site, telling him: "If the temple (*sì*) is completed, the state (*guó*) will be pure (*qīng*); it shall be called *Guoqing Temple*." This is the origin of the name of the famous Guoqing Temple on Mount Tiantai. As the Tiantai school rose to prominence, the connection between the composite figure of Bai Daoyou and the Stone Bridge was reinforced.

By the Tang dynasty, the Stone Bridge of Mount Tiantai had become a famous landmark, a destination longed for by poets. Many celebrated writers left behind memorable lines about it, such as Meng Haoran (AD 689–740), who wrote, "You ask where I am bound? To Tiantai, to visit the Stone Bridge," and Liu Yuxi (AD 772–842), with his line, "The Qujiang monk I met at Songjiang is off again to see the Stone Bridge at Tiantai." It was during this process in the Tang dynasty that the figure of Bai Daoyou—who had evolved from Tanyou of Dunhuang—had his origins changed, becoming a monk from the "Western Regions" or "Western India" and, furthermore, becoming linked with the arhats. Around AD 825, the Daoist priest Xu Lingfu of Hangzhou completed his *Record of Mount Tiantai*, in which he mentioned that "the eminent monk Bai Daoyou from the Western Regions" had built the Zhongyan Stone Temple on Tiantai. He also separately stated that the Stone Bridge was "the place where arhats dwell." In Xu Lingfu's conception, however, Bai Daoyou and the Stone Bridge were still distinct. But in AD 832, the poet Bai Juyi (AD 772–846) completed his

Record of the Wozhou Mountain Chan Cloister, in which he wrote: “In the landscape of the southeast, Yue is the head, Shan is the face, and Wozhou and Tianmu are the eyebrows and eyes. Only in an extraordinary realm can extraordinary people dwell. Since the Jin and Song, because of the opening of mountain caves, in the beginning there dwelt the arhat monk Bai Daoyou from Western India.” He continued: “Thus Daoyou’s poem says: ‘Linked peaks stretch a thousand li; tall forests border the wide ford. The thatched huts are hidden from view; the crow of a rooster reveals that people are there.’” Here, Bai Juyi not only firmly identifies Bai Daoyou as the one who crossed the Stone Bridge but also misattributes Bo Daoyou’s poem about Mount Ruoye as a description of the Tiantai region. Bai Juyi’s *Record of the Wozhou Mountain Chan Cloister* gained widespread circulation and influence, further cementing the relationship between Bai Daoyou and the Mount Tiantai Stone Bridge.

Bai Daoyou and the arhats were originally unrelated. From Bai Juyi’s *Record of the Wozhou Mountain Chan Cloister*, however, we know that by the ninth century, Bai Daoyou had already become an arhat. By the Song dynasty, this identification was widely accepted. In the painting *Meditation in a Grotto* (B6), in the collection of the Museum of Fine Arts, Boston, Bai Daoyou is depicted draped in a red kasaya with a circular halo behind him, a symbol of his arhat status. He sits in a cave with his legs crossed in the full-lotus posture (*jié jiā fū zuò*), his hands resting naturally on his lap and his eyes closed in serene meditation. He is surrounded by treacherous, swirling currents, and a great serpent (or Nāga) with bared fangs is coiled to strike, yet he remains calm and composed, completely unperturbed.

In *the Biographies of Eminent Monks*, Huijiao states that after Tanyou crossed the Stone Bridge, he met "divine monks" and ate with them in their hermitage. In this account, neither the number of monks nor the name of the hermitage is specified. By the Song dynasty, however, the legend had acquired new details: after Bai Daoyou crossed the Stone Bridge, he came face-to-face with the Five Hundred Arhats, and their dwelling place was called Fangguang Temple. The painting The Stone Bridge on Mount Tiantai, in the collection of the Freer Gallery of Art, depicts this fully developed legend. In the painting, an arched stone bridge soars through the air above a rushing waterfall. On the bridge, Bai Daoyou, now identified as an arhat, inches cautiously forward (to the right). At the far end of the bridge, two figures emerge from the swirling mist: one is an arhat in a red kasaya, and the other is his attendant. Behind them, a magnificent temple is faintly visible. Although the characters on the temple are no longer legible, it is undoubtedly Fangguang Temple. (A privately owned Song- or Yuan-dynasty arhat painting in Japan depicts a temple with the three characters for "Fangguang Temple" clearly written.) Below the bridge, three other arhats gaze upward, their attention fixed on Bai Daoyou as he crosses, their expressions seemingly filled with concern.

Meditation in a Cave from the *"Five Hundred Arhats" series*, Museum of Fine Arts, Boston (MFA)

Stone Bridge of Tiantai Mountain, Freer Gallery of Art, Smithsonian Institution

Starting from the late Tang Dynasty, Arhat worship centered on Tiantai Mountain gradually flourished. Later, the Wuyue kings Qian Liu and Qian Hongchu organized monks to hold ceremonies venerating the Five Hundred Arhats at the Tiantai stone bridge, promoting the spread of Arhat worship. By the Song Dynasty, Arhat veneration ceremonies were extremely popular. These ceremonies, called "Arhat Offerings" (*luohan gong*), also known as "Arhat Assemblies" (*luohan hui*) or "Arhat Feasts" (*luohan zhai*), were not only widespread in monasteries but also entered many households. From emperors and generals down to commoners, people expressed diverse wishes through "Arhat Offerings" concerning this life and the next: peace under heaven, favorable weather, healing from illness and warding off disaster, family safety and health, success in imperial exams, promotion and wealth, bearing sons and safe pregnancy, longevity, happiness in the next life, salvation for the deceased... These varied aspirations reflected both people's yearning for a good life and their resignation to harsh realities.

Song Dynasty "Arhat Offering" ceremonies followed a relatively fixed set of rituals. The first step was setting up the altar and hanging Arhat paintings. Daitoku-ji's Five Hundred Arhats were originally used precisely for "Arhat Offering" ceremonies at Ningbo's East Lake Hui'an Cloister. One painting, Arhat Assembly (D1), depicts an "Arhat Offering" scene in an official's home. In the lower part of the painting, a monk holds a smoking long-handled censer, presiding over the ritual to welcome the Arhats. To his left stand two officials in formal attire, the hosts of this ceremony. One kneels in prayer, the other bows in reverence. Behind them stand two women in long robes, their family members. Interestingly, the outer woman, though joining her palms in worship, seems distracted, turning her head left to look at an infant beside her – likely the baby's mother. The green-robed woman holding the infant is probably a nurse. In the inner room (upper right of the painting), a long altar table is laden with abundant offerings. Four servants, each with their task, arrange the offerings, busy yet orderly. On the wall to the right of the altar hang paintings of Arhats. Enlarging the image reveals Arhats in various postures: some looking up, others bowing their heads in deep thought. From this painting, we can understand the basic ritual of "Arhat Offerings" in a Song Dynasty Ningbo official's household.

Assembly of Arhats (Luohán Huì), preserved at Daitoku-ji Temple (Kyoto)

Although Buddhist paintings, Daitoku-ji's Five Hundred Arhats also provide invaluable visual documentation for studying the social life of Ningbo at that time. In these paintings, we see not only Buddhist rituals but also contemporary clothing, jewelry, residences, furniture, and even details like dining manners and writing brush-holding postures. For instance, today, when writing with a pen, we use a three-finger "single sheath" grip (*dānbāo*), while using a brush requires a five-finger "double sheath" grip (*shuāngbāo*), which calligraphy teachers emphasize as fundamental. However, in the MFA's Guanyin Manifested, the elder is depicted using the three-finger "single sheath" grip to hold his brush. Thus, the Five Hundred Arhats also reflect nuances in the history of calligraphy development in eastern Zhejiang.

The "single-wrap brush grip" (*dānbāo*) depicted in *Manifestation of Guanyin* at the Museum of Fine Arts, Boston.

Particularly fascinating is the glimpse they offer into Song Dynasty Zhejiang tea customs. Zhejiang has a long history of tea drinking, but methods differed across eras. Broadly speaking, Tang Dynasty favored boiling tea (*zhǔchá*), while Song Dynasty popularized whisking tea (*diǎnchá*). Compared to modern steeping, Song Dynasty whisking was highly complex.

First, a tea cake was ground into powder using a mill and stored in a tea caddy. A tea scoop then measured the powder into a tea bowl. Finally, boiling water was poured into the bowl, and a specialized bamboo whisk (*chá-xiǎn*) was used to vigorously stir the mixture into a frothy paste before drinking. Daitoku-ji's *Preparing Tea* (D54) shows the preparatory work. In the lower left, a red-haired, fanged demon attendant in red trousers strenuously grinds tea; several tea processing tools lie before him. In the lower right, a green-clad demon attendant holding a fan has heated the stove (flames visible within), but the pot above is empty, waiting for water. He looks up eagerly towards the upper left, where a blue-clad servant fetches water, hoping he will return soon. The blue servant scoops water directly from a rushing mountain spring with a wooden dipper in his left hand, holding a water bottle in his right. Daitoku-ji's *Drinking Tea* (D56) depicts the act of drinking tea: four Arhats hold red tea stands (*tuō*) supporting black tea bowls; a youth, holding a water bottle in his left hand, pours water into one Arhat's bowl, while using a tea whisk (*cháxiǎn*) in his right hand to stir the contents. On the table behind the youth sits the tea caddy containing the powdered tea. Though the drinkers are Arhats, the scene realistically portrays the tea-drinking customs of mortals at that time.

Preparing Tea from Daitoku-ji Temple Collection

Drinking Tea from Daitoku-ji Temple Collection

Daitoku-ji's Five Hundred Arhats were transmitted to Japan during the Southern Song Dynasty. However, long before that, Japanese monks visiting China had already introduced the Tiantai stone bridge and the Five Hundred Arhats to Japan. According to Japanese scholars' statistics, throughout the Song Dynasty, at least 12 Japanese monks performed "Arhat Offerings" at the Tiantai stone bridge, including renowned figures like Jōjin (1011-1082), Eisai (1141-1215), Shunjō (1166-1227), and Dōgen (1200-1253).

Particularly noteworthy is Mujaku Jōshō (1234-1306), who not only performed offerings at the bridge but also brought the Tiantai Stone Bridge Eulogy Scroll back to Japan (See pp. 54-56 of this book). Furthermore, some Chinese monks who went to Japan also introduced Tiantai in various forms. The Wenzhou monk Daikyū Shōnen (1215-1289) wrote a preface for the Tiantai Stone Bridge Eulogy Scroll. The Fuzhou monk Seisetsu Shōchō (1274-1339), arriving in Japan during the early Yuan Dynasty, wrote the poem Stone Bridge: "A thousand-foot flying cliff spans the chasm's face,

Tiantai's stone bridge, as the sacred site of the Five Hundred Arhats, ignited the imagination of the Japanese. Even some Japanese literati who had never visited Tiantai wrote poems or painted pictures on the theme. The painter Tesshū Tokusai (?-1366) wrote this Stone Bridge poem:

"Once laid across a myriad-ren cliff,

At its firmest, toughest point, slippery as moss.

Donkeys and horses cross it routinely –

Which sentient being can swallow it?"

The literary figure Gidō Shūshin (1325-1388) wrote in Inscription on a Wall Painting of Arhats:

"Tiantai's five hundred Venerables,

Holding alms bowls, what year crossed eastward over the sea?

Once taking the wrong turning, return they cannot,

Skirting walls, clinging to cliffs, their spiritual powers lost."

Stone Bridge of Mount Tiantai by Soga Shōhaku

After their transmission to Japan, Daitoku-ji's Five Hundred Arhats from Ningbo also exerted influence on Japanese painting. Japanese artists like Kitsuzan Minchō (1352-1431), Gion Nankai (1676-1751), Soga Shōhaku (1730-1781), and Kanō Kazunobu (1816-1863) all created paintings centered on the Tiantai stone bridge theme. Traditional Japanese Noh theater also includes plays based on the stone bridge. Even in contemporary Japanese art, works featuring the stone bridge persist. Artist Satō Jun, born in Osaka in 1970, created a Stone Bridge Painting. Remarkably, some major Japanese department stores even hang stone bridge-related paintings for promotional purposes, though rendered in a modern style.

While the Tiantai Mountain stone bridge is a unique natural landscape, some Japanese temples, seeking to enhance their own status, endeavored to replicate it. At Hōkō-ji (方广寺) in Hamamatsu City, Shizuoka Prefecture, an artificial stone bridge and statues of the Five Hundred Arhats were constructed. At Nihon-ji on Mount Nokogiri in Chiba Prefecture, a stone bridge was also built, though surrounded by over 1500 Arhat statues. At Rakan-ji in Nakatsu City, Ōita Prefecture, a natural cave is called the "Stone Bridge," and entering this cave, one finds Five Hundred Arhat statues placed beneath the cliff face. These stone bridges and Arhat statues enrich the cultural significance of these temples, becoming important components of modern tourist attractions that draw numerous visitors.

"Stone Bridge" (Shakkyō) at Rakan-ji Temple, Nakatsu City

Transmitted from Zhejiang to Japan via the Maritime Silk Road, Daitoku-ji's Five Hundred Arhats have become a vital part of modern Japanese cultural heritage. In 2009, the Nara National Museum held the special exhibition "Sacred Ningbo: The Source of 1300 Years of Japanese Buddhism" and published an exhibition catalogue. This catalogue not only reproduced all 94 known paintings of Daitoku-ji's Five Hundred Arhats but also presented systematic research. The Nara National Museum, in collaboration with the Tokyo National Research Institute for Cultural Properties, conducted research on the donor inscriptions on the paintings, publishing the Research Report on the Inscriptions of Daitoku-ji's Five Hundred Arhats in 2011. In 2014, a full-color Daitoku-ji's Five Hundred Arhats was published. Thus, Daitoku-ji's Five Hundred Arhats have gained increasing academic attention.

Though renowned overseas, it is regrettable that Daitoku-ji's Five Hundred Arhats remain relatively unknown in their birthplace, Ningbo. Even those aware of them have had no opportunity to see them. From July 1st to October 7th, 2023, the "Compiling Magnificent Legacies—'China Through the Ages: Paintings and Calligraphy' Achievements Exhibition · Ningbo Special Exhibition" held at the Ningbo Art Museum displayed high-definition replicas of the 12 Five Hundred Arhats paintings held by the MFA and the Freer Gallery. This finally allowed the citizens of Ningbo to feast their eyes on the masterpieces of their ancestral painters, further inspiring their love for Ningbo. Visitors from across the country also enthusiastically traveled to Ningbo to experience its rich and diverse historical culture. The summer of 2023 in Ningbo was exceptionally hot, but the cultural wave stirred by the "Compiling Magnificent Legacies" exhibition was even more intense. This fact reminds us that the outstanding cultural heritage painstakingly created by Zhejiang's ancestors belongs not only to Zhejiang but also to the whole nation, and indeed, to the world.

Chapter 13. A Cornucopia of Foreign Goods in Zhejiang

13.1 Introduction

Through the Maritime Silk Road, Zhejiang's products kept flowing steadily to overseas markets, while a rich variety of foreign goods poured into the province from every corner of the globe.

During the Wuyue Kingdom (AD 907–978), well-established maritime routes connected Zhejiang to diverse overseas regions, facilitating the import of many foreign goods. Historical records show that large quantities of Buddhist scriptures printed on the Korean Peninsula were shipped to Zhejiang. Furthermore, excavations in 2000–2001 in the crypt of Leifeng Pagoda, a structure built by Qian Hongchu (AD 929–988), the last king of Wuyue, uncovered a Japanese copper coin, the Jōeki Shinpō, first minted in AD 859. The kingdom's connections also extended to the Arabian Peninsula. In AD 919, a Wuyue naval fleet of over 500 warships, led by the founding king Qian Liu, decisively defeated the rival Wu Kingdom at the Battle of Langshan River. A key factor in this triumph was a formidable new weapon acquired from the Arab world: an incendiary system that used an "iron tube"

The Japanese copper coin "Jōyaku-shinhō" excavated from the Leifeng Pagoda underground palace in Hangzhou.

to launch "fire oil" (huǒyóu), a petroleum-based mixture that incinerated enemy ships. This weapon was none other than the famed "Greek Fire" of the Mediterranean, a technology developed in the 7th-century Byzantine Empire.

Building on this dynamic foundation, Zhejiang's Maritime Silk Road would reach its zenith during the subsequent Song Dynasty (960–1279). The Baoqing Siming Zhi, a local gazetteer of Ningbo completed in 1228, meticulously documented the vast range of goods imported through the port. From the Goryeo Kingdom (Korea) came silver, ginseng, musk, safflower, poria mushroom, linen, pine nuts, pine pollen, chestnuts, dates, hazelnuts, almonds, wild ginger, licorice, saposhnikovia root, atractylodes rhizome, seaweed, mother-of-pearl inlay, feathers, lacquerware, tiger pelts, and bronze wares. From Japan came gold, mercury, deer antlers, sulfur, and various types of timber. Southeast Asia and the Indian Ocean region were the primary sources for a long list of spices and medicinal herbs—including cloves, agarwood, sandalwood, fennel, ambergris, lakawood, myrrh, and asafoetida—as well as betel nuts, coral, tortoiseshell, amber, ivory, pepper, borax, and rosewater. In 1982, an excavation of the crypt at Ningbo's Tianfeng Pagoda uncovered a cache of Southern Song artifacts imported via the Maritime Silk Road from as far as Southeast Asia and the Indian Ocean. Among them were a giant clam shell (tridacna), revered as one of the "Seven Treasures" of Buddhism, and two glass bottles containing spices, which reportedly still emitted a faint fragrance when their caps were opened.

The Baoqing Siming Zhi made special note of the superior quality of certain Japanese goods, observing that their five-colored paper was better than China's own ("that which China cannot match") and their bronze wares more refined ("bronze wares are especially finer than China's"). Japanese timber, prized for its strength and smooth finish, was considered top-grade by the Chinese, fueling a significant trade often intertwined with religious patronage. The Japanese monk Myōan Eisai (1141–1215), who lived at Ningbo's Tiantong Temple after arriving in Zhejiang in 1168, found its Thousand Buddha Pavilion dilapidated and the monastery lacking funds for repair. Upon his return to Japan, Eisai arranged for a shipment of massive logs to be sent "on a great ship across the whale-tossed waves" to Ningbo, enabling the pavilion's restoration. Decades later, in 1242, when a fire devastated Hangzhou's Jingshan Temple, a Hangzhou-born merchant based in Hakata, Japan, named Xie Guoming, shipped 1,000 planks of timber to aid the reconstruction. Japanese wood was also sought by the Song elite for crafting high-end coffins, but the cost was so exorbitant that they were beyond the reach of not only commoners but even the great writer Lu You (1125–1210).

The people of the Song dynasty called Japanese folding fans Wō shàn and prized them as rare treasures. The Song art historian Deng Chun, in his Huaji (Continuation of Painting), described them as "most exquisite" (shèn jīngmiào), with copper rings and yellow silk tassels on their handles. Their surfaces, painted with landscapes, figures, pines, bamboos, and flowers, were "also delightful" (yì kěxǐ). Even in Ningbo, a major port for Japan trade, these fans were so scarce that an official in the Maritime Trade Superintendency could only manage to acquire two. The allure of Japanese fans also sparked the imagination of poets. The Northern Song literary figure Su Zhe (1039–1112) composed a poem titled On Secretary Yang's Japanese Fan: "The fan is from Japan, yet the wind is not Japan's wind. / The wind does not issue from the fan; whence, then, does it come? / The wind itself does not know, so we must ask the vast void. / If the void is the fount of wind, it becomes one with all things. / If all things share this nature, the object is not the wind's origin. / Just hold this Japanese fan, and a wind comes from the infinite." This philosophical verse inspires boundless contemplation on the nature of the world.

Another Japanese specialty cherished by Chinese literati was the sword, also imported primarily through Ningbo. The Song poet Mei Yaochen (1002–1060) composed a poem titled On Scholar Qian Junyi's Japanese Sword. The Qian Junyi of the title was Qian Gongfu (1021–1072) of Wujin, Changzhou, who acquired a Japanese broadsword while serving as the chief administrator of Mingzhou (modern Ningbo). Mei's poem vividly describes the blade and its cultural significance:

"The Japanese broadsword gleams a fluorescent blue, / Its sharkskin-wrapped hilt speckled like stars. / From eastern shores its scabbard crossed the vast sea, / Its ship's sail furled at a bay in Yue... / The high official of

Kuaiji, newly famed, / Regrets not possessing this marvel sooner. / Returning to the Tianlu Pavilion to show his friends, / Its radiance once flashed toward the isles of Fusang. / In candlelight, demons and sprites flee its glow... / In antiquity, civil affairs required martial readiness; / Today's flowing robes are hardly worth mentioning. / The legendary blades Ganjiang and Tai'e are no more; / Let us wipe this clean, admire it together, and cast regrets aside."

Prior to the 16th century, the innumerable foreign goods that entered Zhejiang via the Maritime Silk Road were overwhelmingly rare and expensive luxuries, accessible only to the upper echelons of society: royalty, nobles, and powerful merchants. The common people had little contact with these imports; most would never see more than a few such items in their entire lives. After 1600, however, a rising tide of globalization wove Zhejiang's sea lanes into the fabric of new global shipping routes. This new epoch heralded the arrival of American crops previously unknown in China, which would go on to profoundly reshape Zhejiang's agriculture, daily life, and social customs.

Among the world's ancient civilizations, those of the Americas developed in isolation, cultivating a unique portfolio of agricultural crops. The arrival of Columbus in 1492 shattered this separation between the Eurasian and American worlds. As Europeans began the large-scale transfer of Old World products to the Americas, they also initiated the reverse flow of

American crops to Eurasia, often along established maritime trade routes. Located on the western coast of the Pacific, Zhejiang was one of the first regions in China to feel the impact of this new wave of globalization and to receive crops from the Americas. The following sections introduce several of these crops that had a monumental impact on society and daily life in Zhejiang.

13.2 The Sweet Potato

The sweet potato was a staple food for the indigenous peoples of the Americas. After Columbus's arrival in 1492 under the sponsorship of the Spanish crown, the Americas became a sphere of Spanish influence. In late 1520, Magellan's expedition rounded the southern tip of South America into the Pacific, eventually reaching Luzon (the modern Philippines). Spaniards subsequently traveled from the Americas to Luzon, establishing colonial rule there in the late 16th century and introducing the American sweet potato. Luzon had frequent and close trade relations with China, and many merchants from Fujian and Guangdong settled there. In the late 16th century, Fujianese expatriates brought the crop back to their home province for cultivation. The late-Ming historian Tan Qian (1594–1658) noted in his Zaolin Zazu that it was indeed the vines that were brought back, a claim highly credible given the plant's method of propagation.

Zhejiang was also one of the first regions in China to adopt the sweet potato, with the earliest cultivation occurring in the Zhoushan archipelago.

The 1595 Gazetteer of Mount Putuo states that the sweet potato "comes from Japan and is very sweet and delicious." This account is incorrect, as the crop was not introduced to Japan until the early 17th century. A more plausible explanation lies in the history of Shuangyu Port in Zhoushan. Between 1524 and 1548, Portuguese, Japanese, and Southeast Asian traders operated a major international smuggling hub there, defying Ming maritime bans. It was likely during this period of intense, unregulated trade that the sweet potato was transmitted from Luzon to Zhoushan, probably by Portuguese or other Southeast Asian sailors. The local chroniclers, unaware of the complex maritime networks of the era, may have mistakenly attributed the crop's origin to the Japanese merchants who were also active at the port.

After this new foreign crop arrived in Zhoushan from Luzon, local growers worked to refine its cultivation while jealously guarding their methods. Consequently, yields were low, and the sweet potato acquired an air of mystery. Li Rihua (1565–1635) of Jiaxing, Zhejiang, wrote of receiving a sweet potato from an elderly monk from Sichuan. He described it as resembling a purple radish with a sweet taste when cooked. The monk told Li that this variety grew under the rocks of Mount Putuo and was a "rare medicine in this world," so uncommon that only high-ranking monks had the chance to taste it. Li was deeply moved by the privilege of sampling it. His account reveals how unfamiliar the sweet potato remained at the time. As late as 1678, the editors of the Gazetteer of Taicang Prefecture in neighboring Jiangsu wrote, "It is said that Mount Putuo has many sweet potatoes, but unfortunately the monks are unwilling to share their cultivation methods with others."

Although Zhoushan was the first place in Zhejiang to cultivate the sweet potato, its influence on surrounding areas was limited; the crop did not even spread to the nearby mainland districts of Yinxian and Xiangshan. A second, more influential route of introduction was from the neighboring province of Fujian. In the early Kangxi reign (1662–1722), a native of Fujian brought cultivation techniques to Yinxian, resulting in a bumper harvest that first year and triggering the crop's rapid diffusion. Wenzhou's cultivation methods were also introduced from Fujian. By the early 18th century, having arrived in Zhejiang's coastal regions via several pathways, the sweet potato had become a major crop. The 1758 Gazetteer of Xiangshan County offers a description: "The sweet potato can be planted in barren soil and sand. It can be eaten raw or cooked and is beneficial to people... The method is to plant one tuber, cut its vines, plant the cuttings horizontally, and cover them with ash. Each segment will then take root and sprout, thus propagating abundantly." This passage shows that cultivation techniques were already quite sophisticated by this time.

In the early Qing dynasty, sweet potatoes were grown mainly along Zhejiang's coast and were rarely seen inland. Beginning in the late 18th century, cultivation spread throughout the province, driven largely by migrants from coastal areas like Wenzhou and Taizhou moving inland to reclaim and farm hilly land. Local gazetteers reflect this trend. The 1829 Gazetteer of Wukang County notes, "Sweet potatoes, now established and planted by people from Wenzhou, were formerly unknown here." The 1873 Gazetteer of Anji County states, "Our county had no sweet potatoes until settlers from Wenzhou and Taizhou came to reclaim the hillsides and began to plant this crop." By the late 19th century, sweet potatoes were even widely grown in the Hangjiahu Plain, a traditional center of rice production. The 1892 Gazetteer of Jiashan County reports, "Sweet potatoes are now widely planted by migrants from Wenzhou and Taizhou residing in the county." As recorded in the *Jiaxing County Chronicle* of 1897: "The sweet potato is now widely cultivated by those reclaiming wasteland in Wenzhou and Taizhou." From the late Qing period onward, the sweet potato became a staple food for the people of Zhejiang.

The widespread cultivation of the sweet potato provided a vital new food source for Zhejiang, a province with limited arable land but abundant hills, thereby creating the material conditions for significant population growth. It also spurred the development of related side businesses and handicrafts. People processed sweet potatoes into dried strips, brewed them into alcohol, ground them into flour, and made them into snacks like chips. In eras of scarcity, the sweet potato was not only a lifesaving food but also a rare source of pleasure. Furthermore, because the tubers and vines served as excellent fodder for pigs, cattle, and sheep, their cultivation boosted animal husbandry. To process the crop, people invented tools like specialized slicers and graters, which in turn stimulated the growth of related crafts. While it was hailed as a sweet "miracle medicine" upon its introduction, consuming it as a staple over long periods was found to cause bloating and digestive discomfort.

Since the era of Reform and Opening-Up began, the rapid rise in living standards has seen the sweet potato transition from a staple food to an occasional delicacy. Thus, this American crop, introduced to Zhejiang via the Maritime Silk Road, became deeply woven into the province's history, its story reflecting both periods of hardship and moments of triumph.

13.3 The Chili Pepper

In ancient and medieval Europe, Asian spices like black pepper were highly coveted necessities. In 1453, the Ottoman Empire captured Constantinople, a pivotal crossroads between East and West, and seized control of the main trade routes. This caused the price of spices in European markets to skyrocket, compelling Europeans to seek new sea routes to Asia for its riches. On October 12th, 1492, Columbus completed his first transatlantic voyage and landed in the Americas. He was thrilled to discover a type of "pepper" with an "extremely pungent taste," which he brought back to Europe, promoting it as a "healthful" food. In fact, what Columbus had found was not true pepper (Piper nigrum) but the American chili pepper (Capsicum), a plant previously unknown in Europe.

After their introduction to Europe, chili peppers were brought to India by the Portuguese in the early 16th century. As for their arrival in China, scholars have proposed several possible routes: overland from India to Tibet, from Burma to Yunnan, or by sea from Macau to Guangdong or from Japan via Korea. Recent research, however, suggests that chili peppers first reached China via the Maritime Silk Road, arriving in Zhejiang's Zhoushan archipelago during the period when Shuangyu Port flourished as a smuggling hub (1524–1548). This appears to be the earliest route of introduction into the country.

The earliest known Chinese reference to the chili pepper appears in Zunsheng Bajian (Eight Discourses on Nurturing Life), published in 1591 by Gao Lian, a Hangzhou native and Ming-dynasty scholar of drama, book collecting, and wellness. In this encyclopedic work on healthy living, Gao classifies flowers into three grades. He places the fanjiao (foreign pepper) in the middle grade of "excellent specimens," alongside lilies, winter jasmine, and poppies. He notes that plants in this category serve to "adorn the four seasons," indicating that chili peppers were initially grown for their aesthetic appeal, not for consumption. Gao also provides another name for the plant, dishanhu (ground coral), and accurately describes its fruit as shaped like an inverted brush tip, turning from green to red like coral as it ripens. His mention that this "ground coral" was also grown in Fengyang (in modern Anhui province) shows that the plant had already spread from Zhejiang to neighboring regions.

Throughout the late Ming Dynasty, the chili pepper remained an ornamental plant. Intriguingly, in his monograph on flowers, Huashi Zuobian, Wang Lu of Jiaxing specifically warned that the seeds of "ground coral" were "poisonous, extremely spicy, and must not be eaten." By the early Qing Dynasty, however, two major changes had occurred in Zhejiang. First, the plant became widely known as làqié (spicy eggplant), a name still commonly used by locals today. Second, it began to be used as a culinary seasoning. The 1671 Gazetteer of Shanyin County records: "Laqie is red, shaped like a water caltrop, and can be used as a substitute for pepper." Later gazetteers from the Kangxi and Qianlong reigns also adopted this name. In his 1688 horticultural treatise Huajing (Mirror of Flowers), the long-time Hangzhou resident Chen Haozi still described the chili as an ornamental, but added, "Its flavor is extremely spicy and is widely used. Ground into a fine powder, it is used in winter as a substitute for pepper."

By the 18th century, this American crop had been fully integrated into Chinese medicine. The Hangzhou physician Zhao Xuemin included the chili pepper, which he called laqie, in his 1765 medical work Bencao Gangmu Shiyi (Supplement to the Compendium of Materia Medica). Zhao noted that it was commonly grown in vegetable gardens and used as both a condiment and a medicine. From a medicinal standpoint, he classified it as "pungent, bitter, and intensely hot in nature," with the ability to "warm the body's core, move qi downward, disperse cold, eliminate dampness, relieve melancholy, clear phlegm, aid digestion, kill parasites, and detoxify." It could be used to treat "vomiting, choking, diarrhea, dysentery, and beriberi." He described various treatments, such as applying the skin or a chili paste to frostbite, or chewing the pepper and applying it to snakebites. At the same time, Zhao cautioned that because of its "hot nature and spicy flavor," over-consumption could harm the eyes, cause toothaches and a swollen throat, and aggravate hemorrhoids. This account accurately summarizes the chili's medicinal properties, therapeutic effects, and side effects, demonstrating a sophisticated understanding among physicians of the era.

13.4 Corn (Maize)

Of the world's three major staple crops, rice originated in China, wheat in West Asia, and corn (maize) in the Americas. As far back as 7,000 years ago, the Indigenous peoples of the Americas were already cultivating corn as a dietary cornerstone. When Columbus arrived in the Americas, he was deeply impressed by its sweet, delicious flavor and brought a pouch of kernels back to Spain as a gift for the king. Corn rapidly gained favor in Western Europe and from there began its gradual spread across Asia.

By the mid-16th century, corn had arrived in China through three primary routes: overland from Central Asia into the northwest, from India and its neighboring regions into the southwest, and via the Maritime Silk Road to the southeastern coast. Despite its arrival, corn was still a novelty during the Ming Dynasty. In the celebrated novel The Plum in the Golden Vase (Jin Ping Mei), which gained popularity around 1600, the opulent protagonist Ximen Qing serves cornmeal pastries as a rare delicacy to impress his honored guests. During the ensuing Qing Dynasty, corn cultivation steadily expanded, and by the 19th century, it was being planted all across the nation.

Zhejiang was one of the first regions in China to cultivate corn. The Hangzhou writer Tian Yiheng, in his work Liuqing Rizha, completed between 1567 and 1572, referred to it as yùmài, or "imperial wheat." He explained that the name derived from its status as a grain presented to the emperor for his personal use. Because it came from the West, it was also known as fānmài, or "foreign wheat." Tian also offered a precise botanical description: "Its stalk and leaves resemble millet, its tassels are like rice panicles, its ear is long and fist-like, its silks are like red velvet, and its kernels are large and glossy white, similar to those of the Gorgon fruit. The flower blooms at the top while the fruit forms at the nodes—truly a remarkable grain." He also noted, "This species has made its way to my hometown, and many people are planting it," which confirms that corn was being cultivated in the Hangzhou area by the mid-16th century.

In the late Ming and early Qing periods, however, corn cultivation in Zhejiang was limited, with few mentions in local records. Not until the mid-

18th century did the crop's cultivation spread throughout the province, a trend driven by an influx of migrants who came to farm reclaimed land. Farmers from Anhui were particularly instrumental, leasing hilly terrain in Zhejiang's mountainous regions—such as modern-day western Hangzhou, Lishui, and Quzhou—to plant corn. Encouraged by these newcomers, as well as by migrants from Fujian and Jiangsu, local farmers also learned to cultivate the crop. The local gazetteer for Xuanping County (now part of Lishui) noted that the area had no corn until the late 18th century, when "people from Anhui came to lease and reclaim the land, and the local inhabitants began to imitate them in planting it." As corn cultivation spread, its dietary importance grew. The 1787 Gazetteer of Yinxian County referred to it as liùgǔ, or the "sixth grain," signifying its ascent into the ranks of primary food crops alongside the traditional "five grains" such as rice and millet. By the 19th century, its cultivation was even more widespread. The Kaihua County gazetteer of the era noted, "In recent years, it is planted everywhere," while the Jiangshan County gazetteer stated, "It is widely planted in mountain villages." In addition to feeding people, corn proved to be excellent fodder for livestock and poultry, including cattle, sheep, pigs, chickens, ducks, and geese. A Jinhua local gazetteer lauded it in a single, powerful phrase: "Sufficient to avert famine, it benefits both humans and livestock."

Because corn was introduced to Zhejiang at different times, through various channels, and into regions with distinct dialects, it acquired a multitude of local names. Besides common terms like "imperial wheat" (yùmài), "foreign wheat" (fānmài), and "sixth grain" (liùgǔ), local gazetteers recorded many others: "encounter millet" (yùsù) in Wuyi County; "Guangdong reed" (Guǎngdōng lú) and "jade reed" (yùlú) in Tiantai County; "waist millet" (yāosù) in Shengzhou; and "Guanyin millet" (Guānyīn sù) and "deer-antler millet" (lùjiǎo shǔ) in Huzhou. These diverse names reflect the unique historical path of corn's adoption and spread across Zhejiang.

13.5 The Pumpkin

The ancient Indigenous peoples of the Americas gained extensive experience cultivating pumpkins and developed a wide array of culinary uses. They consumed both the flesh and the seeds, processed the pulp into flour, and even brewed pumpkin-based beverages. After Columbus and other explorers introduced the pumpkin to Europe, however, it was used mainly for ornamental and medicinal purposes. Only from the mid-16th century onward did it become widely adopted as a food.

As Portuguese and Spanish traders arrived in Asia, they brought the pumpkin with them, and by the mid-16th century, it had reached China's coastal regions. A mention in the 1551 Gazetteer of Shanyin County confirms its early introduction to Zhejiang. The celebrated Ming physician Li Shizhen (c. 1518–1593) noted in his masterwork, Compendium of Materia Medica (Bencao Gangmu): "The pumpkin came from the nanfan (southern barbarian lands), passed into Fujian and Zhejiang, and is now also found near Yanjing (Beijing)." Though Li's understanding of its origins was vague, his account reflects its introduction to China via the Maritime Silk Road, with Zhejiang as one of the earliest entry points. The crop spread so quickly that it reached the Beijing area in less than fifty years. Li himself was quite familiar with its characteristics, noting that "its flesh is thick and yellow, and cannot be eaten raw." He added that when cooked, its flavor resembled that of Chinese yam, tasted even better with pork, and could also be fried with honey.

As one of the first regions to adopt the pumpkin and a province where it was widely cultivated, Zhejiang's Ming-era local gazetteers are rich with information about the crop; one scholarly count found 21 distinct references. These records show that pumpkins entered Zhejiang through several routes. For example, Wenzhou's pumpkins were introduced mainly from Fujian, while those in the plains of northern Zhejiang arrived either directly from overseas or by way of Jiangsu. The pumpkin also went by various names. A local text from Huzhou, written during the Kangxi reign, explains: "Fānguā ('foreign melon'), also known as nánguā ('southern melon'), is said to have come from foreign lands. Poor families use it as a substitute for rice, so it is commonly called fànguā ('meal melon')."

Over time, the people of Zhejiang developed various methods for preparing pumpkin and integrated this foreign crop with local ingredients to create distinctive new dishes. By the mid-16th century, residents of Shaoxing were already cooking with it. In the late 17th century, people around Hangzhou were mixing pumpkin with flour to make cakes and had observed that summer-ripened pumpkins had the best flavor, followed by those from the autumn harvest. The 1874 Gazetteer of Huzhou Prefecture summarized several preparation methods: pumpkin could be boiled, stir-fried, mixed with rice flour to make balls, or combined with wheat flour and deep-fried into a dish called fangua tianji, or "foreign melon frogs."

One particularly interesting account comes from the early Qing scholar Gao Shiqi of Hangzhou (1645–1703). In his botanical work Beishu Baoweng Lu, he described a gourmet recipe, advising that older pumpkins were best. He suggested cooking them in the same style as red-braised pork: using very little water and steaming them slowly over a low fire until completely tender. This method, he promised, would yield a flavor that was "sweet, rich, and extremely fragrant." This was, of course, a refined preparation method befitting a member of the social elite like Gao. For the common people, the pumpkin was a fundamental food that could fill an empty stomach. A Ming-era Zhejiang gazetteer noted it was called fànguā ("meal melon") because it was "easy to feel full after eating." Even in Huzhou, a region famed as a "land of fish and rice," local records stated, "Poor families use it as a substitute for rice, so it is commonly known as 'meal melon.'" It became a lifesaving crop during famines. As early as the Kangxi reign, residents of Dongyang were processing pumpkin into dried strips to store for lean years. Throughout Zhejiang's long and arduous history, countless people survived by substituting pumpkin for grain. After its introduction, the pumpkin also became an ideal feed for pigs, a use explicitly recorded in the 1681 Gazetteer of Dongyang County.

After the pumpkin's introduction, physicians in Zhejiang also discovered its medicinal value. They observed that while the stems of most melons detach upon ripening, the pumpkin's stem remains "firmly attached." This led to the stem being regarded as an effective remedy for preventing miscarriage. Zhao Xuemin's Supplements to the Compendium of Materia Medica (Bencao Gangmu Shiyi) includes a recipe for a "Miraculous Decoction" made from pumpkin stem. The simple method involved boiling the stem with an ox's nose and consuming the broth, which was said to ensure the fetus would "never abort." Zhao also offered a theoretical explanation based on traditional Chinese medicine: a fetus is "nourished by the liver's blood," and because the pumpkin "is yellow in color and sweet in flavor, it contains the essence of the central Spleen-Earth element, which can generate liver qi and enrich liver blood, thus making it effective for protecting a pregnancy." The Supplements to the Compendium of Materia Medica also recorded pumpkin pulp as a medicine. Zhao Xuemin described it as an excellent remedy for scalds and burns. The method was to seal the pulp and seeds in a jar during the heat of the sixth lunar month. If someone suffered a burn, the pulp could be applied to the wound to provide pain relief that was "as effective as magic." In some areas today, pumpkin pulp is still used as a folk remedy for burns.

The pumpkin also provided creative inspiration for Zhejiang's artists. In his Guochao Huazheng Lu, completed in the first half of the 18th century, the Jiaxing scholar Zhang Geng mentioned a "Pumpkin Painting." Another Qing scholar from Jiaxing, Zhu Yizun (1629–1709), penned a poem titled Inscription on an Ink Wash Painting of a Pumpkin: "Trailing tendrils, climbing vines, untended in the wild. / A flower peeks from under a thatched eave, / And soon green and yellow fruits pile high. / This year grain is dear and the people starve, / In every village, they have stripped the elm bark bare. / Let this grant the old farmer a full belly, / And his whole family, wife and children, will beam with joy." Believed to be the earliest known ode to the pumpkin, this poem highlights the crop's crucial role during famines and the simple happiness it brought to common people.

Virtually every part of the pumpkin is a treasure: the leaves serve as pig feed, the flesh as food, the stem as medicine, and the seeds as a delightful snack. Although it is unclear when people in Zhejiang began roasting pumpkin seeds, written records of the practice appear by the 19th century. The 1874 Gazetteer of Huzhou Prefecture notes that pumpkin seeds "can also be roasted and eaten as a snack." Some scholars believe this may be the earliest reference to roasted pumpkin seeds in Chinese literature. Shortly after, the 1906 Gazetteer of Fuyang County also states that pumpkin seeds "are also edible."

Today, roasted pumpkin seeds are a common snack for people across

Zhejiang during holidays and leisure time, often enjoyed alongside peanuts and sunflower seeds. Peanuts and sunflowers are, in fact, also American crops introduced via the Maritime Silk Road. Peanuts are recorded in a 1608 local gazetteer from Xianju County, while Chen Haozi provided an accurate description of the sunflower in his Huajing (Mirror of Flowers). Other American crops that arrived in Zhejiang by the same route include potatoes, tomatoes, green beans, pineapples, and jicama. It is easy to imagine how much less varied our cuisine would be without them. Without peanuts, pumpkin seeds, and sunflower seeds, our festivities and leisure time would lose much of their flavor. Finally, any discussion of the impact of American crops on daily life must include tobacco.

13.6 Tobacco

Quan Zuwang (1705–1755), a distinguished representative of Zhejiang culture during the Qing Dynasty, once wrote the Ode to Danbagu. In this long poem, he expressed his bewilderment over a plant called danbagu that had suddenly become popular everywhere. No one seemed to know its origins, and no mention of it could be found in any existing literature. Quan himself speculated that “Danba” might be a small country near Luzon (the modern-day Philippines). In reality, danbagu was not a place, but a phonetic transliteration of a foreign word like “tobacco”—the very plant we know by that name today.

Archaeological research shows that the Indigenous peoples of the

Americas were using tobacco more than 10,000 years ago. They used it in various forms—as a powder, decoction, juice, or paste—and consumed it as food or drink, or by chewing, licking, sniffing, or smoking. They also discovered its analgesic properties, using it to treat ailments like toothaches and earaches. The word "tobacco" derives from a Caribbean indigenous language, though its original meaning is debated: some believe it referred to a roll of tobacco leaves (a cigar), while others think it meant a smoking pipe. Tobacco also featured prominently in Native American mythology and art.

Just days after Columbus first reached the Americas in 1492, his crew members were astonished to find villagers—both men and women—lighting and smoking the leaves of a strange plant. During the 16th century, Europeans carried tobacco across the Atlantic from the Americas to Europe, and simultaneously across the Pacific to Asian ports like Luzon in the Philippines. In this way, tobacco spread rapidly around the globe.

Tobacco was first brought to China around 1600 by people from Fujian returning from Luzon. From Fujian, it spread to the neighboring provinces of Guangdong and Zhejiang, acquiring a variety of phonetically similar names, such as danbagu, danbugui, and damubagu. Though written with different characters, their sounds all trace back to the Native American word "tobacco," providing linguistic evidence of its introduction via the Maritime Silk Road. Of course, literary figures with a fondness for tobacco also gave it more elegant names, like "fragrant grass" (fencao), "benevolent grass" (rencao), "lovesickness grass" (xiangsi cao), and "soul-reviving smoke" (fanhun yan). There was even the provocative moniker, "the grass that infuriates famous doctors" (qisi mingyi cao). China's first specialized treatise on tobacco, titled Record of Golden Silk (Jinsi Lu), was written by Wang Shihan (1707–1780), a native of Hangzhou.

After its introduction to Zhejiang, tobacco spread through urban and rural areas with incredible speed. The late-Ming, early-Qing scholar Zhang Dai (1597–1689) of Shaoxing wrote in his Dream Recollections of Tao'an: "When I was a child, I did not know what tobacco was, but within ten years, everyone—old and young, children and women—was smoking; tobacco stalls lined every major street and small alley." Quan Zuwang himself was an avid smoker who, in his Ode to Danbagu, favorably compared tobacco to wine and tea: "To relieve sorrow, there is wine; to quench thirst, there is tea. What completes this trio? Tobacco is best of all." In Quan Zuwang's view, tobacco was profoundly versatile: "It can make the sober drunk and the drunk sober, so it is perfect for lovers of wine. It can make the hungry feel full and the full feel hungry, making it a friend to the stomach. It can make the idle feel busy and the busy feel idle, rendering it an ideal daily companion." For these reasons, he argued, "sages and eccentrics use it to express their feelings, while scholars and officials use it to aid their inspiration." Ultimately, it took the world by storm: "What a fine plant, that it spreads without legs, reaching every corner under Heaven."

Just as Indigenous Americans used tobacco as medicine, so too did physicians in Zhejiang during the Ming and Qing dynasties. In the Complete Works of Jingyue, by the Ming-dynasty Shaoxing physician Zhang Jingyue (1563–1640), "smoke" (tobacco) is even given its own dedicated entry. Drawing on traditional Chinese medical theory, he concluded that tobacco was "pungent in flavor, warm in qi, and slightly hot in nature." In his view, its qi "ascends to warm the heart and lungs, and descends to warm the liver, spleen, and kidneys. After use, it warms the entire body, causing slight perspiration and a sudden strengthening of the primordial yang." He believed it could treat a wide range of illnesses with remarkable speed. For external conditions, he wrote, "it excels at expelling all yin evils, cold toxins, mountain miasmas, and pathogenic wind-dampness... truly a divine remedy that works in an instant." For internal conditions, it could "strengthen stomach qi, improve appetite, dispel cold stagnation, relieve bloating... stop nausea, vomiting, and cholera... resolve depression, stop pain... and unblock the triple burner, with immediate effect." Zhang Jingyue wrote that when he first encountered tobacco, he was skeptical of its effects, but after smoking it several times, he became convinced that it truly possessed such rapid therapeutic power. However, he also cautioned that because tobacco's "nature is one of pure yang," it would have a "miraculous effect" on people with an excess of yin energy, but was unsuitable for those with an excess of yang. Some people would faint after smoking to excess, a phenomenon Zhang Jingyue called "drunkenness." He used Chinese medical theory to argue that even fainting had no negative side effects: "Its yang qi is so strong and fierce that a person cannot withstand it, and thus one becomes drunk upon inhalation. While it can disperse pathogenic evils, it must also consume qi—this is its nature. However, the tobacco's qi dissipates easily, and one's own qi quickly recovers. Its yang nature remains within and soon generates new qi. Thus, there is replenishment within its consumption, which is why so many people enjoy using it and no harm has yet been observed." This type of medical theory provided a scientific-sounding rationale that undoubtedly fueled tobacco's popularity, exacerbating the harm it caused to individual health and social stability. Like the rest of the country, Zhejiang only came to a widespread recognition of the dangers of tobacco after the era of Reform and Opening-Up, subsequently implementing gradual province-wide measures to control and prohibit smoking.

The far-reaching Maritime Silk Road connected Zhejiang to the distant Americas, enabling a great number of American crops to be introduced to the region. More importantly, these crops took root, flowered, and bore fruit in Zhejiang's soil, becoming an integral part of its society and economy while profoundly shaping the daily lives of its people. The imprint of the Maritime Silk Road can therefore be seen everywhere throughout the course of Zhejiang's historical development.

Chapter 14. The Modern Value of Zhejiang's Maritime Silk Road Culture

Located at the forefront of China's foreign relations, Zhejiang holds a pivotal place in the history of the ancient Maritime Silk Road. General Secretary Xi Jinping has hailed Ningbo—alongside ports like Quanzhou, Guangzhou, Colombo, Jeddah, and Alexandria—as a "living fossil" of this ancient route. In addition to Zhejiang, other coastal provinces and cities in China had various forms of connection to the ancient Maritime Silk Road. Like a multicolored ribbon adorning China's long coastline, each of these places displayed its own unique splendor in different historical periods. Compared to other coastal provinces and cities, Zhejiang's Maritime Silk Road exhibits five distinct characteristics:

First, Ancient Origins and a Profound Heritage.

Zhejiang is a primary cradle of China's maritime culture. As early as the prehistoric era, the ancestors of its people ventured into the ocean. China's oldest known dugout canoe and its earliest shell mound sites, both dating back 8,000 years, were discovered along the Zhejiang coast. During the subsequent Hemudu Culture (5000–3300 BC), people used simple seafaring tools to cross the ocean and visit islands like Zhoushan. The segmented stone adze, an artifact originating from the Hemudu Culture, later spread throughout the Western Pacific. This profound ancient maritime culture laid a solid cultural foundation for the later emergence of Zhejiang's Maritime Silk Road.

Second, Uninterrupted Continuity and Sustained Development.

Among the cities of China's ancient Maritime Silk Road, ports like Hepu, Dengzhou, and Yangzhou rose to prominence relatively early and were already prosperous during the Han and Tang dynasties. However, due to natural silting, these places have lost their importance, and some are no longer ports at all. Only Guangzhou has continuously maintained its status as a foreign trade port from the Qin and Han dynasties to the present day. Similarly, Ningbo, a key city on Zhejiang's Maritime Silk Road, has seen its role continue uninterrupted since its rise in the Tang Dynasty. This sustained development is also evidenced by the ancient shipwrecks discovered in Ningbo. To date, six such wrecks have been found: a Tang-dynasty dragon boat (discovered in 1973), a Northern Song wooden boat (1978), a Southern Song wooden boat (2003), a Yuan-dynasty shipwreck (2014), a

Ming-dynasty wooden boat (1994), and the Xiaobaijiao Qing-dynasty shipwreck (2008). Thus, shipwrecks from every dynasty from the Tang to the Qing have been found in Ningbo. While shipwrecks have been discovered in other Chinese Maritime Silk Road cities, none form a continuous and complete series like Ningbo's. This unbroken succession of shipwrecks from the Tang to the Qing is a testament to the continuity of Zhejiang's Maritime Silk Road.

Third, a River-Sea Nexus Connecting to the World.

The Eastern Zhejiang Canal, situated on the Ningbo-Shaoxing Plain, emerged as early as the time of King Goujian of Yue. In the early 7th century, Emperor Yang of the Sui Dynasty mobilized the nation's resources to construct the Grand Canal, connecting northern and southern China. On June 22nd, 2014, at the 38th session of the World Heritage Committee in Doha, Qatar, the "Grand Canal of China" was successfully inscribed on the World Heritage List. This UNESCO World Heritage site is composed of three main sections: the Sui-Tang Grand Canal, the Beijing-Hangzhou Grand Canal, and the Eastern Zhejiang Canal. Hangzhou and Ningbo are not only key cities along the Grand Canal but also its primary outlets to the sea. This canal system connected Zhejiang to the nation's main transportation network, greatly expanding the commercial reach of its ports and providing the abundant goods and vast inland markets that fueled the prosperity of its Maritime Silk Road.

Fourth, Anchored in the East China Sea, with a Reach to the Southern Seas.

Zhejiang is situated in the central part of the East China Sea, facing Japan and the Korean Peninsula across the water. Natural factors like ocean currents and monsoon winds facilitated maritime navigation. In the age of wooden sailing ships, a voyage from Ningbo, Zhejiang's main port, could reach the Korean Peninsula or the Japanese archipelago in as few as six to ten days with favorable winds and currents. Due to its advantageous position in East Asian maritime affairs, Ningbo historically served as China's primary hub for connecting to the Korean Peninsula and Japan. Ports like Ningbo, Hangzhou, and Wenzhou also established connections with Southeast Asia and the Indian Ocean via the Maritime Silk Road, as evidenced by the Arab residential quarters that appeared in Hangzhou and Ningbo during the Song and Yuan dynasties. However, compared to its relations with Japan and the Korean Peninsula, Zhejiang's trade ties with Southeast Asia and the Indian Ocean region were of secondary importance and often indirect.

Fifth, Rebirth Through Fire and a Successful Transformation.

During the Qing Dynasty, due to government suppression and ruinous policies, Zhejiang's Maritime Silk Road stagnated. The outbreak of the First Opium War in 1840 then shattered the deluded dream of the "Celestial Empire." In 1842, under the cannons of invading British forces, the Qing government signed the Treaty of Nanjing and was forced to open five cities—

Guangzhou, Fuzhou, Xiamen, Ningbo, and Shanghai—as treaty ports. On January 1st, 1844, Ningbo was formally opened, and the river's north bank outside the city wall was designated a residential area for foreigners. From then on, Zhejiang's Maritime Silk Road began its transformation into a network of modern international shipping routes, driving change throughout society. During this reluctant, humiliating, and painful transition, the ignorant and arrogant Qing government remained willfully blind and deaf. Deceiving itself and ignoring the powerful tide of globalization, it stubbornly refused to engage with the world, repeatedly missed opportunities to modernize, and was ultimately consumed by the fires of the 1911 Revolution. In stark contrast to the Qing government, the people of Zhejiang did not resist the currents of history. Instead, they met this era of transformation with an open mind, readily adopting advanced Western technologies and culture. With steadfast resolve, they strove to keep pace with global trends, forged anew in the crucible of conflict and change. In 1855, merchants in Ningbo pooled their capital to purchase the Baoshun, a foreign-built steamship. This acquisition, the first of its kind by Chinese interests, inaugurated the modernization of China's maritime transport. Throughout this transition, successive generations of Zhejiang's people, filled with aspiration, departed from their homes in villages, towns, and remote mountain islands. They ventured to Shanghai, Hong Kong, and destinations abroad, achieving remarkable success in diverse fields and propelling Zhejiang's transformation from a traditional society into a modern one.

In concert with the continued development of the Maritime Silk Road, the people of Zhejiang, together with migrants from other provinces and foreign nationals, co-created a vibrant and multifaceted "Maritime Silk Road Culture," profoundly enriching the heritage of the region. Today, as a global transformation unseen in a century accelerates and a new era of globalization dawns, China has extended a global invitation to jointly build the "21st Century Maritime Silk Road." In this context, Zhejiang is actively pioneering new paths for Chinese-style modernization. Compared to its ancient predecessor, Zhejiang's modern international exchange unfolds against a vastly different backdrop: the age of wooden sailing ships has given way to an era of colossal, satellite-navigated container vessels; the ancient routes operated within a tributary system, whereas today's commerce is conducted within an international order founded on peaceful coexistence; in antiquity, sea lanes were the sole, two-dimensional channel for overseas contact, while today's connections are three-dimensional, encompassing not only maritime routes but also aviation, satellite communications, and digital networks; the ancient Silk Road was comparatively simple, focused primarily on the trade of goods, whereas today's international economic engagement is a complex ecosystem that includes finance, investment, and foreign exchange; and the societal impact of the ancient routes was gradual and localized, whereas Zhejiang's contemporary economic ties are instantaneous and global in their reach. A major event in a distant corner of the world can swiftly affect Zhejiang; likewise, an incident at a single enterprise in Zhejiang can instantly disrupt a global supply chain.Yet, despite these profound historical differences, Zhejiang's "Maritime Silk Road Culture" retains an irreplaceable modern value in the province's ongoing pursuit of Chinese-style modernization. This value has two components: an implicit spiritual legacy and an explicit practical utility. The spiritual legacy is manifest in four key areas:

1. A Fearless Pioneering Spirit

Facing a vast and mysterious ocean, the ancient people of Zhejiang fearlessly braved the unknown, carving out the Maritime Silk Road through tempestuous seas. Even after routes were established, navigating the turbulent ocean remained fraught with peril. Therefore, from its inception to its maturity, the Maritime Silk Road demanded a spirit of intrepid exploration and relentless progress—the very same spirit required today to advance the great project of Chinese-style modernization.

2. A Spirit of Inclusive Openness

When ancient mariners ventured across the great waves and arrived in foreign lands, they encountered entirely different cultures and customs, and they returned with goods wholly unfamiliar to them. Such journeys would have been impossible for the narrow-minded, the conservative, or the short-sighted. The Maritime Silk Road was thus built upon a foundation of openness and inclusivity toward other cultures—a mindset that remains essential for the construction of a modern China.

3. A Spirit of Eclectic Innovation

Through the ancient Maritime Silk Road, a diverse array of foreign cultures flowed into Zhejiang. This included material goods, such as Goryeo porcelain, Japanese fans, Southeast Asian spices, and crops from the Americas, as well as spiritual traditions like Buddhism and Islam. The overland Silk Road also brought exotic goods from the Western Regions, most notably the lion.

The Tang Dynasty celadon seated lion unearthed in Ningbo.

Introduced to China from the Western Regions during the Han dynasty, the lion appeared in Zhejiang by the 3rd century, as seen on Yue ware ceramics excavated in the Ningbo area. Rather than rejecting these foreign influences, the people of Zhejiang actively absorbed and integrated them with local traditions, creating new and even more brilliant cultural forms. In the material sphere, New World crops like the sweet potato and potato became fully integrated into Zhejiang's agriculture. The processed sweet potato and bean-flour products developed in Zhejiang, which do not exist in the Americas, have become signature specialties of certain local townships. Carved wooden and stone lions became a characteristic local craft, and today these figures adorn cities and villages alike. The lion dance is a fixture of local festivals and is even performed by the Zhejiang diaspora abroad. The foreign lion, through cultural fusion and innovation, has become an indelible part of Zhejiang's own heritage. The Tiantai school of Buddhism stands as a paramount example of this synthesis of foreign and native cultures. This spirit of innovation—of creating new cultural forms by absorbing and integrating the foreign with the local—holds profound practical significance for the project of Chinese-style modernization.

4. A Scientific Spirit and the Pursuit of Truth

Safe passage across the turbulent, open sea required more than just sturdy vessels. Navigators needed a comprehensive set of skills: the ability to select favorable weather, maintain a true course, and avoid hidden reefs and shoals. Failure meant disaster. In essence, the Maritime Silk Road was built upon a foundation of science and technology, including shipbuilding, navigation, meteorology, and hydrology. Without a scientific spirit—a relentless pursuit of truth—the technologies essential for seafaring could never have been developed. Regrettably, the creators of these innovations were largely anonymous artisans and laborers, their names lost to history. Yet, among Zhejiang's celebrated cultural elites, there were also outstanding figures who embodied this scientific spirit. Zhao Rushi (1170–1231), a Song-dynasty official from Taizhou, authored the Zhu Fan Zhi (Records of Foreign Peoples) while serving as the maritime trade superintendent in

Quanzhou. Seeking to remedy his countrymen's limited knowledge of the world, he conducted extensive research on foreign lands. Crucially, he cast aside the narrow prejudices of the court and reported truthfully that foreign lands possessed advanced civilizations and unique products, and that some peoples, like those of Daqin (the Roman Empire), were "tall, fair-skinned, and bore a resemblance to the Chinese." Later, the Ming-dynasty scholar Li Zhizao of Hangzhou, though steeped in Confucian tradition, met the influx of modern Western culture not with suspicion but with humility and diligent study, earning the sincere admiration of Western scholars for his profound mastery of their knowledge. Today, as we face a new technological and industrial revolution, Zhejiang's exploration of Chinese-style modernization requires a deep commitment to science, education, and innovation. We must prioritize the role of technology in developing new productive forces. At the heart of this endeavor lies the scientific spirit.

The implicit spiritual values of Zhejiang's Maritime Silk Road Culture, embedded like genetic code within the province's heritage, provide the spiritual impetus for its modernization. Its explicit practical value, in turn, offers concrete, actionable paths for this project, primarily in three areas:

1. A Foundation for Academic Research

The culture of Zhejiang's Maritime Silk Road—with its deep roots, rich substance, and distinct character—is an indispensable component of the province's history and a key area of focus for scholars worldwide. In-depth research not only reveals the nuances of Zhejiang's cultural history and clarifies its contributions to Chinese civilization, but it also illuminates its role in the broader sweep of world history. Such scholarship can foster academic prosperity, promote deeper engagement with the international academic community, and position Zhejiang as a leading center for research, helping it to take its place on the world's academic stage.

2. A Rich Resource for Cultural Development

The long history of the Maritime Silk Road forged a brilliant and diverse cultural legacy in Zhejiang. Although an immeasurable portion of this heritage was lost to natural disasters and human conflict, a great deal has survived. This extant heritage can be divided into two categories: "immovable," such as architecture (historic residences, temples), stone carvings, archaeological sites, and tombs; and "movable," including ceramics, textiles, jade, woodcarvings, metalwork, paintings, calligraphy, maps, books, and manuscripts. This diverse inheritance is a rich resource for Zhejiang's contemporary cultural development. This heritage can be exhibited in museums and galleries, while its motifs can inspire new applications in fashion, product design, and artisan crafts. Its narratives can be adapted into traditional films or reimagined as modern digital content, such as online videos and 3D animation. For Zhejiang, whether the goal is to build a cultural powerhouse or to develop new productive forces, the heritage of the Maritime Silk Road is an invaluable treasure.

3. A Powerful Vehicle for International Communication

Zhejiang's Maritime Silk Road was a conduit to the wider world, traversed by countless envoys, merchants, sailors, and monks from China and abroad, all of whom left their mark in foreign lands. Remnants of this culture can be found across the Korean Peninsula, the Japanese archipelago, Southeast Asia, the Middle East, North Africa, and the West. These scattered relics are an integral part of Zhejiang's historical legacy. By leveraging this overseas heritage, we can better tell the story of Zhejiang and of China, thereby strengthening the international reach and influence of our culture and fostering a favorable external environment for modernization. At the same time, these relics can deepen the connection that overseas Zhejiangese feel for their ancestral home, inspiring them to participate more enthusiastically in its development.

In the history of China's ancient Maritime Silk Road, Zhejiang gradually moved from the periphery to the forefront, pioneering the transition from the age of sail to the age of steam. Today, the Ningbo-Zhoushan Port has become the world's largest by cargo throughput. The entire province is embracing the world with an open spirit, steadfastly forging a new path in the Zhejiang practice of Chinese-style modernization. In this great endeavor, the cultural heritage of the Maritime Silk Road, tempered and refined by the ages, will play a unique and irreplaceable role. It will inspire all people of Zhejiang, both old and new, to deepen their love for this fertile land and to commit themselves more actively to the project of modernization, thereby creating an even more brilliant "Maritime Silk Road Culture" for a new era.

Afterword

Throughout this book, a central fact has been repeatedly emphasized: from the Tang dynasty onward, Ningbo Port served as a primary gateway for China's foreign relations, a vital hub connecting the maritime world of East Asia, and an irreplaceable nexus of the Maritime Silk Road. As this book was going to press, on January 17th, 2025, the China News Service reported that for the 16th consecutive year, the Ningbo-Zhoushan Port had ranked first in the world for annual cargo throughput. This report underscores Ningbo's enduring importance as a key port in the international maritime network, from the age of sail to the age of the container ship. It is for this reason that Ningbo has adopted "A Port Connecting the World" as its official city slogan.

Ningbo's historical and contemporary prominence as an international port stems from its exceptionally favorable natural conditions. Yet, no matter how superior these conditions may be, they cannot automatically become a resource for social progress unless they are developed and utilized by human enterprise. Left untapped, they can even become a burden. The setbacks in Ningbo Port's history vividly illustrate this point. The most telling example is the "Canton System," or single-port trade policy, implemented by the Qianlong Emperor.

In the early Qing dynasty, the court implemented a strict maritime ban to suppress anti-Qing resistance along the coast. After unifying Taiwan in

1683, the government lifted the ban and established four maritime customs houses—in Jiangsu, Zhejiang, Fujian, and Guangdong—to serve as windows for foreign trade. The Zhejiang Customs office was located in Ningbo. At the time, the primary European merchants trading on the China coast were the British. Although they made several voyages to Ningbo in the late 17th century, their main base of operations remained in Guangzhou (Canton). In the mid-18th century, exasperated by the strict regulations and rampant extortion of officials at the Canton customs house, British traders shifted their operations to Ningbo for three consecutive years: 1755, 1756, and 1757.

The arrival of the British was welcomed by the local populace, as it brought considerable commercial benefits. For Canton, however, this diversion of trade meant a loss of profit. Consequently, the officials and merchants who held a monopoly on foreign trade there repeatedly petitioned the court, vehemently opposing British access to Ningbo. The Qianlong Emperor was well aware that the goods most desired by the British, such as silk and tea, were produced primarily in the Jiangsu-Zhejiang region. He understood that allowing trade at Ningbo would reduce costs for the British while stimulating development in China's eastern provinces. Facing this dispute between the two provinces, the emperor identified the crux of the matter: "If many British traders go to Zhejiang, the foreign merchants in Guangdong will lose profit, and the livelihood of the people there will also be affected." Based on this understanding, in the spring of 1757, the Qianlong Emperor decided to raise the duties at the Zhejiang customs house, hoping to make trade there unprofitable and force the British to return to Canton.

To his surprise, the British persisted, indicating their willingness to trade at Ningbo even under the new, higher tax rates. This development prompted deliberations within the Qing government over adjusting its foreign trade policy. The emperor himself even entertained the bold idea of making Ningbo an open port on par with Canton. To this end, he transferred Yang Yingju, the experienced Viceroy of Liangguang who was familiar with Canton's maritime affairs, to the post of Viceroy of Min-Zhe to oversee the opening of the port. After inspecting Ningbo, however, Yang not only proposed that duties at Zhejiang be set at double the rate of Canton's but also argued that opening Ningbo would pose a threat to national coastal defense. For the supreme ruler of the Qing, national security was the paramount concern. The Qianlong Emperor therefore accepted Yang's counsel, abandoned the idea of opening Ningbo, and resolved to concentrate all foreign trade in Canton. In December 1757, the emperor issued a formal edict prohibiting British merchants from trading at Ningbo. With this, the Qing government's foreign trade policy shifted from a multi-port system to the single-port Canton System.

The Canton System secured Guangzhou's monopoly on foreign trade but dealt a devastating blow to Ningbo. Research shows that with British ships concentrated in Canton, revenue at the Guangdong customs house rose steadily from 210,000 taels of silver in 1737 to over 400,000 by 1755. Meanwhile, with no British ships calling at Ningbo, revenue at the Zhejiang customs house stagnated at around 90,000 taels. Thus, Ningbo, a natural deep-water port perfectly suited to be a gateway to the world, was cut off from the West by the Qing's self-imposed policy of isolation and began a gradual decline. The Canton System made Zhejiang its greatest victim, but more importantly, it caused China to miss a crucial opportunity to engage with the world.

In the end, of course, the Canton System failed to secure the dynasty's coastal defenses. The collapse of that very security marked the beginning of the Qing dynasty's downfall. In 1840, the Opium War erupted, and the coast of Ningbo was one of its main theaters. From October 13rd, 1841, to May 7th, 1842, British forces occupied the city of Ningbo. In August 1842, the defeated Qing government was forced to abandon the Canton System and, under the Treaty of Nanking, agree to open five port cities: Guangzhou, Xiamen, Fuzhou, Ningbo, and Shanghai. The sealed gates of the Qing dynasty were thrown open, and the ancient Maritime Silk Road was transformed into a network of modern international shipping lanes.

On February 18th, 1844—the first day of the first lunar month in the 24th year of the Daoguang Emperor—Ningbo was formally opened as a treaty port. With that, the natural advantages of Ningbo's port could once again be realized, and the city began its journey of modern transformation. In the years that followed, Ningbo not only drove the modernization of Zhejiang but also played a pivotal role in the modernization of China as a whole. From this, it is clear that the fate of Ningbo Port is determined by national policy. Under a policy of openness, it thrives; under a policy of closure, it inevitably declines.

Today is the second day of the Lunar New Year, a time of celebration in the traditional Chinese calendar. On this festive occasion, I extend my sincere wishes for the continued and growing prosperity of Ningbo Port, and for Zhejiang to ride the winds of reform and opening, cleaving the waves of progress as it forges fearlessly ahead.

Bibliography

Feng, Chengjun 冯承钧, trans. 2014. *Make Boluo xingji* 《马可波罗行纪》. Annotated by Sha Hai'ang 沙海昂. Shanghai: Shanghai shudian chubanshe.

He, Gaoji 何高济, trans. 1981. *Eduolike dongyou lu* 《鄂多立克东游录》. By Odoric of Pordenone. Beijing: Zhonghua shuju.

Jiang, Jing 江静. 2011. *Furi Song seng Wuxue Zuyuan yanjiu* 《赴日宋僧无学祖元研究》. Beijing: Shangwu yinshuguan.

Jiang, Leping 蒋乐平. 2014. *Kuahuqiao wenhua yanjiu* 《跨湖桥文化研究》. Beijing: Kexue chubanshe.

Jin, Guoping 金国平, and Wu Zhiliang 吴志良. 2006. "Liusan yu Putaoya de Zhongguo Ming Qing ciqi" 流散于葡萄牙的中国明清瓷器. *Gugong bowuyuan yuankan* (Palace Museum Journal), no. 3: 16–31.

Kimata, Yasuhiko 木宫泰彦. 1980. *Rizhong wenhua jiaoliu shi* 《日中文化交流史》. Translated by Hu Xinian 胡锡年. Beijing: Shangwu yinshuguan.

Lin, Shimin 林士民. 1985. "Ningbo xiancun Riben guo Dazaifu Hakata-tsu huaqiao keshi zhi yanjiu" 宁波现存日本国太宰府博多津华侨刻石之研究. *Wenwu* (Cultural Relics), no. 7: 57–67.

Liu, Hengwu 刘恒武. 2009. *Ningbo gudai duiwai wenhua jiaoliu: Yi lishi yicun wei zhongxin* 《宁波古代对外文化交流——以历史遗存为中心》. Beijing: Haiyang chubanshe.

Makita, Tairyō 牧田諦亮. 1955. *Sakugen nyūminki no kenkyū* 『策彦入明记の研究』. Kyoto: Hōzōkan.

Moule, Arthur Christopher, and Paul Pelliot, eds. and trans. 1938. *Marco Polo: The Description of the World*. London: G. Routledge.

Mungello, D. E. 1994. *The Forgotten Christians of Hangzhou*. Honolulu: University of Hawaii Press.

Nagaoka, Ryūsaku 长冈龙作. 2022. "Riben Qingliangsi zang Shijia Rulaixiang tainei de xinyang yu shijieguan" 日本清凉寺藏释迦如来像胎内的信仰与世界观. Translated by Li Yinguang 李银广. *Meishu daguan* (Art Panorama), no. 2: 88–95.

Nara National Museum 奈良国立博物馆. 2009. *Seichi Ninpō: Nihon Bukkyō 1300-nen no genryū* 《圣地宁波——日本仏教 1300 年 の 源流》. Nara: Nara National Museum.

Qin, Dashu 秦大树. 2007. "Shiyi Nanhai, buque Zhongtu: Tan Jingliwen chenchuan de chushui ciqi" 拾遗南海，补阙中土——谈井里汶沉船的出水瓷器. *Gugong bowuyuan yuankan* (Palace Museum Journal), no. 6: 89–101.

Sun, Guoping 孙国平, and Wang Yonglei 王永磊. 2020. "Cong Jingtoushan yizhi kan Ningbo dili huanjing yu haiyang wenhua de guanxi"

从井头山遗址看宁波地理环境与海洋文化的关系. *Ningbo tongxun* (Ningbo Communication), no. 18: 48–50.

Xie, Mingliang 谢明良. 2005. *Maoyi taoci yu wenhua shi* 《贸易陶瓷与文化史》. Taipei: Yunchen wenhua shiye gufen youxian gongsi.

Xu, Jing 徐兢 (Song). 1971. *Xuanhe fengshi Gaoli tujing* 《宣和奉使高丽图经》. Taipei: Shangwu yinshuguan.

Yamaguchi, Osamu 山口修. 1993. "'Chōnen nyū Sō guhō junreikō narabini zuizō zōryūki' kō" 「『奝然入宋求法巡礼行并瑞像造立记』考」. *Bukkō Daigaku Butsugakukai kiyō* (Journal of the Buddhist Society, Bukkyo University), inaugural issue: 1–24.

Zhao, Yinzai 赵胤宰. 2006. "Lüelun Hanguo Baiji gudi chutu de Zhongguo taoci" 略论韩国百济故地出土的中国陶瓷. *Gugong bowuyuan yuankan* (Palace Museum Journal), no. 2: 90–100.

Zhou, Daguan 周达观 (Yuan). 2000. *Zhenla fengtu ji jiaozhu* 《真腊风土记校注》. Annotated by Xia Nai 夏鼐. Beijing: Zhonghua shuju.

Glossary

Table 1: Key Dynasties and Periods

China	Dates	Japan	Dates	Korea	Dates
Han Dynasty	202 BC–AD 220			Three Kingdoms	57 BC–AD 668
Six Dynasties	AD 222–589			(Silla, Baekje, Goguryeo)	
Sui Dynasty	AD 581–618				
Tang Dynasty	AD 618–907	Heian Period	AD 794–1185	Unified Silla	AD 668–935
Five Dynasties	AD 907–960			Goryeo Dynasty	918–1392
Wuyue Kingdom	AD 907–978				
Song Dynasty	960–1279	Kamakura Period	1185–1333		
Yuan Dynasty	1271–1368				
Ming Dynasty	1368–1644	Muromachi Period	1336–1573		

China	Dates	Japan	Dates	Korea	Dates
Qing Dynasty	1644–1912	Edo Period	1603–1868		

Alauddin (阿拉丁, *Ālādīng*): A Muslim master who constructed the Zhenjiao (True Religion) Mosque in Hangzhou between 1314 and 1320, during the Yuan dynasty. His work is a testament to the significant Islamic presence in Zhejiang established through the Maritime Silk Road.

Aleni, Giulio (艾儒略, *Ài Rúlüe*) (1582–1649): An Italian Jesuit missionary who worked in China during the late Ming dynasty. He authored the *Chronicle of Foreign Lands*, a work that introduced world geography to Chinese readers. The 1623 Hangzhou edition included a preface by the local scholar Xu Xuchen.

Amoghavajra (不空, *Bùkōng*) (AD 705–774): An influential monk in Tang China and a master of Esoteric Buddhism. A portrait of him was among the gifts sent from China to the Japanese monk Enchin in AD 862, facilitated by Zhejiang merchants.

An Lushan Rebellion (安史之乱, *Ān Shǐ zhī luàn*) (AD 755–763): A devastating rebellion against the Tang dynasty led by the general An Lushan. The conflict severely weakened the Tang empire, leading to a decline in central authority and shifts in maritime trade patterns.

An Shigao (安世高, *Ān Shìgāo*) (fl. c. AD 148–180): A Parthian monk who was one of the first Buddhist missionaries in China. According to historical records, he traveled to Kuaiji (modern Shaoxing) in Zhejiang, where he died, marking the early arrival of Buddhism in the region via the Maritime Silk Road.

An Tao (安焘, *Ān Tāo*) (1034–1108): A Northern Song official who led a major diplomatic mission to the Goryeo Kingdom (Korea) in 1078. His embassy departed from Mingzhou (Ningbo) aboard two specially constructed "divine ships," highlighting Ningbo's role as the primary port for official exchanges with Goryeo.

Ashoka Temple (阿育王寺, *Āyùwáng Sì*): A renowned Buddhist monastery in Ningbo, Zhejiang. It provided sanctuary to the Tang-dynasty monk Jianzhen after his failed attempts to reach Japan. It was also a key site for cultural exchange, visited by many foreign monks.

Baekje (百济, *Bǎijì*): One of the Three Kingdoms of ancient Korea (18 BC–AD 660). Located on the southwestern Korean Peninsula, it maintained close diplomatic and trade relations with China's southern dynasties and was one of the earliest importers of Zhejiang's Yue ware ceramics.

Baisha Ferry (白沙渡, *Báishā Dù*): A historic ferry crossing on the Qiantang River in ancient Jiande County, Zhejiang. It was here that the 14th-century European traveler Odoric of Pordenone witnessed cormorant fishing, an account that he introduced to Europe.

Baishuiyang (白水洋, *Báishuǐyáng*): Literally "White Water Ocean," the historical name for the sea between the mouths of the Qiantang and Yangtze Rivers. It was a key segment of the northern sea route from Zhejiang.

Batu Hitam Shipwreck: Also known as the Belitung Shipwreck. An Arab or Indian ship discovered off Indonesia's Belitung Island, dated to c. AD 826. Its cargo of over 60,000 Chinese ceramics, including Yue ware from Zhejiang, provides crucial evidence of the westward trade along the Maritime Silk Road during the Tang dynasty.

Bayan (伯颜, *Bóyán*) (1236–1295): A distinguished Mongol general and chancellor of the Yuan dynasty. He led the Yuan forces that conquered the Southern Song capital of Hangzhou in 1276, an event recounted with folkloric embellishments in *The Travels of Marco Polo*.

Baoyun Temple (宝云寺, *Bǎoyún Sì*): A temple founded in Ningbo in AD 968 for the Goryeo monk Yitong. It became a major center for the revival of the Tiantai School of Buddhism during the Song dynasty, shifting the school's focal point from Mount Tiantai to Ningbo.

Bianjing (汴京, *Biànjīng*): The capital of the Northern Song dynasty, located in modern-day Kaifeng, Henan. It was the destination for diplomatic missions from Goryeo and Japan that landed in Zhejiang and traveled north via the Grand Canal.

Bodhisattva (菩萨, *púsà*): In Mahayana Buddhism, an enlightened being who postpones their own nirvana to help all sentient beings achieve enlightenment. Guanyin is a prominent example revered along the maritime routes.

Bohai Kingdom (渤海国, *Bóhǎi Guó*) (AD 698–926): A kingdom located in modern-day northeast China and the northern Korean Peninsula. Merchants from this kingdom, such as Li Yanxiao, were active in the maritime trade with Zhejiang and Japan during the Tang dynasty.

Canton System (一口通商, *yīkǒu tōngshāng*) (1757–1842): A trade policy of the Qing dynasty that restricted all foreign maritime commerce to the single port of Guangzhou (Canton). This policy ended the multi-port system and severely curtailed the development of Zhejiang's ports, such as Ningbo.

Chan Buddhism (禅宗, *Chánzōng*): A school of Mahayana Buddhism that developed in China and emphasizes meditation and direct insight. Known as Zen in Japan, its teachings were transmitted between Zhejiang and Japan by monks such as Lanxi Daolong and Wuxue Sogen.

Chang'an (长安, *Cháng'ān*): The capital city of the Tang dynasty, located in modern-day Xi'an. It was the political and cultural center of China and the destination for many Japanese monks and envoys who traveled through Zhejiang.

Changya (淐雅, *Chāngyǎ*): A monk at Kaiyuan Temple in Taizhou during the Tang dynasty. He was a close friend of the Japanese monk Enchin and maintained correspondence with him via Zhejiang merchants after Enchin's return to Japan.

Chegwan (谛观, *Dìguān*) (d. c. AD 970): A monk from the Goryeo Kingdom who traveled to the Wuyue Kingdom in AD 960, bringing a collection of lost Tiantai School scriptures. He became a disciple of the Tiantai patriarch Yiji and remained on Mount Tiantai, where he authored an important introductory text on Tiantai doctrine.

Chōnen (奝然, *Chōnen*) (938–1016): A Japanese monk who made a pilgrimage to Song China from AD 983 to AD 986, traveling via the port of Taizhou in Zhejiang. He commissioned a famous replica of the legendary Sandalwood Image of Śākyamuni, which he brought back to Japan, where it is now enshrined at Seiryō-ji temple in Kyoto.

Cirebon Shipwreck: A 10th-century shipwreck discovered off the coast of Cirebon, Indonesia. Its cargo included over 300,000 pieces of Yue ware from Zhejiang, demonstrating the massive scale of Zhejiang's ceramics exports during the Wuyue Kingdom period.

Dadu (大都, *Dàdū*): The capital of the Yuan dynasty, located in modern-day Beijing. It was the seat of Kublai Khan's court and the city where Marco Polo resided for many years.

Daitoku-ji (大徳寺, *Daitoku-ji*): A Rinzai Zen temple in Kyoto, Japan. It is the current home of 82 of the original 100 scrolls of the *Five Hundred Arhats* paintings, which were created in Ningbo during the Southern Song dynasty.

Danrin-ji Temple (檀林寺, *Danrin-ji*): A temple constructed in Kyoto, Japan, during the 9th century. The Zhejiang Chan monk Yikong was invited by the Japanese Empress Dowager to be its founding abbot.

Daoyu (道育, *Dàoyù*) (fl. AD 892–938): A monk from the Silla Kingdom who resided on Mount Tiantai for over forty years. He was known for his extreme asceticism and compassion but never learned to speak Chinese.

Dazaifu (太宰府, *Dazaifu*): The administrative and military center of Kyushu, Japan, for much of the 1st millennium. It was the primary point of contact for foreign envoys and merchants arriving from China and Korea, and it housed the official guesthouse, the Kōrokan.

Daxiu Zhengnian (大休正念, *Dàxiū Zhèngniàn*) (1215–1289): A Zen monk from Wenzhou, Zhejiang, who traveled to Japan in 1269. He served as abbot of several major temples in Kamakura, including Kenchō-ji and Engaku-ji, and founded the Daxiu school of Zen.

Deshao (德韶, *Désháo*) (AD 891–971): A Chan master from Zhejiang who became the National Preceptor of the Wuyue Kingdom. He was instrumental in reviving the Tiantai School by persuading the king to send a mission to Goryeo to retrieve lost scriptures.

Dharma (法, *fǎ*): A core concept in Buddhism with multiple meanings, including the cosmic law and order, and the teachings of the Buddha. The transmission of the Dharma was a primary motivation for the travels of monks along the Maritime Silk Road.

Dōgen (道元, *Dōgen*) (1200–1253): A seminal Japanese Zen monk and founder of the Sōtō school. He traveled to Song China in 1223, studying at major Zhejiang monasteries like Tiantong Temple under the master Rujing.

Dōsen (道璿, *Dōsen*) (AD 702–760): A Chinese monk from Luoyang who was invited to Japan in AD 736. He resided at Daian-ji Temple in Nara and, recognizing the scholarship of Jianzhen's disciple Situo, invited him to lecture on the Vinaya.

Edo Period (江戸時代, *Edo jidai*) (1603–1868): The period of Japanese history under the rule of the Tokugawa Shogunate. During this time, a wooden statue of the Hangzhou merchant Xie Guoming was created and enshrined at Jōten-ji in Hakata.

Eisai (栄西, *Eisai*) (1141–1215): A Japanese monk who founded the Rinzai school of Zen in Japan. He made two trips to China, studying at Zhejiang's Tiantong Temple. He is also credited with introducing tea cultivation to Japan.

Enchin (円珍, *Enchin*) (AD 814–891): A Japanese monk of the Tendai school who traveled to Tang China from 853 to 858. He formed close relationships with Zhejiang merchants like Li Da and Zhan Jingquan, who facilitated his travels and correspondence. He is considered the founder of the

Jimon branch of Tendai Buddhism.

Enjō-ji Temple (園城寺, *Enjō-ji*): Also known as Mii-dera, the head temple of the Jimon school of Tendai Buddhism in Ōtsu, Japan. It preserves important historical documents, including correspondence between Enchin and the Zhejiang merchants Li Da and Zhan Jingquan.

Enni Ben'en (円爾弁円, *Enni Ben'en*) (1202–1280): A Japanese monk who traveled to Song China to study Zen Buddhism. He was a disciple of the master Wuzhun Shifan. With the patronage of the Hangzhou merchant Xie Guoming, he founded Jōten-ji temple in Hakata upon his return to Japan.

Fazai (法载, *Fǎzāi*): A monk from Lingyao Temple in Quzhou, Zhejiang, who accompanied Jianzhen on his final voyage to Japan in AD 753. He was appointed by Jianzhen as the second abbot (jōza) of Tōshōdai-ji temple in Nara.

Feng Fang (丰坊, *Fēng Fǎng*) (c. 1500–1570): A renowned scholar and calligrapher from Ningbo during the Ming dynasty. He wrote a preface for the poetry collection of the Japanese monk Sakugen Shūryō, a testament to the deep cultural exchanges that occurred through the tribute missions.

Five Dynasties and Ten Kingdoms Period (五代十国, *Wǔdài Shíguó*) (AD 907–979): A period of political turmoil in China between the fall of the Tang and the founding of the Song. During this era, Zhejiang was ruled by the independent Wuyue Kingdom, which actively promoted maritime trade.

Folangji (佛郎机, *fólángjī*): The early Chinese name for the Portuguese, derived from the Arabic term for Europeans (*Franj*). They first arrived on the coast of Zhejiang in the 1520s and established a smuggling base at Shuangyu Port.

Ganpu (澉浦, *Gănpŭ*): An important port on Hangzhou Bay during the Song and Yuan dynasties, located in modern Haiyan County. Both Marco Polo and the *shibosi* records attest to its role in international trade.

gangshou (纲首, *gāngshŏu*): A term for a merchant-captain or the leader of a trading fleet during the Song and Yuan dynasties. The prominent Hangzhou merchant Xie Guoming, who led the Chinese community in Hakata, held this title.

Goryeo Dynasty (高丽, *Gāolí*) (918–1392): A Korean kingdom that unified the peninsula. It maintained close diplomatic and commercial ties with China's Song and Yuan dynasties, with Ningbo serving as the designated port of entry for its official missions.

Grand Canal (大运河, *Dà Yùnhé*): A vast network of waterways connecting northern and southern China. The Eastern Zhejiang Canal section linked Hangzhou and Ningbo, connecting Zhejiang's maritime ports to the empire's inland commercial and political centers.

Guangzhou (广州, *Guăngzhōu*): A major port in southern China, also known as Canton. During the Tang dynasty, it was the sole port with a *shibosi*. In the Qing dynasty, it became the only port open to foreign trade under the Canton System.

haijin (海禁, *hǎijìn*): A series of maritime prohibitions or "sea bans" imposed by the Ming and early Qing governments. These policies banned private overseas trade and restricted foreign contact to official tribute missions, leading to the rise of smuggling and piracy.

Hakata (博多, *Hakata*): A major port city in Kyushu, Japan (part of modern Fukuoka). From the Song dynasty onward, it was a key destination for Chinese merchants from Zhejiang and Fujian and housed a significant Chinese expatriate community known as the Tōbō.

Hangzhou (杭州, *Hángzhōu*): The provincial capital of Zhejiang. It served as the capital of the Wuyue Kingdom and the Southern Song dynasty (when it was known as Lin'an). A major terminus of the Grand Canal, it was a center of commerce and culture, famously described by Marco Polo as "Quinsai," the "Celestial City."

Han Dynasty (汉朝, *Hàn Cháo*) (202BC–AD 220): A foundational dynasty in Chinese history. During this period, the Maritime Silk Road was in its nascent stages, with foreign goods like Roman glass beads reaching Zhejiang indirectly.

Heian Period (平安時代, *Heian jidai*) (AD 794–1185): A period of Japanese history characterized by the flourishing of court culture in the capital,

Heian-kyō (modern Kyoto). During this time, direct sea routes from Zhejiang were established, and private trade flourished.

Hemudu Culture (河姆渡文化, *Hémǔdù Wénhuà*) (c. 7000–5300 BC): A Neolithic culture centered in the Yuyao area of Zhejiang. Archaeological finds, including wooden paddles and ceramic boat models, provide some of the earliest evidence of shipbuilding and maritime activity in China.

Huayan School (华严宗, *Huáyánzōng*): A school of Chinese Buddhism based on the *Avataṃsaka Sūtra*. It was influential during the Tang dynasty, but the book's glossary draft mistakenly overemphasizes its importance relative to the Tiantai and Chan schools central to Zhejiang's story.

Huiyin Temple (惠因寺, *Huìyīn Sì*): A Buddhist temple in Hangzhou that became a major center for the Huayan School during the Northern Song. It was patronized by the Goryeo prince and monk Yitian, who studied there and donated funds for its scripture pavilion, earning it the nickname "Goryeo Temple."

Jianzhen (鉴真, *Jiànzhēn*) (AD 688–763): A venerable Tang-dynasty monk who, after five failed attempts, successfully traveled to Japan in AD 753 to transmit the Buddhist precepts. Several of his attempts involved Zhejiang, where he took refuge and planned his voyages, underscoring the province's key role on the sea route to Japan. He founded the Ritsu school in Japan.

jinshi (进士, *jìnshì*): The highest and final degree in the imperial civil service examinations in China. Achieving this rank brought great honor and was the ambition of the scholar-gentry class. The son of the merchant Zhou Liangshi became the first *jinshi* from Ninghai County.

Jingtoushan Site (井头山遗址, *Jǐngtóushān Yízhǐ*): An archaeological site in Yuyao, Ningbo, dated to over 8,000 years ago. As China's earliest known shell-mound settlement, its discovery pushed back the timeline of Zhejiang's maritime history. A well-preserved wooden paddle found there proves the inhabitants possessed watercraft.

Jingshan Temple (径山寺, *Jìngshān Sì*): A major Chan (Zen) monastery in Hangzhou. It was a destination for many Japanese monks, including Enni Ben'en, and was the home temple of the master Wuzhun Shifan.

Jōten-ji (承天寺, *Jōten-ji*): A Rinzai Zen temple in Hakata, Japan, founded in 1242. Its establishment was funded by the Hangzhou merchant Xie Guoming for the Japanese monk Enni Ben'en upon his return from studying in China.

Kaesong (开城, *Kāichéng*): The capital city of the Goryeo Kingdom in Korea. It was the destination for Chinese diplomatic missions, such as those led by An Tao and Xu Jing, that departed from Ningbo.

Kaiyuan Temple (开元寺, *Kāiyuán Sì*): A prominent Tang-dynasty monastery in Taizhou, Zhejiang. It hosted many foreign monks, including the Japanese monk Enchin and the Korean monks who studied under the Tiantai patriarchs. Jianzhen's disciple Situo was also from this temple.

Kamakura Period (鎌倉時代, *Kamakura jidai*) (1185–1333): A period of Japanese history marked by the rule of the Kamakura shogunate. During this time, Zen Buddhism flourished, and many Japanese monks traveled to Zhejiang to study, while Chinese monks like Lanxi Daolong traveled to Kamakura to teach.

kanhe (勘合, *kānhé*): Tally certificates issued by the Ming court to foreign states permitted to engage in tribute trade. Japanese missions had to present these official credentials upon arrival in Ningbo to prove their legitimacy.

Kōrokan (鸿胪馆, *Kōrokan*): A state-run guesthouse in Dazaifu, Japan, for lodging foreign envoys and merchants during the Tang and Song periods. Chinese merchants from Zhejiang were confined here while conducting official trade.

Kuahuqiao Site (跨湖桥遗址, *Kuàhúqiáo Yízhǐ*): A Neolithic site in Xiaoshan, Hangzhou, where the oldest known dugout canoe in Asia, dated to over 7,000 years ago, was unearthed.

Kublai Khan (忽必烈, *Hūbìliè*) (1215–1294): The fifth Khagan-Emperor of the Mongol Empire and the founder of the Yuan dynasty in China. He employed Marco Polo and sent a diplomatic mission accompanied by the

Polo family from Quanzhou.

Kumārajīva (鸠摩罗什, *Jiūmóluóshí*) (AD 344–413): A Kuchean Buddhist monk and prolific translator of Buddhist scriptures into Chinese. Legend connects him to the famous Sandalwood Image of Śākyamuni, which was said to have been brought to China with him.

Lanxi Daolong (兰溪道隆, *Lánxī Dàolóng*) (1213–1278): A Chan (Zen) monk from Sichuan who studied at Jingshan Temple in Hangzhou and Tiantong Temple in Ningbo. He traveled to Japan in 1246, where he became the founding abbot of Kenchō-ji in Kamakura and was a key figure in establishing "pure Zen" in Japan.

Li Churen (李处人, *Lǐ Chǔrén*): A 9th-century Chinese merchant who pioneered a direct sea route from Zhejiang to Japan. In AD 842, he built a new ship in Japan and sailed from the Gotō Islands to Wenzhou in just six days.

Li Da (李达, *Lǐ Dá*): A 9th-century merchant from Wuzhou (modern Jinhua), Zhejiang. He frequently traded with Japan and maintained a close friendship with the Japanese monk Enchin, exchanging poems and gifts.

Li Rihua (李日华, *Lǐ Rìhuá*) (1565–1635): A scholar-official and connoisseur from Jiaxing, Zhejiang. His writings provide valuable information on the introduction of New World crops, noting that the sweet potato was initially a rare and mysterious plant in the region.

Li Yanxiao (李延孝, *Lǐ Yánxiào*): A 9th-century merchant from the Bohai

Kingdom. In AD 858, his ship carried the Japanese monk Enchin and the Zhejiang merchants Li Da and Zhan Jingquan from Taizhou to Japan.

Lin'an (临安, *Lín'ān*): The name of Hangzhou when it served as the capital of the Southern Song dynasty (1127–1279). It was the home of the merchant Xie Guoming.

Liampo: The 16th-century Portuguese name for the port of Ningbo, specifically referring to the illegal international trade emporium at Shuangyu Port in the Zhoushan archipelago.

Longquan Celadon (龙泉青瓷, *Lóngquán qīngcí*): A type of green-glazed ceramic produced in Longquan, Zhejiang, and surrounding areas, primarily from the Song to the Ming dynasties. It became a major export commodity on the Maritime Silk Road, with vast quantities found in shipwrecks like the Sinan wreck and at archaeological sites across Asia and Africa.

Lu Yundi (路允迪, *Lù Yǔndí*): A Northern Song official who led a diplomatic mission to the Goryeo Kingdom in 1123. A member of his retinue, Xu Jing, wrote a detailed account of the voyage from Ningbo, the *Xuanhe Fengshi Gaoli Tujing*.

Mangi: The name used by Marco Polo in *The Travels* to refer to Southern China, the former territory of the Southern Song dynasty. The term is a transliteration of the derogatory Chinese word *manzi* (蛮子).

Marco Polo (c. 1254–1324): A Venetian merchant who traveled across Asia and served in the court of Kublai Khan. His book, *The Travels of Marco Polo*, contains a famous and detailed description of Hangzhou (which he called Quinsai), praising it as the "finest and noblest city in the world."

Maritime Silk Road (海上丝绸之路, *Hǎishàng Sīchóu zhī Lù*): A vast network of maritime trade and communication routes connecting China with Southeast Asia, the Indian Ocean, the Arab world, and Europe, flourishing from the Han dynasty until the modern era. Zhejiang was a key hub, particularly on the East Sea Route to Japan and Korea.

Martini, Martino (卫匡国, *Wèi Kuāngguó*) (1614–1661): An Italian Jesuit missionary who worked in Zhejiang during the turbulent Ming-Qing transition. He authored the *Novus Atlas Sinensis* (1655), the first comprehensive atlas of China published in Europe, which included a detailed map and description of Zhejiang. He died and was buried in Hangzhou.

Ming Dynasty (明朝, *Míng Cháo*) (1368–1644): The dynasty that succeeded the Mongol-led Yuan. The Ming court implemented strict maritime prohibitions (*haijin*) and a formal tribute trade system, designating Ningbo as the sole official port for exchange with Japan.

Mingzhou (明州, *Míngzhōu*): The historical name for Ningbo from the Tang to the Yuan dynasties. Under this name, the city rose to become a principal port on the Maritime Silk Road.

Nanking, Treaty of (南京条约, *Nánjīng Tiáoyuē*) (1842): The treaty that ended the First Opium War. It forced the Qing government to abandon the Canton System and open five ports, including Ningbo, to foreign trade, marking the transformation of the ancient Maritime Silk Road into modern international shipping lanes.

Neolithic Era: The New Stone Age. In Zhejiang, this period is represented by cultures like Hemudu and Kuahuqiao (dating back 8,000-7,000 years), which provide the earliest evidence for shipbuilding and the exploitation of marine resources in the region.

Nihon Kiryaku (日本纪略, *Nihon Kiryaku*): A Japanese historical chronicle that contains the earliest known record of Zhejiang merchants on the Maritime Silk Road: the arrival of Zhou Guanghan and Yan Shengze from Yuezhou in Japan in AD 819.

Ningbo (宁波, *Níngbō*): A major port city in Zhejiang. Known as Mingzhou in earlier periods, it was consistently a principal port on the Maritime Silk Road from the Tang dynasty onward, serving as the designated gateway for official missions to and from Japan and Korea.

Odoric of Pordenone (c. 1286–1331): An Italian Franciscan friar who traveled through Asia, arriving in China via the Maritime Silk Road. His travelogue contains accounts of his journey through Zhejiang, including descriptions of Hangzhou and cormorant fishing on the Qiantang River.

Opium War, First (1840–1842): A conflict between Great Britain and the

Qing dynasty, sparked by trade imbalances and the British opium trade. The war shattered China's isolationist policies and led to the opening of Ningbo and other treaty ports.

Pak In-ryang (朴寅亮, *Piáo Yínliàng*): A Goryeo official and man of letters who led a tribute mission to the Song court in 1079. His fleet was shipwrecked off the Zhejiang coast, and he was rescued by local officials, an event that highlighted the perils of sea travel and the complexities of diplomatic exchange.

Prajna (般若, *Bōrě*): A monk from the Goguryeo Kingdom (Korea) who traveled to China in the late 6th century. He became a disciple of Master Zhiyi on Mount Tiantai and is the first Korean monk known to have been buried there.

shibosi (市舶司, *shìbósī*): A government agency, often translated as Maritime Trade Office or Superintendency, established in major port cities during the Tang, Song, and Yuan dynasties to manage and tax overseas commerce. Zhejiang had four such offices during the Song dynasty, highlighting its central role in maritime trade.

Silla Kingdom (新罗, *Xīnluó*) (57 BC–AD 935): One of the Three Kingdoms of Korea, which later unified the peninsula. The rise of Silla in the 7th century disrupted northern sea lanes, creating an opportunity for Zhejiang's ports to establish direct routes to Japan. Silla merchants were also active traders in East Asia.

Sinan Shipwreck: A Yuan-dynasty Chinese ship that sank off the coast of Korea around 1323 while en route to Japan. Its vast cargo included over 12,000 pieces of Longquan celadon from Zhejiang and artifacts bearing inscriptions that strongly link its port of origin to Ningbo.

Situo (思托, *Sītuō*): A monk from Kaiyuan Temple in Taizhou, Zhejiang, who was a loyal disciple of Jianzhen. He accompanied his master on all six attempts to reach Japan. An expert in architecture and sculpture, he is credited with creating the famous hollow dry-lacquer portrait statue of Jianzhen at Tōshōdai-ji.

Song Dynasty (宋朝, *Sòng Cháo*) (AD 960–1279): A Chinese dynasty divided into the Northern Song (AD 960–1127) and Southern Song (1127–1279). The Song court generally encouraged overseas trade, establishing multiple *shibosi* in Zhejiang and propelling the region's Maritime Silk Road into a golden age of prosperity.

South Sea Route: One of the two main branches of the Maritime Silk Road, extending from the southern coast of China to Southeast Asia, the Indian Ocean, and beyond. While originating in Guangdong, its influence and trade networks extended to Zhejiang.

Sui Dynasty (隋朝, *Suí Cháo*) (AD 581–618): The dynasty that reunified China after the Northern and Southern Dynasties period. The Sui emperor Yangdi commissioned the construction of the Grand Canal, which was crucial for linking Zhejiang's ports to the interior.

Sakugen Shūryō (策彦周良, *Sakugen Shūryō*) (1501–1579): A learned Japanese Zen monk who led two tribute missions to Ming China (1539 and 1547), both of which passed through Ningbo. His detailed diaries, the *Record of the First Voyage* and *Record of the Second Voyage*, provide invaluable firsthand accounts of Ningbo's cityscape, society, and its role in the tribute trade system.

Sandalwood Image of Śākyamuni: A legendary statue believed to be the first image of the Buddha, carved from sandalwood during his lifetime. A famous replica, commissioned by the Japanese monk Chōnen and carved in Taizhou, Zhejiang, in AD 985, was brought to Japan and is now the central icon of Seiryō-ji temple in Kyoto.

Seiryō-ji (清凉寺, *Seiryō-ji*): A Buddhist temple in Kyoto, Japan. It is the home of the renowned wooden statue of Śākyamuni commissioned by the monk Chōnen in Taizhou. The statue's distinct style, known as "Seiryō-ji style," was widely copied throughout Japan.

Sesshū Tōyō (雪舟等杨, *Sesshū Tōyō*) (1420–1506): One of Japan's most celebrated ink wash painters. He traveled to Ming China with a tribute mission in 1467 and spent time in Zhejiang, creating works such as the *Map of Ningbo Prefecture* that provide a unique visual record of the region.

Shuangyu Port (双屿港, *Shuāngyǔ Gǎng*): An anchorage in the Zhoushan archipelago that, from c. 1524 to 1548, became a major international smuggling emporium operated by Portuguese traders (who called it Liampo),

Chinese merchants, and Japanese pirates in defiance of Ming maritime prohibitions. It was destroyed by the Ming official Zhu Wan in 1548.

Tang Dynasty (唐朝, *Táng Cháo*) (AD 618–907): A golden age in Chinese history. During this period, direct sea routes were established between Zhejiang and Japan, and ports like Mingzhou (Ningbo) became primary gateways for international trade and cultural exchange.

Taizhou (台州, *Tāizhōu*): A major port city on the coast of Zhejiang. From the Tang dynasty onward, it was a key departure point for merchants and monks traveling to Japan and Korea, and the home of the influential Kaiyuan and Guoqing temples.

Tiantai, Mount (天台山, *Tiāntāi Shān*): A sacred mountain in Zhejiang, renowned for its natural beauty and as a major center of Chinese Buddhism. It is the birthplace of the Tiantai School and a destination for pilgrims from across East Asia.

Tiantai School (天台宗, *Tiāntāizōng*): The first major indigenous school of Chinese Buddhism, founded by the master Zhiyi (AD 538–597) on Mount Tiantai. Its teachings, based on the *Lotus Sutra*, spread to Korea and Japan and were a central element of the cultural exchange along the Maritime Silk Road.

Tōbō (唐房, *Tōbō*): Literally "Tang Quarters," the name for the Chinese residential and commercial enclave in Hakata, Japan, during the Song and

Yuan dynasties. It was home to a thriving community of merchants, many of whom were from Zhejiang and Fujian.

Tōdai-ji (東大寺, *Tōdai-ji*): A landmark Buddhist temple complex in Nara, Japan. The Japanese monk Chōnen, who commissioned the Seiryō-ji Śākyamuni statue, was from this temple.

Tōshōdai-ji (唐招提寺, *Tōshōdai-ji*): A temple in Nara, Japan, founded by the Chinese monk Jianzhen in AD 759. It is the head temple of the Ritsu school in Japan and houses the famous dry-lacquer portrait statue of its founder, created by his Zhejiang disciple Situo.

Udayana (優填王, *Yōutián Wáng*): A king of ancient India who, according to legend, commissioned the first-ever statue of the Buddha, carved from sandalwood. All subsequent "Sandalwood Images" are considered to be replicas or spiritual descendants of this original.

Valignano, Alessandro (范礼安, *Fàn Lǐ'ān*) (1539–1606): An influential Italian Jesuit who served as the Visitor of Missions in the East. He was instrumental in developing the Jesuit strategy of cultural accommodation and dispatched missionaries like Michele Ruggieri and Matteo Ricci to China.

Wang Geon (王建, *Wáng Jiàn*) (AD 877–943): The founder of the Goryeo Kingdom in Korea. He advocated for adopting Chinese institutions while rejecting those of the Khitans, laying the groundwork for close diplomatic ties with the Song dynasty.

Wang Pan (王泮, *Wáng Pàn*): A Ming-dynasty official from Shaoxing, Zhejiang. While serving as the prefect of Zhaoqing in Guangdong, he gave crucial support to the Jesuit missionaries Michele Ruggieri and Matteo Ricci, allowing them to establish their first mission in the Chinese interior in 1583.

Wang Xizhi (王羲之, *Wáng Xīzhī*) (AD 303–361): Hailed as the "Sage of Calligraphy," a master calligrapher of the Eastern Jin dynasty from Shaoxing, Zhejiang. An original work by him was among the treasures the monk Jianzhen carried to Japan.

Wang Xianzhi (王献之, *Wáng Xiànzhī*) (AD 344–386): A renowned calligrapher and the seventh son of Wang Xizhi. Three of his original works were also taken to Japan by Jianzhen.

Wenzhou (温州, *Wēnzhōu*): A major port city on the coast of southern Zhejiang. It was an active hub for trade with Japan during the Tang dynasty and the departure point for Zhou Daguan's Yuan-dynasty mission to Cambodia.

wokou (倭寇, *wōkòu*): Literally "Japanese pirates," a term for pirates who raided the coasts of China and Korea. During the Ming dynasty, these groups were often multinational, including Chinese merchants who turned to smuggling and piracy in defiance of the government's maritime prohibitions (*haijin*).

Wu Zetian (武则天, *Wǔ Zétiān*) (r. AD 690–705): The only female emperor in Chinese history. A patron of Buddhism, she commissioned a series of large silk paintings, one of which was later gifted by a Wenzhou monk to the Japanese monk Enchin.

Wuan Puning (无庵普宁, *Wú'ān Pǔníng*) (1197–1276): A Chan (Zen) monk who studied under Wuzhun Shifan in Zhejiang. He traveled to Japan in 1260 and served as the second abbot of Kenchō-ji in Kamakura. The lineage he established is known as the Wu'an School.

Wuxue Sogen (无学祖元, *Wúxué Zǔyuán*) (1226–1286): A Chan (Zen) monk from Ningbo who studied at Jingshan Temple. He traveled to Japan in 1279 at the invitation of the Kamakura regent Hōjō Tokimune and founded the influential Engaku-ji temple.

Wuyue Kingdom (吴越国, *Wúyuè Guó*) (AD 907–978): An independent kingdom that ruled Zhejiang and surrounding areas during the Five Dynasties and Ten Kingdoms period. Founded by Qian Liu, its rulers actively promoted maritime trade and Buddhism, contributing to the prosperity of the region's ports and the revival of the Tiantai School.

Xie Guoming (谢国明, *Xiè Guómíng*) (fl. 1233–1253): A prominent merchant-captain (*gangshou*) from Lin'an (modern Hangzhou) who became the leader of the Chinese expatriate community in Hakata, Japan. A devout Buddhist, he was a key patron of the Japanese monk Enni, founding Jōten-ji temple for him in 1242. He is still revered in Fukuoka today.

Xie Lingyun (谢灵运, *Xiè Língyùn*) (AD 385–433): A celebrated poet and Buddhist intellectual of the Southern Dynasties period from Shangyu, Zhejiang. He was a key figure in creating the Southern Edition of the *Nirvana Sutra*, a text later taken to Japan by Jianzhen.

Xingzai (行在, *Xíngzài*): Literally "temporary imperial residence," the official name for Hangzhou when it served as the capital of the Southern Song dynasty. The name signaled the court's intention to one day recapture its northern territories. Marco Polo's term "Quinsai" is a transliteration of this name.

Xu Gongyou (许公宥, *Xǔ Gōngyòu*): A 9th-century private merchant who traded between Zhejiang and Japan. He worked in collaboration with his brother, the official Xu Gongzhi, and maintained close ties with the Zhejiang monk Yikong after he moved to Japan.

Xu Jing (徐兢, *Xú Jīng*) (1091–1153): A Northern Song official who accompanied an embassy to the Goryeo Kingdom in 1123. His detailed account of the voyage, the *Xuanhe Fengshi Gaoli Tujing*, is a priceless source on Song-dynasty shipbuilding, navigation techniques (including the compass), and the sea route from Ningbo to Korea.

Yan Shengze (严圣则, *Yán Shèngzé*): A 9th-century merchant from Yuezhou (modern Shaoxing). Along with Zhou Guanghan, he is one of the earliest Zhejiang merchants mentioned in historical records, arriving in Japan aboard a Silla vessel in AD 819.

Yelikewen (也里可温, *yělǐkěwēn*): The Yuan-dynasty term for Christianity, specifically the Church of the East (Nestorianism). A *Yelikewen* church named Dapuxing Temple was established in Hangzhou during this period.

Yeongwang (灵光, *Língguāng*): A monk from the Silla Kingdom who traveled to China in the late 6th century to study under the Tiantai founder Zhiyi. He is credited with being one of the first to transmit Tiantai teachings back to the Korean Peninsula.

Yikong (义空, *Yìkōng*): A 9th-century Chan monk from Yanguan, Zhejiang. In AD 847, he was invited to Japan by the Empress Dowager and became the founding abbot of Danrin-ji Temple in Kyoto, playing a key role in the early transmission of Chan Buddhism to Japan.

Yitian (义天, *Yìtiān*) (1055–1101): A Goryeo prince who became a monk. He traveled to Song China in 1085 to study Buddhism, visiting Hangzhou and Mount Tiantai. Upon his return, he founded the Goryeo Tiantai School, establishing a major Buddhist tradition on the Korean Peninsula.

Yitong (义通, *Yìtōng*) (AD 927–988): A monk from the Goryeo Kingdom who traveled to China and studied on Mount Tiantai. He later settled in Ningbo, where he founded Baoyun Temple and trained a new generation of masters. He is revered as the sixteenth patriarch and a key figure in the revival of the Tiantai School.

Yue ware (越窑, *Yuè yáo*): A type of high-fired ceramic, primarily celadon, produced in the kilns of eastern Zhejiang from the Eastern Han to the Song dynasties. It was one of China's earliest mature porcelains and a major export commodity on the Maritime Silk Road, traded extensively in East Asia, Southeast Asia, and the Arab world.

Yuezhou (越州, *Yuèzhōu*): The historical name for the region around modern Shaoxing, Zhejiang. During the Tang dynasty, it was a major center for the production of Yue ware ceramics and the hometown of some of the earliest merchants recorded trading with Japan.

Yuan Dynasty (元朝, *Yuán Cháo*) (1271–1368): The dynasty established by the Mongol leader Kublai Khan. The Yuan court maintained an open policy toward foreign trade, and Zhejiang's Maritime Silk Road continued to prosper. It was during this period that Marco Polo and Odoric of Pordenone visited the region.

Zhan Jingquan (詹景全, *Zhān Jǐngquán*): A 9th-century merchant from Wuzhou (modern Jinhua), Zhejiang, who was active in the Japan trade. A devout Buddhist and skilled poet, he maintained a deep friendship with the Japanese monk Enchin, acting as a courier for correspondence and gifts between China and Japan.

Zhang Rong (张荣, *Zhāng Róng*): A master carver of Buddhist images in the Northern Song capital of Bianjing. For centuries, he was mistakenly credited with carving the famous Seiryō-ji Śākyamuni statue.

Zhang Yanjiao (张延皎, *Zhāng Yánjiǎo*) and **Zhang Yanxi** (张延袭, *Zhāng Yánxí*): Two brothers and master carvers from Taizhou, Zhejiang. In AD 985, they were commissioned by the Japanese monk Chōnen to create the wooden statue of Śākyamuni that is now the central icon of Seiryō-ji temple in Kyoto.

Zhang Youxin (张友信, *Zhāng Yǒuxìn*): A 9th-century Chinese merchant who owned a ship that sailed the direct route between Ningbo and Japan. In AD 847, his vessel made the crossing in a remarkable three days. He was later appointed as an interpreter in the Japanese government at Dazaifu.

Zhao Kuangyin (赵匡胤, *Zhào Kuāngyìn*) (AD 927–976): The founding emperor of the Song dynasty (Emperor Taizu). He reunified much of China and established policies that generally encouraged private maritime commerce, which benefited Zhejiang's ports.

Zhenjiao Mosque (真教寺, *Zhēnjiào Sì*): The "True Religion" Mosque built in Hangzhou between 1314 and 1320 by the Muslim master Alauddin, reflecting the city's role as a cosmopolitan center during the Yuan dynasty.

Zhenla (真腊, *Zhēnlà*): An ancient kingdom located in modern-day Cambodia. The Wenzhou native Zhou Daguan visited Zhenla with a Yuan diplomatic mission in 1296 and wrote a detailed account of its culture and customs.

Zhili (知礼, *Zhīlǐ*) (AD 960–1028): A native of Yin County (Ningbo) and a leading disciple of the Goryeo monk Yitong. He became the seventeenth patriarch of the Tiantai School and was a central figure in its revival during the Song dynasty.

Zhiyi (智顗, *Zhìyǐ*) (AD 538–597): The de facto founder of the Tiantai School of Buddhism. He established his main monastery, Guoqing Temple, on Mount Tiantai in Zhejiang. His teachings had a profound and lasting influence on Buddhism throughout East Asia.

Zhou Daguan (周达观, *Zhōu Dáguān*) (c. 1266–1346): A native of Wenzhou, Zhejiang, who accompanied a Yuan dynasty diplomatic mission to Zhenla (Cambodia) in 1296. His detailed travelogue, *The Customs of Cambodia*, is a vital historical source on the region.

Zhou Wenyu (周文裔, *Zhōu Wényù*) and **Zhou Liangshi** (周良史, *Zhōu Liángshǐ*): A father and son from Ninghai, Zhejiang, who were prominent merchants in the China-Japan trade during the early Northern Song. Zhou Wenyu took a Japanese wife, and their son, Zhou Liangshi, embodied the transnational identity of the merchant class.

Zhoushan (舟山, *Zhōushān*): An archipelago off the coast of Ningbo. Its strategic location made it a key area for maritime trade, navigation, and defense. It was the site of the Shuangyu Port smuggling emporium and an early center for the cultivation of the sweet potato in China.

Zhu Wan (朱纨, *Zhū Wán*) (1494–1550): A Ming-dynasty official appointed Grand Coordinator of Zhejiang. He was known for his uncompromising efforts to enforce the maritime prohibitions (*haijin*). In 1548, he led a campaign that destroyed the international smuggling base at Shuangyu Port.

www.ingramcontent.com/pod-product-compliance
Lightning Source LLC
LaVergne TN
LVHW010556100826
845148LV00014B/2733

* 9 7 9 8 9 0 1 8 6 0 0 8 3 *